Shuichi Hasegawa
Aram and Israel during the Jehuite Dynasty

Beihefte zur Zeitschrift für die alttestamentliche Wissenschaft

Herausgegeben von
John Barton · F. W. Dobbs-Allsopp
Reinhard G. Kratz · Markus Witte

Band 434

De Gruyter

Shuichi Hasegawa

Aram and Israel during
the Jehuite Dynasty

De Gruyter

FSC
www.fsc.org

MIX
Papier aus verantwor-
tungsvollen Quellen
FSC® C016439

ISBN 978-3-11-028335-8
e-ISBN 978-3-11-028348-8
ISSN 0934-2575

Library of Congress Cataloging-in-Publication Data

A CIP catalog record for this book has been applied for at the Library of Congress.

Bibliographic information published by the Deutsche Nationalbibliothek

The Deutsche Nationalbibliothek lists this publication in the Deutsche
Nationalbibliografie; detailed bibliographic data are available in the Internet
at http://dnb.dnb.de.

© 2012 Walter de Gruyter GmbH & Co. KG, Berlin/Boston

Printing: Hubert & Co. GmbH & Co. KG, Göttingen
∞ Printed on acid-free paper

Printed in Germany

www.degruyter.com

To the memory of my father

Tsutomu Sekine (1935–2001)

Acknowledgements

This work is a revised version of my doctoral thesis "Aram and Israel during the Jehuite Dynasty" written under the supervision of Prof. Nadav Na'aman and submitted to the Senate of Tel Aviv University in December, 2010. The work remains substantially the same as the thesis, with only minor changes being made, mainly the addition of new bibliographical data.

To my supervisor, Prof. Nadav Na'aman, without whom I could never have accomplished what I had started, I wish to express my sincerest gratitude for his patient efforts to help me to complete my dissertation. To me, he has been a wonderful as well as a strict teacher, and to all he is certainly one of the best historians of the history of ancient Israel. I also would like to thank the two anonymous reviewers of the thesis for their insightful comments on an earlier version of it. They helped both to improve the current work and to expand my horizons. For the same reason, my thanks go to the anonymous reviewers from the BZAW series who provided me with valuable advice that improved the work.

This work is an ambitious attempt to integrate studies in three disciplines, biblical studies, Assyriology, and archaeology. The starting point of the work was my MA dissertation "Aram and Israel" written under the supervision of Prof. Yutaka Ikeda (Tsukuba). Since then, various people have helped me develop the skills necessary for this work. In the first years of my studies in Tel Aviv, Prof. Shlomo Izre'el and Prof. Ran Zadok (both Tel Aviv), taught me how to tackle the complexity of the sources. The late Prof. Moshe Kochavi and the late Mr. Gil Covo (both Tel Aviv) taught me the significance of archaeology for reconstructing the history of Israel. During my stay in Heidelberg, I benefited immensely from intellectual conversations and discussions with Prof. Oded Lipschits (Tel Aviv), Prof. Manfred Oeming (Heidelberg), and Prof. Jacob. L. Wright (Emory). The staffs of the Tel Rekhesh expeditions and, among them Dr. Yitzhak Paz (Israel Antiquities Authority), have always offered me warm encouragement to complete my work. Prof. Akio Tsukimoto (Rikkyo), to whom I owe invaluable support during the years of my study, especially deserves to be mentioned here. My thanks go to all these people.

I thank the editors of BZAW, who kindly consented to include this work in the series, and Dr. Albrecht Döhnert, Dr. Sabine Krämer, and Ms. Sabina Dabrowski of de Gruyter, who lent me support in publishing this work.

I would like to thank Emiko Sekine, my mother, and Tamiko and Seïichi Hasegawa, my parents-in-law, who have expressed their encouragement and tolerance in every possible way. Last, I must especially express my gratitude to my family, Satoko, my wife, Rene and Noa, my beloved daughters, for their boundless patience. I dedicate this thesis to the memory of my late father, Tsutomu Sekine.

May 2012, Morioka   Shuichi Hasegawa

Table of Contents

List of Tables

List of Maps

Abbreviations

ABD	Freedman, D.N. Ed. 1992. *Anchor Bible Dictionary*. 6 vols. New York
ADAJ	*Annual of the Department of Antiquities of Jordan*
ADP	*Abhandlungen des deutschen Palästinavereins*
AfO	*Archiv für Orientforschung*
AfOB	*Archiv für Orientforschung: Beiheft*
Ahw	von Soden, W. 1965–1981. *Akkadisches Handwörterbuch*. 3 Vols. Wiesbaden
AION	*Annali dell'Istituto Orientale di Napoli*
AJA	*American Journal of Archaeology*
AJBI	*Annual of the Japanese Biblical Institute*
AJSL	*American Journal of Semitic Languages and Literature*
ANESS	*Ancient Near Eastern Studies Supplement Series*
AnOr	*Analecta orientalia*
AnSt	*Anatolian Studies*
AOAT	*Alter Orient und Altes Testament*
AoF	*Altorientalische Forschung*
ARM	*Archives royales de Mari*
ARRIM	*Annual Review of the Royal Inscriptions of Mesopotamia Project*
ASOR	*American Schools of Oriental Research*
ATD	*Das Alte Testament Deutsch*
ATHANT	*Abhandlungen zur Theologie des Alten und Neuen Testaments*
BA	*Biblical Archaeologist*
BARev	*Biblical Archaeology Review*
BASOR	*Bulletin of the American Schools of Oriental Research*
BCSMS	*Canadian Society for Mesopotamian Studies, Bulletin*
BHT	*Beiträge zur historischen Theologie*
BiOr	*Bibliotheca orientalis*

BJS	*Brown Judaic Studies*
BN	*Biblische Notizen (NF)*
BWANT	*Beiträge zur Wissenschaft vom Alten und Neuen Testament*
BZAW	*Beihefte zur Zeitschrift für die alttestamentliche Wissenschaft*
BZNW	*Beihefte zur Zeitschrift für die neutestamentliche Wissenschaft und die Kunde der älteren Kirche*
CAD	1956–. *The Assyrian Dictionary of the Oriental Institute of the University of Chicago.* Chicago
CB	*Coniectanea biblica: Old Testament Series*
CBQ	*Catholic Biblical Quarterly*
CBQMS	*Catholic Biblical Quarterly Monograph Series*
CHANE	*Culture and History of the Ancient Near East*
CRAIBL	*Comptes rendus de l'Académie des inscriptions et belles-lettres*
CTN	*Cuneiform Texts from Nimrud*
DMOA	*Documenta et monumenta Orientis antiqui*
EI	*Eretz-Israel: Archaeological, Historical and Geographical Studies*
FRLANT	*Forschungen zur Religion und Literatur des Alten und Neuen Testaments*
GAG	von Soden, W. 1995. Grundriss der Akkadischen Grammatik. 3rd edition. Rome
GTA	*Göttinger theologischer Arbeiten*
HA-ESI	*Hadashot Arkheologiyot: Excavations and Surveys in Israel*
HAL	Koehler, L. and Baumgartner, W. 1967–1996. *Hebräisches und aramäisches Lexikon zum Alten Testament.* 5 vols. 3rd Ed. Leiden.
HO	*Handbuch der Orientalistik*
HSM	*Harvard Semitic Monographs*
HSS	*Harvard Semitic Studies*
HUCA	*Hebrew Union College Annual*
IEJ	*Israel Exploration Journal*
JAOS	*Journal of the American Oriental Society*
JBL	*Journal of Biblical Literature*
JCS	*Journal of Cuneiform Studies*
JNES	*Journal of Near Eastern Studies*
JSOT	*Journal for the Study of the Old Testament*

JSOTS	*Journal for the Study of the Old Testament: Supplement Series*
JSS	*Journal of Semitic Studies*
KAI 1-3	Donner, H. and Röllig. W. 1962–1964. *Kanaanäische und aramäische Inschriften.* Wiesbaden.
KAT	*Kommentar zum Alten Testament*
KLG I-III	Alt, A. 1953. *Kleine Schriften zur Geschichte des Volkes Israel.* Band I-III. München
LAPO	*Littératures anciennes du Proche-Orient*
LHBOTS	*Library of Hebrew Bible/Old Testament Studies*
MSIATU	*Monograph Series of the Institute of Archaeology, Tel Aviv University*
NABU	*Nouvelles assyriologiques breves et utilitaires*
NEA	*Near Eastern Archaeology*
NEAEHL	Stern, E. Ed. 1993–2008. *The New Encyclopedia of Archaeological Excavations in the Holy Land*, 5 vols. Jerusalem.
OBO	*Orbis biblicus et orientalis*
OIC	*Oriental Institute Communications*
OIP	*Oriental Institute Publications*
OLA	*Orientalia lovaniensia analecta*
OLZ	*Orientalistische Literaturzeitung*
Or	*Orientalia (NS)*
OTE	*Old Testament Essays*
OtSt	*Oudtestamentische Studiën*
PEQ	*Palestine Exploration Quarterly*
I R	Rawlinson, H.C. and Norris, E. 1861. *The Cuneiform Inscriptions of Western Asia, I: A Selection from the Historical Inscriptions of Chaldaea, Assyrian and Babylonia.* London.
III R	Rawlinson, H.C. and Smith, G. 1870. *The Cuneiform Inscritpions of Western Asia, III: A Selection from the Miscellaneous Inscriptions of Assyria.* London.
RA	*Revue d'assyriologie et d'archéologie orientale*
RB	*Revue Biblique*
RHPR	*Revue d'histoire et de philosophie religieuses*
RIMA	*The Royal Inscriptions of Mesopotamia, Assyrian Periods.* 3 vols. Toronto.
RlA	1928–. *Reallexikon der Assyriologie.* Berlin/Leipzig/New York

SAA	*State Archives of Assyria*
SAAB	*State Archives of Assyria Bulletin*
SAAS	*State Archives of Assyria Studies*
SBLDS	*Society of Biblical Literature Dissertation Series*
ScrHier	*Scripta Hierosolymitana*
SEL	*Studi epigrafici e linguistici*
SHANE	*Studies in the History and Culture of the Ancient Near East*
SJOT	*Scandinavian Journal of the Old Testament*
TA	*Tel Aviv: Journal of the Institute of Archaeology of Tel Aviv University*
TLZ	*Theologische Literaturzeitung*
TThSt	*Trierer theologische Studien*
TUAU	Kaiser, O. 1984–. Ed. *Texte aus der Umwelt des Alten Testaments.* Gütersloh.
UF	*Ugarit-Forschungen*
VT	*Vetus Testamentum*
VTS	*Supplements to Vetus Testamentum*
WBC	*World Biblical Commentary*
WO	*Die Welt des Orients*
ZA	*Zeitschrift für Assyriologie*
ZAW	*Zeitschrift für die alttestamentliche Wissenschaft*
ZDPV	*Zeitschrift des deutschen Palästina-Vereins*
ZKTh	*Zeitschrift für katholische Theologie*

Introduction

Subject of the Research

The dynasty of Jehu ruled the Northern Kingdom of Israel for about ninety years, from the late forties of the ninth to the middle of the eighth century BCE. Five kings of this dynasty are known from the biblical text: Jehu, Joahaz, Joash, Jeroboam II, and Zechariah. Two of them, Jehu and Joash, are mentioned in the Assyrian royal inscriptions, and Jeroboam is mentioned on a stamp used by one his officials (Shema').

Assyria had been a dominant power in Syria-Palestine since the time of Shalmaneser III (858–824 BCE). Following the Assyrian withdrawal in the 830s, Aram-Damascus under Hazael and his son, Bar-Hadad, became dominant in the Syro-Palestinian arena for some forty years, until Adad-nērārī III resumed military campaigns to that region.

According to the Bible, Jehu, formerly a high officer, rebelled against Joram, king of Israel of the Omride Dynasty, when the latter fought against the Aramaeans at Ramoth-Gilead, and afterwards usurped the throne (841 BCE). Shortly after Jehu's rebellion, Israel was subjugated by Hazael, king of Aram-Damascus, and an Aramaean hegemony lasted for about thirty to forty years. Only in the early eighth century BCE did Israel overthrow the yoke of Damascus.

It is thus evident that Aram and Assyria had great influence on the history of Israel from the mid-ninth century BCE onward. In investigating the history of the Jehuite Dynasty, one should first discuss, in detail, the relations between these three states.

Sources for the Research

Three kinds of sources are available for the history of the Jehuites: the biblical texts, the extra-biblical texts, and the archaeological data. The biblical texts include (1) 2 Kgs 9-15, which relates the reign of each Israelite and Judahite king; (2) 1 Kgs 20 and the Elisha narrative cycle in 2 Kgs 5-8, which are dated to the time of the Omrides in the Book of Kings; (3) some parts of the books of Hosea and Amos. The extra-biblical texts comprise Assyrian, Aramaic, Moabite, and Hebrew inscriptions. Most of the Assyrian inscriptions discussed in this study are royal inscriptions written during the reigns of Shalmaneser III, Adad-nērārī III, and Shalmaneser IV (*RIMA* 3). The Assyrian Eponym Chronicles form the basis for the Assyrian chronology and the Assyrian campaigns to the west (Millard 1994). The Aramaic inscriptions, such as the Tel Dan (Biran and Naveh 1993; 1995), Zakkur (Gibson 1975: 6-17), Samos (Röllig 1988), Eretria (Charbonnet 1986), and Arslan Tash Inscriptions (Gibson 1975: 4-5), attest to the Damascene hegemony over the Syro-Palestinian kingdoms from the late ninth to the beginning of the eighth century BCE. The Mesha Inscription (Gibson 1971: 71-83) describes relations between the Moabite Kingdom and the Northern Kingdom in the second half of the ninth century BCE. Some other inscriptions (i.e., the Tell Deir ʿAlla Inscription) also may shed light on the Kingdom of Israel in the first half of the eighth century BCE (Lemaire 1977; Hoftijzer and Van der Kooij 1976).

Due to archaeological excavations carried out over the years, more information about the time of the Jehuite Dynasty is available. In this study, I will discuss archaeological information acquired from relevant strata in the excavated sites. The investigated sites include the major cities of the Northern Kingdom, such as Samaria (Reisner, Fisher, and Lyon 1924), Tell el-Farʿah (North) (Chambon 1984), Tel Jezreel (Ussishkin and Woodhead 1992; 1994; 1997), Tel Megiddo (Lamon and Shipton 1939; Finkelstein, Ussishkin, and Halpern 2000; 2006a), Tel Yokneʿam (Ben-Tor and Rosenthal 1978; 1979; 1983), Tel Beth-Shean (James 1966; Mazar 1993; 2006), Tel Rehov (Mazar 1999), Tel Hazor (Yadin et al. 1958; 1960; 1961; Ben-Tor 1989; Ben-Tor and Bonfil 1997) and Tel Dan (Biran 1994; Biran, Ilan, and Greenberg 1996; Biran and Ben-Dov 2002); also some small sites and border sites such as Tell eṣ-Ṣafi (Boas and Maeir 1998; Maeir 2001), Tel ʿEn Gev (Tsukimoto, Hasegawa, and Onozuka 2009), Tel Kinrot (Fritz 1990; 1993; Fritz and Münger 2002; Pakkala, Münger, and Zangenberg 2004), and Bethsaida (et-Tell) (Arav 1995; 1999; 2004; 2009).

Aims of the Research

In the late nineteenth century, a new critical approach to the Bible, based on documentary and literary criticism, was adopted in the academic world of biblical research. Wellhausen (1885) hypothesised that what we read in different parts of the Hebrew Bible might have been a projection of the reality that prevailed at the time the text was written. In other words, the biblical narrative about ancient Israel is not accurate contemporaneous history, but rather historiography. His view was gradually accepted by the academic world, inevitably giving rise to a form-critical perspective of the Hebrew Bible. With the advance of this line of research since the 1970s, the historicity of the Patriarchal narratives has basically been discounted and attributed to a later period (Thompson 1974; Van Seters 1975). Accumulating archaeological data soon refuted even the historicity of the "conquest of the land" story in the Book of Joshua (Finkelstein 1988; Finkelstein and Na'aman 1994). By the 1990s, the reliability of the biblical descriptions of the United Monarchy was being heatedly debated (see for example, Fritz and Davies 1996; Handy 1997). Due to these problems involved with the historical credibility of the biblical text, it is generally accepted today that extra-biblical texts and archaeological data are essential for reconstructing the history of ancient Israel. For some periods, they carry even more weight than the biblical texts.

A critical approach has also developed in the study of biblical sources for the Jehuite Dynasty. This approach contributes to the clarification of the genre, origin, and date of the biblical texts relating to this period. Biblical history contains some episodes attributed to the time of the Omride and the Jehuite Dynasties, whose historical credibility has been challenged. Gunkel (1906) pointed out that these stories contain both historical and legendary elements, and it is the historian who must differentiate between them. The date for the integration of these narratives into the Book of Kings is also essential. The integration of the entire Elijah-Elisha narratives into the Book of Kings was ascribed to the Deuteronomist(s) (henceforth Dtr) by some scholars (Šanda 1911; Fohrer 1957; Noth 1967; Hentschel 1977; Campbell 1986). Gradually, the problems of this theory have been recognised, and a number of scholars have attributed parts of the stories to the post-Dtr stage (Hölscher 1923; Miller 1966; Schmitt 1972; Van Seters 1983). The extent of the integrated stories at each stage is, however, in debate. For example, some scholars have attributed only 1 Kings 20 and part of the Elisha stories to the post-Dtr stage (Rofé 1988; 2001; Na'aman 1997a; 2002a; 2006; 2008; Sroka 2006), and others have ascribed the majority to the post-Dtr stage (Stipp 1987; McKenzie 1991; Otto 2001). In addition, since these narratives are supposed to have been handed down orally to the author and to have been woven into the composition long after the related events, one should take a cautious attitude when discussing the historical credibility of these narratives. As early as the 1940s, Jepsen (1941–44) pointed out that the Elisha narratives reflected the historical reality of the Jehuite Dynasty (see Schmitt 1972); he also dated 1 Kgs 20 to the time of the Jehuites (see Whitely 1952; Miller 1966; 1967). The dates of these prophetic stories will be investigated in detail in the course of this research.

The books of Hosea and Amos also contain historical information relating to the Northern Kingdom that reflects perspectives different from those of the Book of Kings. Scholars have agreed that some parts of the Book of Hosea originated in the Northern Kingdom in the late eighth century and were later edited by a Judahite scribe (Wolff 1956). The analysis of the book is limited only to several passages (Hos 1:4; 5:1-2; 6:7-8; 10:14; 12:12), for the contents give little information about political events. Some passages of the Book of Amos (Am 1:3-5; 6:13-14) provide us with clues for understanding the territorial extent of the Northern Kingdom in the mid-eighth century BCE. Due to the literary genre of the books of Hosea and Amos, their historical reliability will also be carefully re-evaluated (Koch 1976; Schmidt 1965; Wolff 1964).

Throughout the years, many works have been published that discuss the history of the Jehuites and their relations with their neighbours. Nevertheless, some of these works are not critical enough. Many biblical texts are still open to different interpretations. Moreover, new texts have recently come to light, new archaeological excavations and surveys have been conducted, and recent discussions of the archaeological data have raised new questions that have not been taken into consideration in previous historical works. In the light of all this recently available data, a new historical study becomes desirable. It is the aim of this research to re-evaluate the biblical and extra-biblical texts, and the archaeological data, in order to write a comprehensive history of Israel's relations with Aram and Assyria in the time of the Jehuite kings.

Hypothesis and Methods

In the early 1990s, scholars began to question the reliability of using biblical texts as sources for writing a history of Israel. Some scholars even suggested that the authors of the biblical history lived either in the Persian or the Hellenistic period, hundreds of years after the events described. Their motives in writing the history were mainly religious and ideological. Hence, large portions of the biblical history are products of an imagination coloured by a heavily biased perspective (Davies 1992; Thompson 1992; 1999; Lemche 1998). The reliability of biblical sources and their contribution to the study of the history of Israel continue to be debated among scholars, and doubts have been expressed about the legitimacy of biblical history from the late tenth to the eighth century BCE.

In this research, I wish to demonstrate that the biblical texts, in fact, do include reliable historical information concerning the political relations of the Jehuite Dynasty with its neighbours. While the present form of the biblical texts, which emerged only in a later period, presents only the biblical history of Israel, distinct from the historical Israel (Kratz 2000; Witte 2005), historical information, however fragmentary, is certainly embedded in the texts and can be gleaned from them. This hypothesis depends on another hypothesis, namely, that some early sources were available to the author of the Book of Kings (Dtr), which he used in his composition, and that these sources were, in part, written shortly after the events they described. A detailed analysis of the texts thus enables us to identify those sources, and to use them in the historical reconstruction (Smelik 1992; Na'aman 2001a).

The biblical texts concerning the Jehuite Dynasty are of three types, classified as follows: (1) an account of each king, written in a formalised style, possibly derived from the chronicles of the kings of Israel (Parker 2006); (2) the narratives of Elijah-Elisha; (3) the texts written by the author (Dtr), in which he filled in the gaps in the account and overlaid it with his own theological and ideological view.

The texts of the first type demonstrate high reliability; the second type are less reliable, due to their literary genre; and those of the third type rather reflect the reality and intellectual thinking of the author during that time.

To differentiate these textual types and evaluate their historical reliability, I will follow the method presented by Smelik (1992: 22-25). He suggested the following three-stage-analysis: (1) analysis of the relevant biblical texts from a literary, theological, and historical perspective; (2) establishment of the general situation in the period, based on the extra-biblical sources; (3) a combination of the results of this analysis in order to reconstruct the historical reality.

At the first stage, each relevant text will be analysed: its context, literary genre, theological and ideological tendencies, and historical reliability. Since a major problem in this study is the analysis of the Elisha narratives, I discuss this corpus in great detail. For instance, the prophetic story in 1 Kgs 20, ascribed to Ahab's days, needs thorough analysis. The image of Ahab here as a weak king, conforms to his image neither in other biblical descriptions nor in the Assyrian royal inscriptions. The Aramaean hegemony as related in 1 Kgs 20 does not harmonise with the historical situation. The many discrepancies may indicate that either the story is fictional or originally describes events in the time of another king.

Like the Bible, extra-biblical texts were also written in order to convey various messages to the audience. Assyrian royal inscriptions are subjective and propagandistic, and must be analysed with great caution (Garelli 1982; Oded 1992; Tadmor 1983; 1997). To give one example: Adad-nērārī III described his campaigns in the Syro-Palestinian region in several inscriptions. In three different inscriptions, he mentioned the tribute paid by the king of Damascus, but details of the tribute are different in each inscription. To understand this difference, it is necessary to take into account the schematic and exaggerated use of numbers in the Assyrian royal inscriptions (De Odorico 1995).

Material culture reflects the external conditions in the land and is sensitive to periods of rise and decline. Layers of sites displaying destruction might illustrate the disastrous results of a conquest, whereas construction of a series of fortified cities and large public and private buildings, or the discovery of prestige artefacts of local and foreign origin, indicate a period of upheaval. Hence, the results of archaeological research are essential for evaluating the results of the political and military conditions during this period.

Above all, the dating of archaeological strata is important for this research. There is a controversy among archaeologists about the dating of the strata at the major sites of the Northern Kingdom. Finkelstein (1996; 1999; 2000; 2005) suggested a low chronology for strata formerly dated to the time of the United Monarchy and the Omride Dynasty. Other scholars rejected his re-dating and continued dating these strata in the tenth and ninth centuries BCE (Ben-Tor 2000; Bunimovitz and Faust 2001).

The chronological debate over the dating of the archaeological strata was initially influenced by historical considerations. Recently, radiocarbon dating is becoming critically important for establishing the chronology of the Iron Age (Sharon et al. 2007). It supplies data that is independent of historical considerations. In this research, I will take into account all these considerations and integrate them into the historical discussion.

A Review of Previous Research on the Subject

No textual sources about the Aramaeans in this period other than the Hebrew Bible had been known before the discovery of the ancient Near Eastern documents. For many years since the beginning of Assyriology, however, the study of Aramaean history has attracted scholars' interest. The elucidation of their language, history, religion, and culture has grown along with the great advance made in Assyriological research (e.g., Schiffer 1911; Kraeling 1918; Dupont-Sommer 1949). In general, scholars have dealt with the origin of the Aramaeans and their history from the second millennium BCE until the Assyrian annexation of the Aramaean kingdoms in the first millennium. In those studies, the scope of investigation varied according to the available sources. No less than five monographs about the Aramaeans have appeared recently. Sader (1987) analysed the Assyrian and Aramaic inscriptions and reconstructed the political and economic history of the Aramaean kingdoms. Pitard (1987) analysed the biblical texts and to some extent the archaeological data, and reconstructed the history of Aram-Damascus. Dion (1997), using the analysis of both textual and archaeological data, discussed the political, social, and cultural history of the Aramaean states in the Iron Age. Lipiński (2000) studied the history and geography of the Aramaean states, and also discussed their society, economy, law, and religion. Finally, Hafthorsson (2006) thoroughly examined the historical and archaeological sources for reconstructing the history of Aram-Damascus in the late ninth century BCE.

Research into the relationship between Aram-Damascus and the kingdoms of Israel and Judah has its own history. The first monograph on this subject was written by Kraeling (1918). He described the history of the Aramaeans in Syria and Mesopotamia from their rise to their fall, and also their relations with Israel. Jepsen (1941–44) significantly contributed to this subject, especially through his ascription of some Elisha narratives to the Jehuite Dynasty. His suggestion has been accepted widely, occasionally with some modifications (Whitley 1952; Miller 1966; 1967; 1968). Unger (1957) wrote the first monograph on the history of Aram-Damascus. Reinhold (1989) published a monograph, in which he discussed the relationship between the Aramaean states and Israel-Judah, particularly emphasising their economic and political relations. Analysing biblical and extra-biblical sources, Galil (2001a) discussed the relations between Assyria, Israel,

Judah, and Aram from the ninth to the seventh century BCE. Stith (2008) collected and analysed biblical and extra-biblical sources for reconstructing the coups of Hazael and Jehu.

Only a few works discuss the Jehuite Dynasty in detail. This is due to the paucity of extra-biblical texts from that period (mid-ninth to mid-eighth century BCE), when Assyria temporarily withdrew from the Syro-Palestinian arena. Another reason for this dearth of works are the complicated biblical texts relating to the Jehuites, in particular the prophetic narratives (see above). Some scholars discussed the history of these narratives by using form-critical and literary critical methods. Campbell (1986), Minokami (1989), and White (1997) suggested that the Dtr had used ancient sources, composed originally in the Northern Kingdom, for his account of Jehu's rebellion. Würthwein (1984) analysed the Elijah-Elisha narratives, suggesting that they were integrated only at the post-Dtr stage. Other scholars attributed some stories to the Dtr history and others to the post-Dtr stage (e.g., Stipp 1987; McKenzie 1991; Otto 2001; 2003). Mulzer (1992) conducted a literary and structural analysis of Jehu's coup narrative in 2 Kgs 8:25-10:36. Lamb (2007) examined the Dtr's view on the dynastic succession reflected in the narratives relating Jehu and his successors. Wray Beal (2007) analysed the story of Jehu's coup in 2 Kgs 9-10 in the framework of the Dtr history.

Knott (1971) studied the history of the Jehuite Dynasty in his doctoral dissertation. He described the history of this period, using the biblical and extra-biblical texts, and to a lesser degree, also the archaeological data. Haran (1967) wrote the history of the Jehuite Dynasty in the time of Jeroboam II, using the biblical text and the Assyrian inscriptions.

Missing in all these works is a detailed updated study focusing on the time of the Jehuite Dynasty and examining all the available written sources and the results of the archaeological excavations and surveys. The present research is aimed at drawing on current methods of historical research to ensure a more accurate picture.

1. Chronology of the Jehuite Kings

Two chronological anchor points are available for dating the reigns of the Jehuites. The first is Jehu's tribute to Shalmaneser III in 841 BCE and the second is the fall of Samaria in 722 BCE. Jehu brought tribute to Shalmaneser III when the Assyrian army conducted a campaign to Syria in 841 BCE.[1] Hoshea, the last king of the Northern Kingdom, paid tribute to Tiglath-pileser III at Sarrabānu, a major city of the Chaldaean tribe of Bit-Shilani, besieged and destroyed in 731 BCE.[2] Pekah, who was murdered by Hoshea, was still on the throne in the years 733–732 BCE, when Tiglath-pileser conducted campaigns against the Syro-Ephraimite coalition.[3] Hence, Hoshea's coup against Pekah and his subsequent enthronement (2 Kgs 15:30) were dated to 731 BCE. This date is confirmed by subtracting the nine years assigned by the biblical chronology to the duration of Hoshea's reign (2 Kgs 17:1) from 722 BCE, the date of Samaria's fall.[4]

The years 841 and 731 BCE could thus serve as safe chronological anchor points. The reigns of all the Jehuite kings and their four successors (Shallum, Menahem, Pekahiah, and Pekah) must be dated in between these dates.

The Book of Kings provides chronological data for each of the Jehuite kings and their successors. The data includes the duration of each king's reign, and his accession year is synchronised with the regnal year of a Judahite king. The chronological data of the Israelite kings are shown in the following table (Table 1).

---

1   This campaign took place in the eighteenth *palû* of Shalmaneser III (*RIMA* III, A.0.102.8, lines 1"-27"; A.0.102.10, Col. iii, line 45b-iv, line 15a; A.0.102.12, lines 21-30a; A.0.102.16, lines 122'b-137'a).

2   Tiglath-pileser's Summ. 9, Rev. lines 9-12 (Tadmor's numbering of Tiglath-pileser III's inscriptions [Tadmor 1994] is applied in this study). Borger and Tadmor 1982: 244-249; Tadmor 1979: 54; 1994: 277-278. For Sarrabānu, see Brinkman 1968: 230.

3   This event is described in the first parts in the descriptions of *Bīt-Humri* in three summary inscriptions (Summ. 4, lines 15'-17'; Summ. 9, Rev. lines 9-11; Summ. 13, lines 18') and in two parallel recensions of an annalistic inscription of Tiglath-pileser III (Ann. 18, line 3'; Ann. 24, line 3').

4   The date of the fall of Samaria has been dated widely to 723/722 BCE, the last year of Shalmaneser IV. See, Olmstead 1904–1905: 179-182; Tadmor 1958: 33-40; Thiele 1983: 163-172; Becking 1992: 21-56.

King	Duration of Reign	Synchronism	Source
Jehu	28 years	No synchronism	2 Kgs 10:36
Joahaz	17 years	23rd year of Jehoash	2 Kgs 13:1
Joash	16 years	37th year of Jehoash	2 Kgs 13:10
Jeroboam II	41 years	15th year of Amaziah	2 Kgs 14:23
Zechariah	6 months	38th year of Azariah	2 Kgs 15:8
Shallum	1 month	39th year of Azariah	2 Kgs 15:13
Menahem	10 years	39th year of Azariah	2 Kgs 15:17
Pekahiah	2 years	50th year of Azariah	2 Kgs 15:23
Pekah	20 years	52nd year of Azariah	2 Kgs 15:27

Table 1. Biblical Chronological Data for the Israelite Kings from Jehu to Pekah

Two major difficulties exist in the above chronology. First, the sum of the years of the ten kings amounts to 134 years and seven months, whereas the time-span between the years 841 and 731 amounts to only 111 years. The gap of twenty-three years and seven months can be reduced by subtracting one year for each king, since it overlaps with the last year of the previous king (except for Jehu, Zechariah, and Shallum). Six years can accordingly be subtracted, but there is still a gap of seventeen years.

The second problem is the inconsistencies in the synchronisms. (1) Joahaz ascended the throne in the twenty-third year of Jehoash and reigned for seventeen years (2 Kgs 13:1). The accession of Joash, son of Joahaz, should thus fall in the thirty-ninth year of Jehoash, but the synchronism dates it to the thirty-seventh year of Jehoash (2 Kgs 13:10). (2) Amaziah ascended the throne in the second year of Joash (2 Kgs 14:1) and Jeroboam II was enthroned in the fifteenth year of Amaziah (2 Kgs 14:23). Azariah son of Amaziah ascended the throne in the twenty-seventh year of Jeroboam II (2 Kgs 15:1). But then thirteen years of inter-regnum lie between the death of Amaziah and the enthronement of Azariah.

Various solutions to these problems have been offered by scholars. The assumption behind some proposed solutions is that the biblical chronology is based on authentic sources. The existence of internal contradictions in synchronisms and in the length of kings' reigns may indicate that the biblical chronographer(s) used diverse kinds of sources without changing the data to achieve a chronological harmony. The present study adopts this assumption and thus avoids suggesting corruptions in the numbers.

The excess of the total years of the reigns can be explained only by co-regencies, although not all the cases are described in the Book of Kings.[5] The "year" counting system must also be considered: (1) when to count the first regnal year; (2) when to count the first calendar year; (3) how to count the length of

---

5   David and Solomon (1 Kgs 1); Jehoshaphat and Jehoram (2 Kgs 8:16); Uzziah and Jotham (2 Kgs 15:5).

reigns; and (4) how to count the synchronistic year. The following principles will
be applied in the present study.

(1) There were two systems of counting the first regnal year in the ancient
Near East: the post-date and the ante-date system. In the post-date system, the
last regnal year of the previous king is counted as the accession year of the new
king and the new king's regnal year is counted from the following year. In the
ante-date system, the last regnal year of the previous king is counted as the first
regnal year of the new king. Judah apparently adopted the post-date system, and
Israel possibly employed the ante-date system.[6]

(2) Judah probably used a Tishri calendar[7] and Israel might have followed a
Nisan calendar.[8] This calendar system will be, with all due reservation, adopted in
the following calculation.

(3) Length of reign was generally counted according to the following principle. A reign covering two calendar years was counted as two years of reign (Pekahiah); yet, if the total length of the actual reign did not reach six months, the
number of months was specified (Zechariah: six months; Shallum: one month).[9]
The accession year (Judah) was counted as a full year. A period of co-regency is
usually included in the period of reign.

(4) Each of the two kingdoms counted its neighbour king's reign by using the
partner's year/calendar system.[10] There are three types of synchronisation: (1) the
beginning of the sole reign with the neighbour king's regnal year, counted from
the beginning of the latter's sole reign (Jehoash); (2) the beginning of the sole
reign with the neighbour king's regnal year, counted from the beginning of the
co-regency (Jeroboam II, Zechariah, Shallum, Menahem, Pekahiah, Pekah, and
Hoshea); (3) the beginning of the co-regency with the neighbour king's regnal
year, counted from the beginning of the sole reign (Joash and Amaziah).

Based on these assumptions, the following dates are calculated. Jehu captured
the throne in 841 and ruled until 814 BCE (twenty eight years), and Joahaz ruled
from 814 to 798 BCE (seventeen years). The inconsistency in the synchronisms
between Joash's accession and Jehoash's thirty-seventh year can be explained by
co-regency. Joash ascended the throne as co-regent in 799/798 BCE, a year before his father died, and ruled until 784 BCE (sixteen years). Jeroboam II must
have begun his reign as a co-regent, possibly in 788/787 BCE, with his reign
ending in 748 BCE (forty one years). Zechariah ruled from 748 to 747 BCE (six

6   Thiele 1983: 47-50; Hughes 1990: 179-181.
7   Thiele 1983: 51-53. For the view that the calendar system in Judah changed sometime from the
     end of the eighth century BCE to the reign of Jehoiakim, see Begrich 1929: 70-72; Hughes 1990:
     165-174; Galil 1996: 9-10.
8   Thiele 1983: 53-54.
9   Cf. 7 days for Zimri (1 Kgs 16:15).
10   An exception is the synchronisms of Azariah's regnal year with the first regnal years of Menahem,
     Pekahiah, and Pekah.

months) and Shallum's reign was in 747 BCE (one month). Menahem ascended the throne in 747 BCE and died in 738 BCE (ten years). Pekahiah succeeded to his father's throne in 738 BCE and was killed in 737 BCE (two years). Pekah seized the throne in 737 BCE and ruled until 731/730 BCE (eight years). The twenty years ascribed to Pekah's reign remain problematic; the chronographer(s) seems to have dated Pekah's enthronement to 750 BCE for unknown reasons.[11] Hoshea was the king of Israel from 731/730 to 723/722 BCE (nine years).

The above chronology leaves some problems with the Judahite kings' synchronisms after Azariah.[12] At any event, the range of error should remain marginal within the chronological anchor points. Thus, it suffices for dating events in the time of the Jehuite Dynasty (Table 2).

King	Year (BCE)	Length of Reign
Jehu	841-814	28 years
Joahaz	814-798	17 years
Joash	799/798-784	16 years
Jeroboam II	788/787-748	41 years
Zechariah	748-747	6 months

Table 2. Chronology of the Jehuite Kings

---

11 Various solutions have been suggested for the twenty years ascribed to Pekah. For the earlier literature, see Na'aman 1986: 75, nn. 9-10. Na'aman (*op. cit.*, 74-82) suggested that Pekah considered himself as a legitimate successor of the Jehuite Dynasty and hence counted the beginning of his rule from the end of the Jehuite Dynasty.

12 Using synchronistic data, the reigns of the Judahite kings will be dated as follows: Athaliah: 841-835 (seven years); Jehoash: 835–797 (forty years); Amaziah: 797–769 (twenty-nine years, including one year of co-regency with Jehoash); Azariah: 785–734/733 (fifty-two years, including sixteen years of co-regency with Amaziah and eight years co-regency with Jotham); Jotham: 751/750–732/731 (sixteen years, including sixteen years co-regency with Azariah and excluding four years of co-regency with Ahaz); Ahaz: 735/734–717/716 (sixteen years, excluding four years co-regency with Jotham); and Hezekiah: 728/727–688/687 (twenty-nine years, including twelve years co-regency with Ahaz). This calculation results in a double co-regency in 735/734–733/732 BCE between Azariah, Jotham, and Ahaz. It also means that Jotham never ruled alone but always had a co-regent or two.

2. The Rise of Jehu (841 BCE)

Four types of textual sources are available for Jehu's rise: (1) the biblical text; (2) Shalmaneser III's inscriptions; (3) the Mesha Inscription; and (4) the Tel Dan Inscription. The biblical text describes in detail Jehu's coup d'état and his extermination of the Baal cult. Shalmaneser III's texts describe the Assyrian western campaigns and Jehu's tribute in 841 BCE. The Mesha Inscription mentions the fall of the Omride Dynasty and the Tel Dan Inscription refers to the author's killing of Joram. These sources were composed from different perspectives and for different purposes. The Bible stresses Jehu's religious devotion to YHWH, which is reflected in his expulsion of the Baal cult in the Northern Kingdom. The Assyrian texts mention Jehu as a tributary king of Shalmaneser III. The Mesha Inscription emphasises Mesha's deeds in contrast to his predecessor's. The Tel Dan Inscription aggrandises the Aramaean victory over Israel and Judah. Due to these differences, each source must first be examined individually and then carefully compared in order to illuminate the historical background for Jehu's rise to power.

2.1. The Jehu Narrative (2 Kgs 9-10)

The rise of Jehu as described in 2 Kgs 9-10 may be presented in five parts: (1) the anointment of Jehu (9:1-13); (2) the conspiracy of Jehu against Joram (vv. 14-16); (3) the murders of Joram (vv. 17-26), Ahaziah of Judah (vv. 27-29), and Jezebel (vv. 30-37); (4) the massacre of the Omride descendants by Jehu (10:1-17); and (5) the extermination of the Baal cult (vv. 18-28). The narrative will be called "Jehu Narrative" (henceforth JN) in the present study.

Omitting the last part (10:29-36), these two chapters, often including 8:28-29, have been included widely in a story complex – the Elisha Cycle stories (1 Kgs 19:19-21; 2 Kgs 2-13).[1] The Elisha Cycle stories relate the deeds of Elisha, a major prophet in the Northern Kingdom. This categorisation is based on the mention of Elisha in 9:1-3, the scene where Elisha orders his disciple to anoint Jehu as the king of Israel. However, this narrative (8:28-10:28) cannot be classified with the other stories as Elisha Cycle stories, where Elisha plays a major role.[2] Elisha

---

1   Benzinger 1899: 129; Eissfeldt 1965: 292.
2   Šanda 1912: 122-123; Montgomery 1951: 399-400; Rofé 1988: 82.

appears only at the beginning of the story and his role is marginal. Hence, the JN will be regarded as an independent story, detached from the Elisha Cycle stories.

Reconstruction of the original story, which was available to the Dtr, is indispensable for the historical analysis of the narrative. The JN can be divided into three redaction layers: (1) text available to the Dtr (henceforth as a layer, pre-Dtr layer, and as an independent story, OJN = Original Jehu Narrative); (2) text that the Dtr wrote and inserted into his source (henceforth Dtr layer or Dtr redaction); (3) later insertions possibly dated either to the Exilic or post-Exilic period.[3]

It is assumed that the pre-Dtr layer bears more authentic information about Jehu's rise. As suggested below (2.1.2.1.), the OJN was probably composed, at the latest, in the early eighth century BCE, still under the Jehuite Dynasty. The assumed time of composition was thus more than 100 years earlier than the Dtr's time.

2.1.1. The OJN and Dtr's Redaction

I will open the discussion by reconstructing the OJN, which the Dtr integrated into his composition. The literary-critical approach helps in discerning different redaction layers in a text. Phrases that employ Dtr's style, language, and theology should be isolated within the JN.[4] Since similar linguistic features alone cannot be decisive factors for grouping a text into multiple layers, the division of the text into redactional layers will be conducted with caution. Redaction layers will be determined only when the underlying coherent theology is distinctly perceived. The following reconstruction may sometimes appear arbitrary, and there admittedly may be different ways in isolating the OJN, yet the emerged OJN shows coherence in literary theme and tendencies (2.1.1.17., 2.1.2.1.).

2.1.1.1. Dtr's Redaction of the Scene of Jehu's Anointment (9:6b-10a)

The passage in vv. 6b-10a is included within the words spoken by Elisha's disciple when he anoints Jehu. The disciple does not follow Elisha's instructions (9:1b-3aαb), which require him to "flee" and not to "linger" after anointing Jehu (v. 3). This incongruence suggests the Dtr's insertions of the two phrases, "God of Israel" and "over the people of YHWH" in v. 6b. Vv. 7-10a, prophesying annihi-

---

3   Possible layers within the OJN are beyond the scope of the present study. It is difficult to establish such multiple layers in the OJN as some scholars, such as Mulzer (1992), did. Otto's suggestion (2001: 55-64, 113, 119-141; 2003: 493-494) that a pre-Dtr editing (called the "Naboth Edition" = 9:21b, 25-27) can be discerned in the OJN is a possibility, but this editing does not affect the aim of the present study.

4   For example, see Burney 1903: xiii-xiv.

lation of the House of Ahab and Jezebel's end, likewise should be excluded from the pre-Dtr layer.[5] Vv. 7b and 10a are denunciations of Jezebel, while vv. 7a, 8-9 are condemnations of the entire House of Ahab. Due to the repeated changes both in the subject and of the target of the disaster, most scholars regarded vv. 7b and 10a as later interpolations, independent of vv. 6b-10 by the Dtr.[6] However, v. 10a can be ascribed to the Dtr redaction together with vv. 7a, 8-9, for they are all based on the story of Naboth's vineyard (1 Kgs 21). V. 7b alone may be a later interpolation, which connects the JN to the story of the extermination of prophets in 1 Kgs 18-19 (Otto 2001: 42-43).[7] By the exclusion of v. 7b, vv. 6b-10a become equivalent to 1 Kgs 21:21-23. The Dtr interpolated these verses in order to connect Jehu's coup to the Elijah Cycle story in 1 Kgs 21, and also to juxtapose the denunciations of Ahab, Jeroboam, and Baasha.

2.1.1.2. The Original Introduction of the JN (8:28-29 vs. 9:14-16)

There are verbatim correspondences between 2 Kgs 8:29a and 2 Kgs 9:15a, and between 8:29b and 9:16b. This fact has led scholars to discuss the original introduction of the JN. Although it is unanimously agreed that at least one of the passages is a secondary insertion to the OJN, the dating of each passage (8:28-29 and 9:14-16) is a matter of controversy.[8] In what follows, the dates of each passage and the literary relations between the two will be examined. First, the two passages are presented.

2 Kgs 8:28-29

וילך את־יורם בן־אחאב למלחמה עם־חזהאל מלך־ארם ברמת גלעד ויכו ארמים את־יורם:
וישב יורם המלך להתרפא ביזרעאל מן־המכים אשר יכהו ארמים ברמה בהלחמו את־חזהאל
מלך ארם ואחזיהו בן־יהורם מלך יהודה ירד לראות את־יורם בן־אחאב ביזרעאל כי־חלה הוא:

2 Kgs 9:14b, 15a, 16aβb

ויורם היה שמר ברמת גלעד הוא וכל־ישראל מפני חזאל מלך־ארם: וישב יהורם המלך
להתרפא ביזרעאל מן־המכים אשר יכהו ארמים בהלחמו את־חזאל מלך ארם כי יורם שכב
שמה ואחזיה מלך יהודה ירד לראות את־יורם:

---

5   Barré 1988: 9, n. 27; Minokami 1989: 53-55; Otto 2001: 41, n. 50 with earlier literature. Noth (1967: 104) suggested that vv. 8b, 9, and 10a are repetitions of 1 Kgs 21:21-22a and 2 Kgs 9:36.

6   Würthwein 1984: 325; Campbell 1986: 36-41; Barré 1988: 11; Minokami 1989: 53-55; Otto 2001: 42, n. 58 with earlier literature.

7   There is a close similarity between 2 Kgs 9:16a and 1 Kgs 18:45b. These two passages are the same except for the subject (Ben-Ruven 2004). 2 Kgs 9:16a: וירכב יהוא וילך יזרעאלה; 1 Kgs 18:45b: וירכב אחאב וילך יזרעאלה. Na'aman (2008: 205) ascribed the latter to an editorial statement.

8   A brief history of the discussion is found in Barré 1988: 11-13; Long 1991: 114-117.

Some scholars suggested that the OJN begins at 2 Kgs 8:28 (not at 9:1), and that 2 Kgs 9:14-16 is secondary for the following two reasons.[9] (1) 9:14-15a interrupts the flow of the story between vv. 13 and 15b. (2) The literary style of 9:14-15a is different from the rest of the JN (Schmitt 1972: 23).[10]

Minokami (1989: 23-29) and Otto (2001: 48), on the contrary, regarded 2 Kgs 8:28b-29 as secondary and suggested that they were composed by the Dtr based on 2 Kgs 9:15a, 16aβb.[11] In a close comparison of the two passages, Otto (*op. cit.*, 47-50) noted the following observations. (1) The spellings of the two kings' names, Joram (יורם) of Israel and Jehoram (יהורם) of Judah, are clearly differentiated in 8:28-29, whereas Joram of Israel is spelled in both forms (יהורם/יורם) in 9:15-16. (2) The filiations of the two kings (Joram and Ahaziah) are precisely mentioned in 8:28-29, in contrast to 9:15-16. (3) The phrase "כי־חולה הוא" in 8:29 has no equivalence in 9:15-16, which probably shows Dtr's tendency to exactness in the former passage. (4) Information about the Aramaean strike of Joram is repeated in 8:28-29,[12] which possibly indicates that the two verses derived from the same source (9:15). It is therefore suggested that 8:28-29, which is a verbatim repetition of 9:15, was composed by the Dtr.[13]

It is notable that 8:28-29 is written in a style similar to that of the so-called "short report" (1 Kgs 16:24; 2 Kgs 8:20-22; 15:10, 14, 19-20, 25; 16:5-18; 17:3-8;

---

9   Würthwein 1984: 328; Mulzer 1992: 215-222. Minokami 1989: 26-29, 69; Long 1991: 114; Mulzer 1992: 219, n. 22; Otto 2001: 47, n. 90; 66; Lehnart 2003: 402, n. 135 with earlier literature. Mulzer (*op. cit.*, 218-222) and Schmitt (1972: 23-24) suggested that 2 Kgs 9:14b-15a, 16aβb are secondary, because the style of vv. 14-15a does not agree with the rest of the JN.

10   Otto (2001: 47) rejected this assumption for the following two reasons. (1) A verb without היה rarely begins a biblical narrative (8:28), especially pre-Exilic narratives from the Northern Kingdom (Gross 1981: 135, n. 13). (2) 8:28-29 concerns neither the theme of the JN nor Jehu, but Joram (Otto, *op. cit.*, 47 with n. 98).

11   Benzinger 1899: 149; Šanda 1912: 95, 121; Montgomery 1951: 396, 400; Noth 1967: 83-84; Steck 1968: 32-33, nn. 1-2; Gray 1977: 543-544; Timm 1982: 138; Campbell 1986: 22, n. 8. Minokami (1989: 26-29) ascribed 2 Kgs 9:14b, 15a, and 15aβ to later insertions. Kittel (1900: 231) suggested that 2 Kgs 9:14a is a redactional insertion. Trebolle Barrera (1984: 122-125, 185-189), comparing the text with the Lucianic recension and Old Latin text, identified v. 14b as Dtr's insertion and suggested that v. 15a was moved from 9:16a (see McKenzie 1991: 71-73). For earlier literature of this theory, see Mulzer 1992: 219, n. 22.

12   ויכו ארמים את־יורם in v. 28 and יכהו ארמים in v. 29.

13   The reference to רמה in 8:29, in contrast to רמת גלעד in 9:14, is exceptional for the Dtr's tendency to relate geographical information precisely. This might show the possibility that the Dtr used another source besides 9:14-16 (Otto 2001: 49-50). The situations in 8:28a and 9:14b are also different. In the former, Ahaziah went to Ramoth-Gilead to fight against Hazael, king of Aram, whereas in the latter, Joram had been on guard at Ramoth-Gilead against Hazael. Otto (*op. cit.*, 50) suggested that this difference reflects two distinct sources for both verses: 8:28a on the basis of the Judahite Chronicle and 9:14b on the basis of the JN. She (*op. cit.*, 50, n. 116) assumed that the situation, in which Ramoth-Gilead belongs to Israel, possibly reflects the territorial situation under Jeroboam II.

21:23-24; 23:33-35; 24:1-2, 10-17).[14] The short report adds historical information on kings to the schematic introductory and closing formulae. These reports are considered to be based on historical sources that were available to the Dtr.[15] This hypothesis is supported by the following fact: 8:28 describes Ahaziah's participation in the battle against Aramaeans. On the other hand, 9:14-16, referring only to Ahaziah's visit to Jezreel, creates an impression that Ahaziah did not participate in the battle (2.1.2.2.2.1). It seems, therefore, that 8:28 is not a complete invention of the Dtr, but rather based on a historical source, most likely a Judahite Chronicle (Otto 2001: 50). By using such a source, the Dtr composed 8:28-29 in order to connect the royal formula of Ahaziah (2 Kgs 8:25-27) to the beginning of the JN (9:1).

The origin of 9:14a has also been discussed. Some scholars regarded the verse as a later interpolation (Kittel 1900: 227-278; Schmitt 1972: 22-23).[16] Long (1991: 117), on the other hand, interpreted v. 14a as "a conventional introduction to the report of conspiracy which follows". He cited the following passages as parallels: 1 Kgs 15:27-30; 16:9-13; 2 Kgs 15:10, 14, 25, 30; and 21:23.[17] However, there are two stylistic differences between 2 Kgs 9:14a and the cited verses. (1) 2 Kgs 9:14a, unlike in the cited verses, employs the hithpaʿel form of the verb קשר. (2) 2 Kgs 9:14a, in contrast with the other reports (1 Kgs 15:27b; 16:9b, and 15b), employs היה to describe the circumstances of the coup (Schmitt, *op. cit.*, 23-24). These differences may indicate that v. 14a was a later interpolation.[18]

It was suggested above that both 2 Kgs 9:14b-15a and 16aβb describe the background for Jehu's coup and were a possible source for 8:28-29. The date of these verses and their function in the OJN will be investigated in the following

---

14   Hoffmann 1980: 33-38; Otto 2001: 48, n. 107.

15   Montgomery (1934; 1951: 33-37) suggested that these reports derived from certain archival sources. Yet, his assumption (1951: 34) that time-expressions, such as בימיו, אז etc. go back to the archival source cannot be supported. Cf. Naʾaman 2002a: 88-90.

16   Schmitt (1972: 23-24), pointing to the stylistic similarity of v. 14a to the other reports on the revolts in the Northern Kingdom, ascribed these verses to the annalistic redaction, which is later than the Dtr redaction. Be that as it may, his ascription of the phrase כל-ישראל to the same redaction (*op. cit.*, 23, n. 38) should be rejected. This expression also appears in other verses (1 Kgs 12:1, 16, 18; 2 Kgs 3:6), which are not formulated in annalistic style. Gray (1977: 541) and Hentschel (1985: 39) regarded v. 14a as a concluding verse of 9:1-13, derived from a "prophetic source".

17   Otto (2001: 66-67), likewise pointing to the common conspiracy motif in 9:14a and 10:9, rejected the Dtr's authorship of v. 14a. Although her ascription of v. 14a to a pre-Dtr source is legitimised, only one single common word (verb קשר), which appears in a different form in each verse (in hithpaʿel in 9:14a and in qal in 10:9), is a weak ground for attributing the two verses to the same redactor. Minokami (1989: 26-29, 69) and Mulzer (1992: 215-219) ascribed even v. 16aβ (together with 14b and 15a) to a secondary interpolation; yet, this theory cannot explain the reason for the addition of the verse. See Otto, *op. cit.*, 67, n. 241.

18   Otto 2001: 66-67.

paragraphs.[19] The integrality of vv. 14b-15a and 16aβb to the OJN is self-evident,[20] and vv. 14-15a were widely thought to be the original introduction of the OJN,[21] which was initially located before 9:1.[22] Although vv. 14-15a interrupt the course of the narrative between vv. 13 and 15b,[23] they do not fit well in the position before 9:1 either.[24] It is thus assumed that 9:14b-15a and 16aβb were based on another unknown source and were integrated by the Dtr to explain the reason for Jehu's advance toward Jezreel.

2.1.1.3. The Anointment of Jehu as Integral Part of the OJN (9:1-13)

The entire passage of 2 Kgs 9:1-13 is usually regarded as secondary because the passage interrupts the course of the narrative between 8:28-29 and 9:14a.[25] However, the verses employ stylistic and thematic elements common to the rest of the narrative.[26] Hence, most of 9:1-13 (9:1-6a, 7b, and 10b-13) constitutes an integral part of the OJN. Only 9:6b-7a and 8-10a can be ascribed safely to the Dtr Redaction.[27] This conclusion conforms well to the hypothetical provenance of the OJN in the court of the Jehuite Dynasty (2.1.2.1.).

---

19 Minokami (1989: 67-95) attributed 9:15b, 16b, 21bα1*, 23b, 27; 10:4-6, 13-14bα to a Judahite editing. However, this editing cannot be clearly perceived. Cf. Otto 2001: 70-71.

20 Otto 2001: 67; Lehnart 2003: 403-404.

21 Otto 2001: 66, n. 229.

22 *Contra* Steck 1968: 32-33, n. 2.

23 Benzinger 1899: 149; Kittel 1900: 230-231; Šanda 1912: 94, 121; Gunkel 1913: 290; Montgomery 1951: 400; Gray 1977: 543-544; Barré 1988: 12.

24 Some scholars suggested that these verses stemmed from a much longer version of the OJN and afterwards the Dtr moved/incorporated them here to explain the reason behind Jehu's advance to Jezreel (Noth 1967: 84; Cogan and Tadmor 1988: 108-109; Otto 2001: 66-68).

25 Würthwein 1984: 328-330; Benzinger 1899: 149; Gray 1977: 537. See Otto 2001: 64, n. 215 with further literature. Cf. Dietrich 1972: 103-109.

26 Olyan (1984: 653) pointed to a "*Leitwort*" – defined as the intentional and multiple rendering of a word in order to accentuate a motif within a text – of the JN – שלום. The word also appears in v. 11. Otto (2001: 64) pointed to another possible *Leitwort* שׁעט of the JN in vv. 11 and 20. Furthermore, she (*op. cit.*, 65, with n. 227) pointed to the same inversed style of verbal clause (9:11, 30b; 10:13), which begins new episodes. According to Eskhult (1990: 50-55), this style appears in the pre-Exilic narratives originating in the Northern Kingdom.

27 McKenzie (1991: 70-71) ascribed vv. 7a, 8-9 to the Dtr and 7b, 10a to a later editor.

2.1.1.4. Naboth's Murder as Legitimisation of Joram's Murder in the OJN (9:21b and 25-26)

The verses, legitimising Joram's murder by Jehu as retribution for Naboth's bloody murder by Ahab, have usually been regarded as part of the OJN.[28] On the other hand, some scholars excluded these verses from the OJN, since 9:25-26 interrupt the flow of the narrative between Joram's murder (v. 24) and Ahaziah's flight (v. 27).[29] In addition to vv. 25-26, v. 21b "they met him at the property of Naboth the Jezreelite", which sets the background for this event in vv. 25-26, has likewise been excluded from the OJN.[30] However, there is no consensus among scholars in terms of division and dating of these verses.[31]

Naboth's murder by Ahab is described in detail in 1 Kgs 21, which is probably a pre-deuteronomistic composition (Otto 2001: 138-143; Pruin 2007: 212; Na'aman 2008: 199-204).[32] This story and the mention of Naboth's murder in 2 Kgs 9:21b, 25-26, despite their similarities, seem to reflect two distinct traditions of the same event (Na'aman, *op. cit.*, 212-213). Thus, knowledge of the story in 1 Kgs 21 need not be presupposed for the composition of 2 Kgs 9:21b, 25-26.[33] The function of the verses is to legitimate Jehu's killing of his lord. It conforms well to the fundamental characters and the raison d'être of the OJN to justify Jehu's rebellion (2.1.2.1.). Therefore, I suggest ascribing vv. 21b, 25-26 to the pre-Dtr author.[34]

---

28   Noth 1967: 84; Montgomery 1951: 402; Dietrich 1972: 50; Olyan 1984: 657-659; Lehnart 2003: 404-405.

29   Schmitt 1972: 25-27; Minokami 1989: 34-43; McKenzie 1991: 73-74; Mulzer 1992: 233-236.

30   The double mention of "kings' sortie" in v. 21 seems redundant. The verb יצא appears twice here: ויצא יהורם מלך־ישראל ואחזיהו מלך־יהודה איש ברכבו ויצאו לקראת יהוא. Cf. Würthwein 1984: 332-333; Minokami 1989: 39; Otto 2001: 56.

31   There are three major views as to the dating of these verses: (1) pre-Dtr (Steck 1968: 33-34; 44-46; Schmitt 1972: 25-27; Bohlen 1978: 282-284; Otto 2001: 55-64); (2) Dtr (Whitley 1952: 148-149; Miller 1967: 314-317; Timm 1982: 141; Na'aman 1997a: 167); and (3) post-Dtr (Würthwein 1984: 332-333; Minokami 1989: 34-42; Mulzer 1992: 302). Olyan (1984: 657-659) regarded v. 26 as an integral part of the OJN because it explains the reason for Joram's death. On the other hand, Otto (*op. cit.*, 56) regarded it as an unnecessary explanation because Jehu is the king anointed by YHWH (9:3, 6, and 12) and thus it is clear that disqualified Joram must die before Jehu, the newly anointed king.

32   Some scholars, on the contrary, suggested that the narrative was a later composition (Rofé 1988: 97-100; Blum 2000: 114-123). For the criticism of this theory, see Na'aman 2008: 200-203.

33   These similarities are enumerated in Na'aman 2008: 212.

34   Whether these verses were integrated into the OJN by a pre-Dtr editor (or editors) is not my concern here. Cf. Otto 2001: 55-64, 113, 119-141; 2003: 493-494.

2.1.1.5. Dtr's Interpolation of the Description of Ahaziah's Burial into the OJN (9:27bβ-29)

V. 28 describes the transfer of Ahaziah's corpse from Megiddo to Jerusalem and its subsequent burial there.[35] The verse has been ascribed to the Dtr, who connects the JN to the reign of Ahaziah of Judah.[36] V. 29 synchronises Ahaziah's reign to Joram's eleventh year.[37] As such, 9:28-29 mention the events in Judah and thus seem to be unnecessary in the OJN, which mainly concerns incidents in the Northern Kingdom.

The expression "they buried him in his tomb with his ancestors in the city of David" (v. 28) is a typical Dtr formula employed for concluding passages of the Judahite kings, and can thus safely be ascribed to the Dtr.

According to the Book of Kings, the Judahite kings were commonly buried in Jerusalem. Even the bodies of kings who died outside Jerusalem were carried back to the city for burial.[38] Hence, burying the king's corpse in Jerusalem must have been important for the author.

The linguistic and stylistic similarity between the three verses (vv. 27bβ-29) is hardly a coincidence. The Dtr, who worked in the late seventh century BCE, was familiar with Josiah's death at Megiddo and the transfer of his corpse to Jerusalem, but not with the murder of Ahaziah, which happened more than 200 years earlier.[39] It is therefore assumed that 2 Kgs 9:28 was composed by the Dtr, who was inspired by 2 Kgs 23:30a; or alternatively, that both 2 Kgs 9:28 and 2 Kgs 23:30a were the Dtr's composition.[40]

Likewise, the mention of Megiddo in v. 27bβ is probably an interpolation by the Dtr, who might have felt it necessary to insert an appropriate city here, where loyal Judahite servants were present to transfer Ahaziah's corpse to Jerusalem.

---

35 The plot of a Judahite king dying in Megiddo, being transported to Jerusalem, and then being buried there shows striking resemblance to that of Josiah's death (2 Kgs 23:30). For this reason, Barré (1988: 15) suggested that vv. 27bβ and 28 were dependent on the account of Josiah's death, and that they were inserted by a post-Dtr editor.

36 Barré 1988: 15, n. 51; Otto 2001: 50-51, n.121 with earlier literature. On the other hand, Schmitt (1972: 24) regarded this verse as a post-Dtr addition. See also Barré 1988: 15, 31. McKenzie (1991: 74-75) ascribed vv. 27b-29 to a post-Dtr editor.

37 It contradicts 8:26, which dates it to Joram's twelfth year (Noth 1967: 84, n. 2).

38 Examples include Jehoash (2 Kgs 12:21-22, although the verses do not contain a description of transferring the body), Amaziah (2 Kgs 14:19-20), and Josiah (2 Kgs 23:29-30).

39 The hypothesis of the double redaction of the Dtr History, which was suggested by Cross (1973), is adopted in the present study. According to the theory, the Dtr History was first redacted in Josiah's reign and then, in the Exilic period. For a new, strong view on the date and the extent of the composition of the Deuteronomistic work, see Kratz 2000; Witte 2005: 68-70.

40 The difference between the two verses is the forms of verbs. In 2 Kgs 9:28, the verbs accompany with direct object marker את, while in 2 Kgs 23:30a, the verbs are with the object suffix of the third person masculine singular הו-.

The selection of Megiddo could have been inspired by the description of Josiah's death at Megiddo (2 Kgs 23:29-30) and by its geographical proximity to the place of the event.[41]

V. 29, on the other hand, cannot be ascribed to the Dtr. This verse lacks typical formulaic elements, such as the mention of source and the king's successor.[42] Contradictory information on Ahaziah's reign in 2 Kgs 8:25 and in 9:29 indicates that 9:29 was inserted after the Dtr's framing of the JN.[43]

2.1.1.6. Jezebel's Death as Fulfilment of Elijah's Prophecy (9:36, 37)

The passage 9:36, 37 is Jehu's speech announcing that Elijah's prophecy concerning Jezebel's death (1 Kgs 21:23b) has been fulfilled. The passage interrupts the course of the story (Minokami 1989: 59-60; Mulzer 1992: 238-243; Otto 2001: 44-45). Despite small differences, 2 Kgs 9:36 and 1 Kgs 21:23b evidently refer to the same prophecy.[44] Considering the Dtr's intention to connect the JN with the prophecy of the annihilation of the House of Ahab (2.1.1.1.), it seems that v. 36 was a Dtr's interpolation.[45] This assumption is supported by a close similarity between v. 36 and 9:10, which is ascribed to the Dtr.[46]

V. 37 is the continuance of Jehu's speech citing another prophecy concerning Jezebel's corpse. Yet, the cited prophecy is missing in the Book of Kings. Some scholars ascribed v. 37, which is an explanation of v. 36, also to the Dtr,[47] while others regarded it as a later interpolation.[48] Due to its lexical similarity to Jer 8:2; 9:21; 16:4; 25:33, the latter view seems to be more plausible.

---

41   Otto 2001: 76, n. 296. It is worth noting that Amaziah's flight to Lachish is also described with
      the same verb in the same form "וינס" (2 Kgs 14:19). This similarity between 2 Kgs 9:27 and
      14:19 may suggest that "וינס" in 9:27 is also a Dtr's interpolation.

42   In a schematic frame, synchronism is generally positioned in the opening formula and not in the
      concluding. For earlier literature, see Otto 2001: 51-52, nn. 127, 129.

43   The synchronistic data in 8:25 is corrected here based on the following calculation. Joram died in
      his twelfth year of reign (2 Kgs 3:1) and Ahaziah died at the same time. Since Ahaziah reigned
      for one year (2 Kgs 8:26), Ahaziah's enthronement was dated to Joram's eleventh year. Otto
      2001: 52, n. 131 with earlier literature.

44   2 Kgs 9:36 reads: וישבו ויגידו לו ויאמר דבר־יהוה הוא אשר דבר ביד־עבדו אליהו התשבי לאמר בחלק
      יזרעאל יאכלו הכלבים את־בשר איזבל .1 Kgs 21:23 reads: ואת־איזבל יאכלו הכלבים לאמר יהוה דבר וגם־לאיזבל
      את־איזבל בחל יזרעאל.

45   Dietrich 1972: 60; Schmitt 1972: 21-23; Timm 1982: 137-138. See Otto 2001: 44, n. 74 for earlier
      literature. McKenzie (1991: 75-76) ascribed vv. 36, 37 to the Dtr but vv. 36aβ and 36b to a
      post-Dtr editor.

46   2 Kgs 9:10 reads: ואת־איזבל יאכלו הכלבים בחלק יזרעאל ואין קבר.

47   Steck 1968: 36-38, 40; Schmitt 1972: 21-23. Minokami 1989: 59-62 ascribed v. 36a to the Dtr,
      and vv. 36b-37 to a later editor.

48   Würthwein 1984: 334; Mulzer 1992: 240-242; Otto 2001: 45. Barré (1988: 16) attributed only v.
      36 to a later redactor.

2.1.1.7. Overlapped Information on Those Who Rear Ahab's Sons in Samaria (10:1a, 6b)

Both verses refer to the people in Samaria who reared the seventy sons of Ahab. A repetition of information was recognised by early scholars,[49] and some excluded the verses from the OJN.[50] However, v. 1a is consistent with the following story, and it is thus unnecessary to delete it from the OJN (Otto 2001: 68).

V. 6b, on the other hand, is possibly a gloss because it is a repetition of the information in 10:1, 2. Additionally, there is inconsistency between v. 1 and v. 6b: in v. 1, the "sons of Ahab" stayed at the "guardians of Ahab" (האמנים אחאב), whereas in v. 6b, they stayed with the "elders of the city" (גדלי־העיר).[51]

2.1.1.8. Dtr's Interpolation of Jehu's Speech (10:10)

Jehu's proclamation of the fulfilment of YHWH's word (10:10) is an interpolation conveying a theological message to the reader.[52] The lexical similarity of the phrase לא יפל מדבר ה' ארצה to the typical Dtr phrase in 1 Kgs 8:56; Jos 21:43; 23:14 suggests Dtr's authorship.[53]

2.1.1.9. Jehu's Extermination of Ahab's House (10:11)

The verse, describing Jehu's massacre of the House of Ahab in Jezreel, can also be ascribed to the Dtr. The characteristic Dtr phrase עד־בלתי השאיר־לו שריד supports its Dtr origin.[54]

---

49   Benzinger 1899: 152. For earlier literature, see Barré 1988: 17, n. 63.

50   Most scholars regarded v. 1a as a later gloss due to the mention of Ahab instead of Joram (Montgomery 1951: 413; Schmitt 1972: 230, n. 210; Würthwein 1984: 335; Barré 1988: 17). On the other hand, Minokami (1989: 55-56) and McKenzie (1991: 76) ascribed it to the Dtr.

51   See Otto 2001: 68 with n. 249 for earlier literature.

52   Steck 1968: 40; Schmitt 1972: 22; Timm 1982: 137-138; Würthwein 1984: 338; Hentschel 1985: 46; Barré 1988: 17-18; Minokami 1989: 62-64. For earlier literature, see Otto 2001: 45, n. 81. Mulzer (1992: 246) suggested that v. 10 consists of two chronologically different parts: vv. 10a and 10b.

53   Burney 1903: 126; Schmitt 1972: 22, n. 30; Weinfeld 1972: 21-23, 350; Otto 2001: 45-46.

54   Schmitt 1972: 23; Sekine 1975: 55; Timm 1982: 135; Würthwein 1984: 337; Barré 1988: 17; Otto 2001: 46, n. 86. See Otto, *op. cit.*, 46-47, n. 89 for earlier literature.

2.1.1.10. The Murder of Ahaziah's Brothers and Jehu's Encounter with Jehonadab (10:12aβ*-16)

The passage can be divided into two parts. The first part (vv. 12aβ*-14) describes the massacre of Ahaziah's relatives. The second part (vv. 15-16) relates Jehu's encounter with Jehonadab, the Rechabite. Most scholars have regarded the passage as secondary.[55] However, Otto (2001: 69) pointed out a thematic coherence in the passage, which may show that vv. 12aβ*-16 is an integral part of the OJN.[56] Since no substantial ground for regarding the passage as a later interpolation has been provided, I would like to follow Otto's view and ascribe the passage to the OJN.[57]

2.1.1.11. Jehu's March to Samaria (10:12aα*, 17aα)

With the exclusion of 10:12aβ*-16 from the OJN, the story relates Jehu's advance toward Samaria (10:12aα*, 17aα), immediately after his annihilation of Ahab's descendants in Jezreel. Hence, some of the scholars who regarded 10:12aβ*-16 as secondary, suggested that 10:12aα*, 17aα are the conclusion of the OJN.[58] However, the following points attest that the OJN does not end with 10:12aα*, 17aα. (1) The end of the story must include the scene of the extermination of the Baal cult (10:18-28), for this is one of the primary themes of the OJN.[59] (2) A biblical narrative does not end with the expression "and he went/came toward ... (ויבא)" (10:12aα*, 17aα). Hence, this phrase is used as a binder between the two individual scenes.[60]

---

55 Stade 1885: 276-278; Schmitt 1972: 25; Würthwein 1984: 338-339; Barré 1988: 18-20; Minokami 1989: 67-95; McKenzie 1991: 76-78.

56 The coherence can be found in the following three points. (1) In v. 13, the *Leitwort* שלם and a reference to Jezebel appear, as in 9:22, 31. (2) In vv. 15-16, Jehu is described as a rebel looking for an ally, as in 9:15b, 32, and 10:6a. (3) Vv. 15-16 are thematically connected with 10:17aα, 18-28, where the "eradication of Baal cult" is the main theme. Schmitt (1972: 28-29) also reached the same conclusion. Mulzer (1992: 253-261), on the other hand, distinguished only ויבא in v. 12 and v. 14bβ as gloss.

57 Šanda 1911: 110; Steck 1968: 61. Barré (1988: 20) suggested that vv. 15-16 was inserted by the Dtr.

58 Würthwein 1984: 338; Minokami 1989: 96-97, 130. McKenzie ascribed vv. 18-28 to the Dtr.

59 Mulzer 1992: 271-273; Otto 2001: 71-72

60 Otto 2001: 72.

2.1.1.12. The Annihilation of Ahab's Descendants (10:17aβb)

The verse describes Jehu's annihilation of Ahab's descendants. Its thematic resemblance to 9:7-10 and formulaic similarity to v. 11a attest to Dtr's authorship.[61]

2.1.1.13. Jehu's Intention to Destroy Baal's Worshippers (10:19b)

The passage explains Jehu's concealed intention to destroy the worshippers of Baal, and interrupts the story related in 10:17-25a. The phrase, "in order to destroy the worshippers of Baal", indicates its Dtr origin.[62] This part was possibly inserted to defend Jehu from reproach, for he declares his intention to serve the Baal more than Ahab (v. 18).[63]

2.1.1.14. Jehu's Invitation to the Baal Cult Sent throughout Israel (10:21aα)

The part, "then Jehu sent throughout Israel", an invitation to the worshippers of Baal, can be ascribed to the Dtr, whose intention was to stress that Jehu's cult reform was not limited to Samaria but was carried out all over Israel. This statement is consistent with v. 28, which can also be ascribed to the Dtr.[64]

2.1.1.15. The Eradication of Baal's Cult (10:25b-27)

The passage describes Jehu's eradication of Baal's cult. An etiological note in 10:27b – "and made it (the house of Baal) a latrine to this day" – does not seem to be the original end of the OJN. A close similarity between the verses 10:18-25a

---

61 Schmitt 1972: 22; Timm 1982: 137-138; Würthwein 1984: 338; Hentschel 1985: 48; Barré 1988: 20, 33; Minokami 1989: 56-57; Otto 2001: 46. The following three points attest that v. 17aβb does not belong to the OJN: (1) repetitious reference to Samaria in 17aα and 17aβ; (2) a Dtr's theme "extermination of the House of Ahab (cf. 1 Kgs 15:29; 16:11)"; and (3) the second reference to the extermination of Ahab's family (already in 10:1-11). In contrast, Dietrich (1972:24, 61) regarded v. 17aβ as part of the OJN and ascribed only v. 17b to the Dtr.

62 Barré 1988: 20-21; Otto 2001: 55. For the Dtr phraseology of the verse, see Weinfeld 1972: 346-347. Some scholars regarded v. 19b as a later gloss (Schmitt 1972: 24-27; Sekine 1975: 56; Mulzer 1992: 262-267). Minokami (1989: 113-114, 116-117) regarded it as part of the OJN.

63 Otto 2001: 55. Schmitt (1972: 24-27) ascribed it to the apologetic editing that pre-dates the Dtr. See also, Sekine 1975: 56; Würthwein 1984: 340. Mulzer (1992: 261-267), on the other hand, regarded 10:19b, 20, 21aα as secondary gloss.

64 Otto 2001: 55. For the view that regards v. 21aα as secondary, see Otto, *op. cit.*, 55, n. 159 with earlier literature. Minokami (1989: 114) included it in the OJN. For the ascription of 10:28 to the Dtr, see 2.1.1.16.

and 2 Kgs 23 has been pointed out (Hoffmann 1980: 97-104).[65] The former describes Jehu's cult reform and the latter describes that of Josiah of Judah. The
verbs used in 10:26, 27 are typical Dtr vocabulary, employed for describing destruction of cult places and cult objects: שרף in v. 26 and נתץ in v. 27.[66] Therefore,
vv. 10:25b-27 can be ascribed to the Dtr.[67]

2.1.1.16. The Conclusion of the OJN (2 Kgs 10:28)

The verse "thus Jehu eradicated Baal out of Israel" was ascribed by some scholars
to the Dtr,[68] while by others to the OJN.[69] I follow the second view, since no
other verse in the text concludes the OJN.

2.1.1.17. Three Compilation Stages of the JN

Based on the above observations, the text of JN (2 Kgs 9:1-10:28) can be divided
into three main redactional layers: (1) pre-Dtr layer;[70] (2) Dtr layer; and (3) later
additions.[71] The first two layers have distinct themes. The primary theme of the
pre-Dtr layer is the justification of Jehu's coup d'état, and the Dtr layer connects
the OJN to the fulfilment of the prophet's words concerning the House of Ahab
and the death of Jezebel. The three layers are presented as follows:

---

65 In both stories, cult objects are taken out of the temples and then burnt, and cult places are
    defiled and made useless (2 Kgs 23:8, 10, 13, 14, 20). The subject of vv. 25b-27 is plural, showing
    that Jehu is not the main figure of the passage. It is notable that the action depicted in the pas-
    sage does not form verbatim repetitions of Jehu's order (vv. 18-25a), but it still preserves this
    structure in terms of vocabulary. See Otto 2001: 54.

66 נתץ "to destroy" is used forty-two times in the Hebrew Bible, twenty-one times of which are
    used with religious objects such as an altar or temple (Ex 34:13; Deut 7:5; 12:3; Jgs 2:2; 6:28, 30,
    31, 32; 8:17; 2 Kgs 10:27 [twice]; 11:18; 23:7, 8, 12, 15; 2 Chr 23:17; 31:1; 33:3; 34:4, 7). However,
    נתץ מצבה appears only here. שרף "to burn" is used with cultic objects in Ex 33:20; Deut 7:5, 25;
    9:21; 1 Kgs 15:13; 2 Kgs 23:4, 6, 11, 15.

67 Also Barré 1988: 21.

68 Schmitt 1972: 19, n. 2; Montgomery 1951: 411; Barré 1988: 22; Otto 2001: 52. For the following
    reasons, they ascribed v. 28 to the same level as the following judgment of Jehu's religious policy
    (vv. 29-31). (1) The Dtr summarises the preceding story of the extermination of Baal's cult (vv.
    18-27) and connects between the story and the judgment. (2) The following judgment (vv. 28-
    31a) has a typical Dtr style, describing a "good" king. It is noteworthy that this expression is oth-
    erwise used only for the Judahite kings: 1 Kgs 15:11 (Asa); 22:43 (Jehoshaphat); 2 Kgs 12:3 (Je-
    hoash); 14:3 (Amaziah); 15:3 (Azariah/Uzziah), 34 (Jotham); 18:3 (Hezekiah); 22:2 (Josiah).

69 Campbell 1986: 103; Mulzer 1992: 271.

70 It includes the possible pre-Dtr editing (9:21b, 25-26).

71 It includes the secondary Dtr editing (9:29, 37).

(1) 2 Kgs 9:1-6a, 10b-27abα*, 30-35; 10:1-6a, 7-9, 12-17aα, 18-19a, 20, 21aβb-25a, 28.

(2) 2 Kgs 9:6b*-7a, 8-10a, 27bβ*, 28, 36; 10:10-11, 17aβb, 19b, 21aα, 25b-27.

(3) 2 Kgs 9:7b, 29, 37; 10:6b.

The Redactional Layers in 2 Kgs 9-10

1. Original

2. Dtr Editing

3. Later Additions

2 Kgs 9

¹ וֶאֱלִישָׁע הַנָּבִיא קָרָא לְאַחַד מִבְּנֵי הַנְּבִיאִים וַיֹּאמֶר לוֹ חֲגֹר מָתְנֶיךָ וְקַח פַּךְ הַשֶּׁמֶן הַזֶּה בְּיָדֶךָ וְלֵךְ רָמֹת גִּלְעָד: ² בֹּאתָ שָׁמָּה וּרְאֵה־שָׁם יֵהוּא בֶן־יְהוֹשָׁפָט בֶּן־נִמְשִׁי וּבָאתָ וַהֲקֵמֹתוֹ מִתּוֹךְ אֶחָיו וְהֵבֵיאתָ אֹתוֹ חֶדֶר בְּחָדֶר: ³ וְלָקַחְתָּ פַךְ־הַשֶּׁמֶן וְיָצַקְתָּ עַל־רֹאשׁוֹ וְאָמַרְתָּ כֹּה־אָמַר יְהוָה מְשַׁחְתִּיךָ לְמֶלֶךְ אֶל־יִשְׂרָאֵל וּפָתַחְתָּ הַדֶּלֶת וְנַסְתָּה וְלֹא תְחַכֶּה: ⁴ וַיֵּלֶךְ הַנַּעַר הַנָּבִיא רָמֹת גִּלְעָד: ⁵ וַיָּבֹא וְהִנֵּה שָׂרֵי הַחַיִל יֹשְׁבִים וַיֹּאמֶר דָּבָר לִי אֵלֶיךָ הַשָּׂר וַיֹּאמֶר יֵהוּא אֶל־מִי מִכֻּלָּנוּ וַיֹּאמֶר אֵלֶיךָ הַשָּׂר: ^{6a*} וַיָּקָם וַיָּבֹא הַבַּיְתָה וַיִּצֹק הַשֶּׁמֶן אֶל־רֹאשׁוֹ וַיֹּאמֶר לוֹ כֹּה־אָמַר יְהוָה

^{6b*} אֱלֹהֵי יִשְׂרָאֵל

^{6b*} מְשַׁחְתִּיךָ לְמֶלֶךְ

^{6b*} אֶל־עַם יְהוָה

^{6b*} אֶל־יִשְׂרָאֵל:

^{7a} וְהִכִּיתָה אֶת־בֵּית אַחְאָב אֲדֹנֶיךָ

^{7b} וְנִקַּמְתִּי דְּמֵי| עֲבָדַי הַנְּבִיאִים וּדְמֵי כָּל־עַבְדֵי יְהוָה מִיַּד אִיזָבֶל:

⁸ וְאָבַד כָּל־בֵּית אַחְאָב וְהִכְרַתִּי לְאַחְאָב מַשְׁתִּין בְּקִיר וְעָצוּר וְעָזוּב בְּיִשְׂרָאֵל: ⁹ נָתַתִּי אֶת־בֵּית אַחְאָב כְּבֵית יָרָבְעָם בֶּן־נְבָט וּכְבֵית בַּעְשָׁא בֶן־אֲחִיָּה: ^{10a} וְאֶת־אִיזֶבֶל יֹאכְלוּ הַכְּלָבִים בְּחֵלֶק יִזְרְעֶאל וְאֵין קֹבֵר

^{10b} וַיִּפְתַּח הַדֶּלֶת וַיָּנֹס: ¹¹ וְיֵהוּא יָצָא אֶל־עַבְדֵי אֲדֹנָיו וַיֹּאמֶר לוֹ הֲשָׁלוֹם מַדּוּעַ בָּא־הַמְשֻׁגָּע הַזֶּה אֵלֶיךָ וַיֹּאמֶר אֲלֵיהֶם אַתֶּם יְדַעְתֶּם אֶת־הָאִישׁ וְאֶת־שִׂיחוֹ: ¹² יֹאמְרוּ שֶׁקֶר הַגֶּד־נָא לָנוּ וַיֹּאמֶר כָּזֹאת וְכָזֹאת אָמַר אֵלַי לֵאמֹר כֹּה אָמַר יְהוָה מְשַׁחְתִּיךָ לְמֶלֶךְ אֶל־יִשְׂרָאֵל: ¹³ וַיְמַהֲרוּ וַיִּקְחוּ אִישׁ בִּגְדוֹ וַיָּשִׂימוּ תַחְתָּיו אֶל־גֶּרֶם הַמַּעֲלוֹת וַיִּתְקְעוּ בַּשּׁוֹפָר וַיֹּאמְרוּ מָלַךְ יֵהוּא:

^{14a} וַיִּתְקַשֵּׁר יֵהוּא בֶּן־יְהוֹשָׁפָט בֶּן־נִמְשִׁי אֶל־יוֹרָם

^{14b} יוֹרָם הָיָה שֹׁמֵר בְּרָמֹת גִּלְעָד הוּא וְכָל־יִשְׂרָאֵל מִפְּנֵי חֲזָאֵל מֶלֶךְ־אֲרָם: ¹⁵ וַיָּשָׁב יְהוֹרָם הַמֶּלֶךְ לְהִתְרַפֵּא בְיִזְרְעֶאל מִן־הַמַּכִּים אֲשֶׁר יַכֻּהוּ אֲרַמִּים בְּהִלָּחֲמוֹ אֶת־חֲזָאֵל מֶלֶךְ אֲרָם וַיֹּאמֶר יֵהוּא אִם־יֵשׁ נַפְשְׁכֶם אַל־יֵצֵא פָלִיט מִן־הָעִיר לָלֶכֶת (לַגִּיד) [לְהַגִּיד] בְּיִזְרְעֶאל: ¹⁶ וַיִּרְכַּב יֵהוּא וַיֵּלֶךְ יִזְרְעֶאלָה כִּי יוֹרָם שֹׁכֵב שָׁמָּה וַאֲחַזְיָה מֶלֶךְ יְהוּדָה יָרַד לִרְאוֹת אֶת־יוֹרָם: ¹⁷ וְהַצֹּפֶה עֹמֵד עַל־הַמִּגְדָּל בְּיִזְרְעֶאל וַיַּרְא אֶת־שִׁפְעַת יֵהוּא בְּבֹאוֹ וַיֹּאמֶר שִׁפְעַת אֲנִי רֹאֶה וַיֹּאמֶר יְהוֹרָם קַח רַכָּב וּשְׁלַח לִקְרָאתָם וְיֹאמַר הֲשָׁלוֹם: ¹⁸ וַיֵּלֶךְ רֹכֵב הַסּוּס לִקְרָאתוֹ וַיֹּאמֶר כֹּה־אָמַר הַמֶּלֶךְ הֲשָׁלוֹם וַיֹּאמֶר יֵהוּא מַה־לְּךָ וּלְשָׁלוֹם סֹב אֶל־אַחֲרָי וַיַּגֵּד הַצֹּפֶה לֵאמֹר

בָּא־הַמַּלְאָ֥ךְ עַד־הֶ֖ם וְלֹא־שָׁ֑ב: 19 וַיִּשְׁלַ֞ח רֹכֵ֣ב סוּס֮ שֵׁנִי֒ וַיָּבֹ֣א אֲלֵהֶ֗ם וַיֹּ֙אמֶר֙ כֹּֽה־אָמַ֣ר הַמֶּ֣לֶךְ
שָׁל֔וֹם וַיֹּ֧אמֶר יֵה֛וּא מַה־לְּךָ֥ וּלְשָׁל֖וֹם סֹ֥ב אֶֽל־אַחֲרָֽי: 20 וַיַּגֵּ֤ד הַצֹּפֶה֙ לֵאמֹ֔ר בָּ֖א עַד־אֲלֵיהֶ֑ם
וְלֹא־שָׁ֔ב וְהַמִּנְהָ֗ג כְּמִנְהַ֤ג יֵהוּא֙ בֶּן־נִמְשִׁ֔י כִּ֥י בְשִׁגָּע֖וֹן יִנְהָֽג: 21 וַיֹּ֤אמֶר יְהוֹרָם֙ אֱסֹ֔ר וַיֶּאְסֹ֖ר רִכְבּ֑וֹ
וַיֵּצֵ֣א יְהוֹרָ֣ם מֶֽלֶךְ־יִשְׂרָאֵ֗ל וַאֲחַזְיָ֤הוּ מֶֽלֶךְ־יְהוּדָה֙ אִ֣ישׁ בְּרִכְבּ֔וֹ וַיֵּצְא֖וּ לִקְרַ֣את יֵה֑וּא וַיִּמְצָאֻ֙הוּ֙
בְּחֶלְקַ֖ת נָב֥וֹת הַיִּזְרְעֵאלִֽי: 22 וַיְהִ֗י כִּרְא֤וֹת יְהוֹרָם֙ אֶת־יֵה֔וּא וַיֹּ֖אמֶר הֲשָׁל֣וֹם יֵה֑וּא וַיֹּ֙אמֶר֙ מָ֣ה
הַשָּׁל֔וֹם עַד־זְנוּנֵ֞י אִיזֶ֧בֶל אִמְּךָ֛ וּכְשָׁפֶ֖יהָ הָרַבִּֽים: 23 וַיַּהֲפֹ֧ךְ יְהוֹרָ֛ם יָדָ֖יו וַיָּנֹ֑ס וַיֹּ֥אמֶר אֶל־אֲחַזְיָ֖הוּ
מִרְמָ֥ה אֲחַזְיָֽה: 24 וְיֵה֞וּא מִלֵּ֤א יָדוֹ֙ בַּקֶּ֔שֶׁת וַיַּ֤ךְ אֶת־יְהוֹרָם֙ בֵּ֣ין זְרֹעָ֔יו וַיֵּצֵ֥א הַחֵ֖צִי מִלִּבּ֑וֹ וַיִּכְרַ֖ע
בְּרִכְבּֽוֹ: 25 וַיֹּ֗אמֶר אֶל־בִּדְקַר֙ שָׁלִשׁ֔וֹ]שָׁלִשֹׁ֔ו[שָׂ֚א הַשְׁלִכֵ֔הוּ בְּחֶלְקַ֖ת שְׂדֵ֣ה נָב֣וֹת הַיִּזְרְעֵאלִ֑י
כִּֽי־זְכֹ֞ר אֲנִ֣י וָאַ֗תָּה אֵ֣ת רֹכְבִ֤ים צְמָדִים֙ אַחֲרֵי֙ אַחְאָ֣ב אָבִ֔יו וַֽיהוָה֙ נָשָׂ֣א עָלָ֔יו אֶת־הַמַּשָּׂ֖א הַזֶּֽה: 26
אִם־לֹ֡א אֶת־דְּמֵ֣י נָבוֹת֩ וְאֶת־דְּמֵ֨י בָנָ֜יו רָאִ֤יתִי אֶ֙מֶשׁ֙ נְאֻם־יְהוָ֔ה וְשִׁלַּמְתִּ֥י לְךָ֛ בַּחֶלְקָ֖ה הַזֹּ֑את
נְאֻם־יְהוָ֑ה וְעַתָּ֗ה שָׂ֧א הַשְׁלִכֵ֛הוּ בַּחֶלְקָ֖ה כִּדְבַ֥ר יְהוָֽה: 27abα* אֲחַזְיָ֤ה מֶֽלֶךְ־יְהוּדָה֙ רָאָ֔ה וַיָּ֕נָס דֶּ֖רֶךְ
בֵּ֣ית הַגָּ֑ן וַיִּרְדֹּ֤ף אַחֲרָיו֙ יֵה֔וּא וַיֹּ֙אמֶר֙ גַּם־אֹת֔וֹ הַכֻּ֖הוּ אֶל־הַמֶּרְכָּבָ֗ה בְּמַעֲלֵֽה־ג֔וּר אֲשֶׁ֖ר
אֶת־יִבְלְעָ֑ם

27bβ* וַיָּ֖נָס מְגִדּֽוֹ

27bβ* וַיָּ֥מָת שָֽׁם:

28 וַיַּרְכִּ֧בוּ אֹת֛וֹ עֲבָדָ֖יו יְרוּשָׁלָ֑מָה וַיִּקְבְּר֨וּ אֹת֧וֹ בִקְבֻרָת֛וֹ עִם־אֲבֹתָ֖יו בְּעִ֥יר דָּוִֽד:
פ

29 וּבִשְׁנַת֙ אַחַ֣ת עֶשְׂרֵ֣ה שָׁנָ֔ה לְיוֹרָ֖ם בֶּן־אַחְאָ֑ב מָלַ֥ךְ
אֲחַזְיָ֖ה עַל־יְהוּדָֽה:
30 וַיָּב֥וֹא יֵה֖וּא יִזְרְעֶ֑אלָה וְאִיזֶ֣בֶל שָׁמְעָ֗ה וַתָּ֨שֶׂם בַּפּ֤וּךְ עֵינֶ֙יהָ֙ וַתֵּ֣יטֶב אֶת־רֹאשָׁ֔הּ וַתַּשְׁקֵ֖ף בְּעַ֥ד
הַחַלּֽוֹן: 31 וְיֵה֖וּא בָּ֣א בַשָּׁ֑עַר וַתֹּ֣אמֶר הֲשָׁל֔וֹם זִמְרִ֖י הֹרֵ֥ג אֲדֹנָֽיו: 32 וַיִּשָּׂ֤א פָנָיו֙ אֶל־הַֽחַלּ֔וֹן וַיֹּ֕אמֶר
מִ֥י אִתִּ֖י מִ֑י וַיַּשְׁקִ֣יפוּ אֵלָ֔יו שְׁנַ֥יִם שְׁלֹשָׁ֖ה סָרִיסִֽים: 33 וַיֹּ֣אמֶר שִׁמְט֑וּהוּ]שִׁמְטֻ֑הוּ[וַֽיִּשְׁמְט֖וּהָ וַיִּ֨ז
מִדָּמָ֤הּ אֶל־הַקִּיר֙ וְאֶל־הַסּוּסִ֔ים וַֽיִּרְמְסֶֽנָּה: 34 וַיָּבֹ֖א וַיֹּ֣אכַל וַיֵּ֑שְׁתְּ וַיֹּ֗אמֶר פִּקְדוּ־נָ֞א אֶת־הָאֲרוּרָ֤ה
הַזֹּאת֙ וְקִבְר֔וּהָ כִּ֥י בַת־מֶ֖לֶךְ הִֽיא: 35 וַיֵּלְכ֖וּ לְקָבְרָ֑הּ וְלֹא־מָ֣צְאוּ בָ֗הּ כִּ֧י אִם־הַגֻּלְגֹּ֛לֶת וְהָרַגְלַ֖יִם
וְכַפּ֥וֹת הַיָּדָֽיִם:
36 וַיָּשֻׁבוּ֮ וַיַּגִּ֣ידוּ לוֹ֒ וַיֹּ֙אמֶר֙ דְּבַר־יְהוָ֣ה ה֔וּא אֲשֶׁ֣ר דִּבֶּ֗ר בְּיַד־עַבְדּ֛וֹ אֵלִיָּ֥הוּ
הַתִּשְׁבִּ֖י לֵאמֹ֑ר בְּחֵ֣לֶק יִזְרְעֶ֔אל יֹאכְל֥וּ הַכְּלָבִ֖ים אֶת־בְּשַׂ֥ר אִיזָֽבֶל:
37)וְהָיָ֣ת( ]וְהָֽיְתָה֩[נִבְלַ֨ת אִיזֶ֜בֶל כְּדֹ֗מֶן עַל־פְּנֵ֥י הַשָּׂדֶ֖ה
בְּחֵ֣לֶק יִזְרְעֶ֑אל אֲשֶׁ֥ר לֹֽא־יֹאמְר֖וּ זֹ֥את אִיזָֽבֶל: פ

2 Kgs 10

1 וּלְאַחְאָ֛ב שִׁבְעִ֥ים בָּנִ֖ים בְּשֹׁמְר֑וֹן וַיִּכְתֹּב֩ יֵה֨וּא סְפָרִ֜ים וַיִּשְׁלַ֣ח שֹׁמְר֗וֹן אֶל־שָׂרֵ֤י יִזְרְעֶאל֙ הַזְּקֵנִ֔ים
וְאֶל־הָאֹמְנִ֖ים אַחְאָ֑ב לֵאמֹֽר: 2 וְעַתָּ֗ה כְּבֹ֨א הַסֵּ֤פֶר הַזֶּה֙ אֲלֵיכֶ֔ם וְאִתְּכֶ֖ם בְּנֵ֣י אֲדֹנֵיכֶ֑ם וְאִתְּכֶ֞ם
הָרֶ֤כֶב וְהַסּוּסִים֙ וְעִ֣יר מִבְצָ֔ר וְהַנָּֽשֶׁק: 3 וּרְאִיתֶ֞ם הַטּ֤וֹב וְהַיָּשָׁר֙ מִבְּנֵ֣י אֲדֹנֵיכֶ֔ם וְשַׂמְתֶּ֖ם עַל־כִּסֵּ֣א
אָבִ֑יו וְהִלָּחֲמ֖וּ עַל־בֵּ֥ית אֲדֹנֵיכֶֽם: 4 וַיִּֽרְאוּ֙ מְאֹ֣ד מְאֹ֔ד וַיֹּ֣אמְר֔וּ הִנֵּ֞ה שְׁנֵ֣י הַמְּלָכִ֗ים לֹ֤א עָֽמְדוּ֙ לְפָנָ֔יו
וְאֵ֖יךְ נַעֲמֹ֥ד אֲנָֽחְנוּ: 5 וַיִּשְׁלַ֣ח אֲשֶׁר־עַל־הַבַּ֣יִת וַאֲשֶׁ֣ר עַל־הָעִ֡יר וְהַזְּקֵנִים֩ וְהָאֹמְנִ֨ים אֶל־יֵה֜וּא
לֵאמֹ֗ר עֲבָדֶ֤יךָ אֲנַ֙חְנוּ֙ וְכֹ֣ל אֲשֶׁר־תֹּאמַ֤ר אֵלֵ֙ינוּ֙ נַעֲשֶׂ֔ה לֹֽא־נַמְלִ֖יךְ אִ֑ישׁ הַטּ֥וֹב בְּעֵינֶ֖יךָ עֲשֵֽׂה: 6a
וַיִּכְתֹּ֣ב אֲלֵיהֶ֣ם סֵ֘פֶר֮ שֵׁנִ֣ית לֵאמֹר֒ אִם־לִ֣י אַתֶּ֗ם וּלְקֹלִי֙ אַתֶּ֣ם שֹׁמְעִ֔ים קְח֞וּ אֶת־רָאשֵׁי֙ אַנְשֵׁ֣י
בְנֵֽי־אֲדֹנֵיכֶ֔ם וּבֹ֧אוּ אֵלַ֛י כָּעֵ֥ת מָחָ֖ר יִזְרְעֶ֑אלָה

6b וּבְנֵ֤י הַמֶּ֙לֶךְ֙ שִׁבְעִ֣ים אִ֔ישׁ אֶת־גְּדֹלֵ֥י הָעִ֖יר מְגַדְּלִ֥ים
אוֹתָֽם:

וַיְהִי כְבֹא הַסֵּפֶר אֲלֵיהֶם וַיִּקְחוּ אֶת־בְּנֵי הַמֶּלֶךְ וַיִּשְׁחֲטוּ שִׁבְעִים אִישׁ וַיָּשִׂימוּ אֶת־רָאשֵׁיהֶם [7]
בַּדּוּדִים וַיִּשְׁלְחוּ אֵלָיו יִזְרְעֶאלָה: [8] וַיָּבֹא הַמַּלְאָךְ וַיַּגֶּד־לוֹ לֵאמֹר הֵבִיאוּ רָאשֵׁי בְנֵי־הַמֶּלֶךְ
וַיֹּאמֶר שִׂימוּ אֹתָם שְׁנֵי צִבֻּרִים פֶּתַח הַשַּׁעַר עַד־הַבֹּקֶר: [9] וַיְהִי בַבֹּקֶר וַיֵּצֵא וַיַּעֲמֹד וַיֹּאמֶר
אֶל־כָּל־הָעָם צַדִּקִים אַתֶּם הִנֵּה אֲנִי קָשַׁרְתִּי עַל־אֲדֹנִי וָאֶהְרְגֵהוּ וּמִי הִכָּה אֶת־כָּל־אֵלֶּה:
עוּ אֵפוֹא כִּי לֹא יִפֹּל מִדְּבַר יְהוָה אַרְצָה אֲשֶׁר־דִּבֶּר יְהוָה עַל־בֵּית אַחְאָב [10]
וַיהוָה עָשָׂה אֵת אֲשֶׁר דִּבֶּר בְּיַד עַבְדּוֹ אֵלִיָּהוּ: [11] וַיַּךְ יֵהוּא אֵת כָּל־הַנִּשְׁאָרִים
לְבֵית־אַחְאָב בְּיִזְרְעֶאל וְכָל־גְּדֹלָיו וּמְיֻדָּעָיו וְכֹהֲנָיו עַד־בִּלְתִּי הִשְׁאִיר־לוֹ שָׂרִיד:
וַיָּקָם וַיָּבֹא וַיֵּלֶךְ שֹׁמְרוֹן הוּא בֵּית־עֵקֶד הָרֹעִים בַּדָּרֶךְ: [13] וְיֵהוּא מָצָא אֶת־אֲחֵי אֲחַזְיָהוּ [12]
מֶלֶךְ־יְהוּדָה וַיֹּאמֶר מִי אַתֶּם וַיֹּאמְרוּ אֲחֵי אֲחַזְיָהוּ אֲנַחְנוּ וַנֵּרֶד לִשְׁלוֹם בְּנֵי־הַמֶּלֶךְ וּבְנֵי
הַגְּבִירָה: [14] וַיֹּאמֶר תִּפְשׂוּם חַיִּים וַיִּתְפְּשׂוּם חַיִּים וַיִּשְׁחָטוּם אֶל־בּוֹר בֵּית־עֵקֶד אַרְבָּעִים וּשְׁנַיִם
אִישׁ וְלֹא־הִשְׁאִיר אִישׁ מֵהֶם: ס
וַיֵּלֶךְ מִשָּׁם וַיִּמְצָא אֶת־יְהוֹנָדָב בֶּן־רֵכָב לִקְרָאתוֹ וַיְבָרְכֵהוּ וַיֹּאמֶר אֵלָיו הֲיֵשׁ אֶת־לְבָבְךָ יָשָׁר [15]
כַּאֲשֶׁר לְבָבִי עִם־לְבָבֶךָ וַיֹּאמֶר יְהוֹנָדָב יֵשׁ וָיֵשׁ תְּנָה אֶת־יָדֶךָ וַיִּתֵּן יָדוֹ וַיַּעֲלֵהוּ אֵלָיו
אֶל־הַמֶּרְכָּבָה: [16] וַיֹּאמֶר לְכָה אִתִּי וּרְאֵה בְּקִנְאָתִי לַיהוָה וַיַּרְכִּבוּ אֹתוֹ בְּרִכְבּוֹ: [17aα] וַיָּבֹא
שֹׁמְרוֹן וַיַּךְ אֶת־כָּל־הַנִּשְׁאָרִים לְאַחְאָב בְּשֹׁמְרוֹן
[17aβb] עַד־הִשְׁמִדוֹ כִּדְבַר יְהוָה אֲשֶׁר דִּבֶּר אֶל־אֵלִיָּהוּ: פ
וַיִּקְבֹּץ יֵהוּא אֶת־כָּל־הָעָם וַיֹּאמֶר אֲלֵהֶם אַחְאָב עָבַד אֶת־הַבַּעַל מְעָט יֵהוּא יַעַבְדֶנּוּ הַרְבֵּה: [18]
[19a] וְעַתָּה כָל־נְבִיאֵי הַבַּעַל כָּל־עֹבְדָיו וְכָל־כֹּהֲנָיו קִרְאוּ אֵלַי אִישׁ אַל־יִפָּקֵד כִּי זֶבַח גָּדוֹל לִי
לַבַּעַל כֹּל אֲשֶׁר־יִפָּקֵד לֹא יִחְיֶה
[19b] יֵהוּא עָשָׂה בְעָקְבָּה לְמַעַן הַאֲבִיד אֶת־עֹבְדֵי הַבָּעַל:
וַיֹּאמֶר יֵהוּא קַדְּשׁוּ עֲצָרָה לַבַּעַל וַיִּקְרָאוּ: [20]
[21aα] וַיִּשְׁלַח יֵהוּא בְּכָל־יִשְׂרָאֵל
[21aβb] וַיָּבֹאוּ כָּל־עֹבְדֵי הַבַּעַל וְלֹא־נִשְׁאַר אִישׁ אֲשֶׁר לֹא־בָא וַיָּבֹאוּ בֵּית הַבַּעַל וַיִּמָּלֵא
בֵית־הַבַּעַל פֶּה לָפֶה: [22] וַיֹּאמֶר לַאֲשֶׁר עַל־הַמֶּלְתָּחָה הוֹצֵא לְבוּשׁ לְכֹל עֹבְדֵי הַבָּעַל וַיֵּצֵא לָהֶם
הַמַּלְבּוּשׁ: [23] וַיָּבֹא יֵהוּא וִיהוֹנָדָב בֶּן־רֵכָב בֵּית הַבָּעַל וַיֹּאמֶר לְעֹבְדֵי הַבַּעַל חַפְּשׂוּ וּרְאוּ
פֶּן־יֶשׁ־פֹּה עִמָּכֶם מֵעַבְדֵי יְהוָה כִּי אִם־עֹבְדֵי הַבַּעַל לְבַדָּם: [24] וַיָּבֹאוּ לַעֲשׂוֹת זְבָחִים וְעֹלוֹת
וְיֵהוּא שָׂם־לוֹ בַחוּץ שְׁמֹנִים אִישׁ וַיֹּאמֶר הָאִישׁ אֲשֶׁר־יִמָּלֵט מִן־הָאֲנָשִׁים אֲשֶׁר אֲנִי מֵבִיא
עַל־יְדֵיכֶם נַפְשׁוֹ תַּחַת נַפְשׁוֹ: [25a] וַיְהִי כְּכַלֹּתוֹ לַעֲשׂוֹת הָעֹלָה וַיֹּאמֶר יֵהוּא לָרָצִים וְלַשָּׁלִשִׁים
בֹּאוּ הַכּוּם אִישׁ אַל־יֵצֵא וַיַּכֻּם לְפִי־חָרֶב
[25b] וַיַּשְׁלִכוּ הָרָצִים וְהַשָּׁלִשִׁים וַיֵּלְכוּ עַד־עִיר בֵּית־הַבָּעַל: [26] וַיֹּצִאוּ אֶת־מַצְּבוֹת
בֵּית־הַבַּעַל וַיִּשְׂרְפוּהָ: [27] וַיִּתְּצוּ אֵת מַצְּבַת הַבַּעַל וַיִּתְּצוּ אֶת־בֵּית הַבַּעַל
וַיְשִׂמֻהוּ לְמַחֲרָאוֹת (לְמוֹצָאוֹת) עַד־הַיּוֹם:
וַיַּשְׁמֵד יֵהוּא אֶת־הַבַּעַל מִיִּשְׂרָאֵל: [28]

2.1.1.18. Genre of the OJN

In view of the OJN reconstructed above, it is appropriate to discuss its literary genre. This account can be classified as a historical story, defined by Long (1984: 6-7) as "a self-contained narrative mainly concerned to recount what a particular event was and how it happened, but with more literary sophistication than is usually evident in simple reports".[72]

Although the present form of the JN is apparently a prophetic story, some elements in this narrative do not conform to those of prophetic stories.[73] The inappropriateness of fitting the OJN into the Elisha Cycle stories was discussed above (2.1).[74]

In sum, I designate the genre of the OJN as a royal historical story with apologetic nature, which is prophetically orientated. The main protagonist of the Narrative is Jehu, and not a prophet. Its connection to the prophet Elisha is marginal, intending to legitimise Jehu's rebellion. This definition is significant for the following historical analysis of the text.[75]

2.1.2. Historical Considerations

In the following sections, the historical authenticity of Jehu's rebellion as described in the OJN will be evaluated.

2.1.2.1. Milieu and Date of the Composition of the OJN

In order to discuss the historicity of the OJN, its milieu/place and date of composition are essential. Three sorts of milieu for the composition of the OJN have been suggested: (1) the royal court of the Jehuite Dynasty;[76] (2) military or official circles around Jehu;[77] and (3) prophetic circles.[78] A conspicuous tendency to legitimise Jehu's coup d'état in the text is the key in determining the milieu of

---

72 Cf. Plein 1966: 15-17; Steck 1968: 32, n. 2; Schmitt 1972: 29.

73 Long (1991: 123) correctly stated, "since the writer-narrator has given such an important role to a prophet, and attached so much of the story's religious and cultural outlook to prophetic oracles and their fulfilment, one might be justified in refining the designation to prophetic story, a special type of historical narrative".

74 Steck (1968: 32-33, n. 2) suggested that the contemptuous attitude toward Elisha's disciple, as reflected in the words of the generals (9:11), seems unsuitable to a prophetic story. Lehnart (2003: 422, n. 192; 468-469), on the contrary, suggested that this contempt plays only a secondary role in the story and thus does not present the author's view toward prophets as a group. Cf. Hentschel 1977: 53-54, n. 190; Campbell 1986: 22, n. 8; Mulzer 1992: 223, 241, 341.

75 Campbell (1986: 105) defined the JN as "theologically inspired history", and Rofé (1988: 79-88) as "prophetic historiography". Gray (1977: 535-536) suggested that the JN consists of two different sources which were collected and edited by a prophetic compiler.

76 Minokami 1989: 154; Na'aman 1997b: 125; Irvine 2001: 106-112.

77 Steck 1968: 47; Schmitt 1972: 31.

78 Montgomery 1951: 399; Campbell 1986: 22-23, 99-101.

composition.[79] This tendency is reflected especially in the following two points. (1) Jehu is anointed by YHWH's order (9:3, 12). (2) Jehu's rebellion is supported by prophets (9:1-3), military captains (9:13), and pious worshippers of YHWH (= Jehonadab; 10:15-16). The mention of these supporters shows the propagandistic and apologetic nature of the OJN aiming to legitimate Jehu's rebellion. Hence, the author of the narrative must have been sympathetic to the coup. A person who could have held such a view would have been someone close to the royal court of the Jehuite kings, and/or someone who (retrospectively) saw Jehu's acts favourably from a religious perspective. The sophisticated style and structure of this narrative show that a well-educated author, probably a scribe in the royal court, composed, or at least, embellished the original story.[80]

In order to establish the date of the composition, two elements in the narrative must be taken into account. (1) Details of Jezebel's sins and the background of Jehonadab are not described in the narrative. It indicates that the original readers must have known the background of these characters.[81] (2) The narrative justifies Jehu's rebellion from a religious viewpoint. This justification is summarised in Jehu's words in 9:22: "what peace can there be, so long as the many whoredoms and sorceries of your mother Jezebel continue?" The "whoredoms" here clearly refer to Jezebel's religious "whoredoms" as denunciated in 1 Kgs 16:31-33.[82] As such, the story claims that the Baal worship introduced by Jezebel was the major reason for Jehu's rebellion. That the revolution culminates in cultic reform (10:18-25a) also emphasises the religious aspect of Jehu's coup. The manifold justifications of Jehu's coup in the story indicate the necessity to justify Jehu's rebellion at the time of the composition of the OJN, possibly due to a counterargument. For this reason, most scholars have dated the composition of the OJN to the time of the Jehuite Dynasty.

Some scholars have dated the composition of the OJN to Jehu's or Joahaz's reign,[83] and some have dated it to the reigns of the last Jehuites.[84] According to the view of the former, it was essential to justify Jehu's coup soon after the rebellion. And according to the opinion of the latter, the issue of the legitimacy of the Jehuite Dynasty surfaced in the later years of the Dynasty.[85] Although an exact

---

79 Šanda 1912: 123; Steck 1968: 32, n. 2; Schmitt 1972: 31; Minokami 1989: 154; Otto 2001: 105. For another view, see Würthwein 1984: 327, 329-330.

80 Otto (2001: 75-96) pointed to a sophisticated construction of the JN. Wellhausen (1905: 279) called the JN "a glittering jewel (= ein blitzendes Juwel)".

81 Otto 2001: 109-110.

82 Cf. Nah 3:4.

83 Šanda 1912: 123; Minokami 1989: 154. Cf. Montgomery 1951: 399; Alt 1953: 283; Steck 1968: 32, n. 2; Schmitt 1972: 29-30.

84 Joash or Jeroboam II (Jepsen 1934: 73-74); Jeroboam II (Miller 1967: 321-322; Irvine 2001: 106-112; Otto 2001: 110-111).

85 Vogelstein 1945: 12; Tadmor 1961: 248; Ottosson 1969: 234.

date cannot be obtained, an analogy may help to date the composition. Tadmor (1983) discussed similar legitimation of kingships in the Assyrian royal inscriptions of Esarhaddon (681–669 BCE) and Ashurbanipal (668–627 BCE). They both fought against their brothers over the thrones. The legitimising compositions were not written at the beginning of their reigns, but much later, when they appointed their successors to the throne.[86] The apology of Hattušili III (mid-twelfth century BCE) who usurped the throne was also composed after nearly a decade of his accession to the throne.[87] In light of these analogies, I suggested dating the composition of the OJN to sometime in the early years of the Jehuite Dynasty, probably during the reigns of Jehu or Joahaz, when the Aramaeans oppressed Israel (Chapter 4). Yet, unlike the royal Assyrian inscriptions, the OJN had probably been revised after its composition, in order to conform to the historical reality of the later years of the Jehuite Dynasty.

2.1.2.2. Historicity of the Detailed Description

In the following sections, the historicity of each scene in the OJN will be evaluated. It should be noted that the authenticity of most of the details cannot be verified. Therefore, attention will be directed to the historical information of each scene that illuminates the background of Jehu's rise. The Tel Dan Inscription, which is the most important extra-biblical source for comparison, will be referred to minimally, for the inscription will be thoroughly examined in the next section (2.2.).

2.1.2.2.1. Historicity of 2 Kgs 9:1-13

The historicity of Jehu's anointment (9:1-13) cannot be evaluated. The story, possibly composed by a pro-Jehuite author(s), attempted to legitimise Jehu's kingship by connecting his anointment to Elisha. The only reliable historical information here is the general situation of Jehu's rise. The conspiracy began among the Israelite army officials when they camped at Ramoth-Gilead.

2.1.2.2.2. Historical Setting of 2 Kgs 9:14-16

The passage seems to contain authentic information on the general background for Jehu's coup. The first piece of information is the patronym of Jehu (v. 14a):

---

86   Cf. Irvine 1995: 500, n. 17.
87   Tadmor 1983: 54-55.

"Jehu, son of Jehoshaphat, son of Nimshi".[88] The same patronym also appears in 9:2, which is possibly based on this information. Jehu's filiation is mentioned differently in 1 Kgs 19:16; 2 Kgs 9:20; only Nimshi is mentioned as Jehu's "father". It has been suggested that the name Nimshi may be either a clan name or the name of his real father or grandfather.[89] Some scholars have considered that Jehoshaphat mentioned in 9:14a might be a later addition because this name was not mentioned in the Syriac version and was put after Nimshi in the Lucianic recension.[90] Yet, the name should be retained as the *lectio difficilior*, since no cogent reasons for inserting it could be found.[91] Thus, Jehu could have been a son of Jehoshaphat, son of Nimshi. Inscriptions containing either the phrase לנמש "of Nimshi", or the word including a component נמש, have been discovered at Tel 'Amal,[92] Samaria (an ostracon),[93] Khirbet Tannin,[94] and Tel Rehov,[95] and they are dated to the tenth-ninth centuries BCE.[96] This suggests that the name Nimshi was a popular name in the Northern Kingdom at that time.

2.1.2.2.2.1. Did Ahaziah of Judah Take Part in the War at Ramoth-Gilead?

The time when Ahaziah, King of Judah, came to visit the wounded Joram in Jezreel is not mentioned. With only 2 Kgs 9:16, readers might assume that Ahaziah came from Jerusalem and that he did not participate in the battle of Ramoth-Gilead. This lack of specification about Ahaziah's initial location in the OJN shows that the place of his departure was not important for the author. It raises the question whether Ahaziah participated in the battle of Ramoth-Gilead, as conveyed by 8:28.

The Tel Dan Inscription gives us a clue with respect to this issue. Hazael boasts in the inscription that he killed both Joram of Israel and Ahaziah of Judah.[97] Even if this is an exaggerated expression, it is hard to believe that Hazael invented the deaths of these two kings if he had nothing to do with them. Therefore, we may safely assume that the two kings were indeed killed in a war against

---

88   The name Jehu is also attested in Shalmaneser III's inscriptions as ^{m}*iu-ú-a* DUMU ^{m}*hu-um-ri-i.*

89   Šanda 1912: 93; Gray 1977: 540; Na'aman 2008: 213.

90   Šanda 1912: 93; Thiel 1992: 670.

91   Mulzer 1992: 43-46; Otto 2001: 29, n. 2; Lamb 2007: 27-29.

92   Lemaire 1973: 559.

93   Lemaire 1977: 37, 53.

94   Lemaire 1985a: 13-17, esp. 13-15.

95   Mazar 2003a: 178-181.

96   Two seal impressions dating to later periods also bear the name Nimshi. See Avigad and Sass 1997: 128 (no. 266); 218 (no. 574); Lemaire 1999: 106*.

97   Lines 7-8 of the inscription.

Hazael, or at least in the course of the subsequent events (for more detail, see 2.2.6.2.).

2.1.2.2.3. Literary Elements in the Description of Joram's Murder (2 Kgs 9:17-25)

The OJN relates that Jehu killed Joram at Jezreel; the Tel Dan Inscription, however, claims that the murder of Joram was accomplished by its author – Hazael. The discrepancy between these two accounts requires an extensive discussion on the Tel Dan Inscription (see 2.2.6.2 below).

The narrative of Joram's murder is formed in a highly sophisticated style. Its plot is similar to the story of 1 Sam 19:19-24, where Saul sent messengers to Naioth in Ramah to take David. In both stories, the King first sends two/three messengers, and finally must appear himself on the main stage. The plot is also similar to the story of 2 Kgs 1:9-14, where Ahaziah of Israel sent captains of fifty to Elijah three times; the first and the second captains did not return. This may well attest to a folkloristic character in the story. Such elements in a narrative should not be taken as evidence against the historicity of the described event as a whole, but caution is required when using its details for reconstructing the event.

2.1.2.2.4. Historicity of the Murder of Ahaziah (2 Kgs 9:27-29)

The verse relates the murder of Ahaziah, King of Judah. Three toponyms, Beth-haggan, the ascent of Gur, and Megiddo, are explicitly mentioned. Since Beth-haggan and the ascent of Gur appear only here, it is difficult to assume that these toponyms are pure inventions of the author(s). Hence, the story is possibly based on a historical event; yet, the historicity of Ahaziah's murder by Jehu cannot be verified.

V. 27 describes Ahaziah's flight from Jehu. Ahaziah's itinerary is puzzling: he fled by the way of Beth-haggan, was shot at the ascent of Gur, which is at Ibleam, and then fled to Megiddo to die there. Beth-haggan is often identified with modern Jenin, and Ibleam is identified with modern Khirbet Bel'ameh, two kilometres south of Jenin.[98] The ascent of Gur cannot be located with certainty.[99] Given that these identifications of toponyms are correct, it is unclear why Ahaziah, after he was wounded near Ibleam, which is further southward to Beth-haggan, proceeded

---

98   Smith 1894: 356; Abel 1938: 317; Montgomery 1951: 402; Gray 1977: 548; Würthwein 1984: 332; Cogan and Tadmor 1988: 111.

99   On the basis of an incorrect reading of the Ta'anach Letter 2 (line 5) by Hrozný (1904), Montgomery (1951: 402) suggested that modern Gurra, close to Ta'anach, might preserve the name. However, it is now clear that Gurra is actually not mentioned in the Ta'anach Letter. See Rainey 1999; Horowitz and Oshima 2006: 132-134, for earlier literature.

to Megiddo, far northwest of Ibleam. Scholars have suggested different solutions for this incomprehensible itinerary. Gray (1977: 548), for example, explained it by a geographical cause: the wounded Ahaziah gave up his journey toward Samaria, fearing that his pursuer would catch him on the ascending slope.[100] Na'aman (2006: 163-164) suggested a conflation of sources. None of the suggested solutions can be substantiated, and this puzzling itinerary remains open.[101]

2.1.2.2.5. Historicity of the Murders of Jezebel, "Sons of Ahab", and "Brothers of Ahaziah" (2 Kgs 9:30-35; 10:1-14)

All the murders described in 2 Kgs 9:30-35 and 10:1-14 really may have happened, but their historicity cannot be verified for lack of sources. In what follows, I will briefly discuss the narrative's historical probability based on indirect evidence and conjectures.

It seems logical to assume that Jehu killed Jezebel, the queen, when he arrived in Jezreel. The murder is justified by referring to Jezebel's "whoredoms", which is a major pretext for Jehu's coup d'état in the Narrative.

The historicity of the murder of the Samarian princes (10:1-11) is supported by Hos 1:4, which refers to "the blood in Jezreel" that was shed by the Jehuite Dynasty (2.1.3.). According to 10:8-9, the seventy princes' heads were brought to the gate of Jezreel and shown to the people (העם). This appalling scene accords well with the mention of the bloodguilt of the Jehuite Dynasty. It is likewise logical to assume that Jehu exterminated Ahaziah's brothers (10:12-14), who could eventually be potential avengers.

2.1.2.2.6. Historicity of the Rest of the Events in the OJN (2 Kgs 10:15-17aα, 18-27)

Similar to the murders of the House of Ahab, there is no other source to verify the historicity of Jehu's encounter with Jehonadab (10:15-17aα), nor the slaughters of the worshippers of Baal (10:18-27).[102] These scenes show the propagandis-

---

100 See also Kittel 1900: 233. Stade (1889: 542) suggested that Jehu was blocked from travelling southward. Hentschel (1985: 44) explained that Ahaziah headed to the closest big town.

101 Omitting Megiddo in 2 Kgs 9:27, the itinerary of Ahaziah's flight will be clear. Ahaziah fled southward from Jezreel, where Joram was slain; Ahaziah passed the Beth-haggan; and then at the "ascent of Gur", the pursuer caught up to him and shot him. Cf. Hasegawa 2006.

102 2 Kgs 10:15-17aα, which describes the involvement of Jehonadab son of Rechab in Jehu's cult reform, is not directly related to the present research. With regard to Rechabites, see Cogan and Tadmor (1988: 114); Charlesworth (1992: 632-633) with earlier literature. They could be a fictional link between the extinction of the Baal cult and the involvement of the ascetic Rechabites

tic object of the OJN to legitimise Jehu's coup by emphasising his devotion to YHWH. However, since the latter part of the narrative consists of an important part of the Jehu Narrative, which justifies Jehu's coup d'état by emphasising the aspect of religious reform, it is possible that Jehu actually exterminated the Baal worshippers (whoever they actually were) and destroyed the Baal temple. Although the place of this incident is not mentioned, the story might possibly refer to the Baal temple which Ahab built in Samaria (1 Kgs 16:32).

2.1.3. Hosea 1:4

The Book of Hosea is a collection of the words of the prophet dated by the editor of the book to the time of Jeroboam II (1:1). Yet the contents of the prophecies are dated at the end of Jeroboam's reign, on the eve of Samaria's fall.[103] The majority of the text in the book could be ascribed to Hosea himself, or to his followers, although the book has been subjected to later redactions.[104]

Hos 1:4 mentions the punishment of "the house of Jehu" (בית יהוא) for the "blood in Jezreel" (דמי יזרעאל). דמים is the bloodguilt of a murderer (Ex 22:1, 2; 2 Sam 16:7, 8), and possibly refers to Jehu's extermination of the Omride descendants and the Judahite king (2 Kgs 10:7, 14).[105] The verse condemns what is justified in the OJN, and regards it as a criminal and punishable (ופקדתי) deed.[106] This accusation of the extermination of the Omrides contradicts YHWH's command, spoken through Elisha's disciple (2 Kgs 9:7a). Since the reference to the House of Ahab in 9:7a was a Dtr's interpolation (2.1.1.1.), this denunciation of the Jehuite Dynasty in Hos 1:4 must have derived from an independent tradition, possibly from the prophetic circle of Hosea.

That another biblical source gives a negative assessment of the Jehuite Dynasty supports the historicity of Jehu's rebellion and his extermination of the Omride descendants. Mention of Jezreel as the place of the bloodguilt indicates that the massacre of the members of the Omrides took place there, as described in 2 Kgs 10:11 (2.1.1.9.).

---

in this event – "probably a gesture to rally all conservative elements in Israel and convince them that his coup d'état was more than the fulfilment of personal ambition" (Gray 1977: 559).

103 Hos 1:4 dates Hosea's activity before the fall of the Jehuite Dynasty, and 13:1-14:1 before the fall of Samaria.

104 See for example, Emmerson 1984; Macintosh 1997: lxx-lxxii. For various theories on the composition and redactions of the book, see Yee 1987: 1-25.

105 Caquot 1961: 127-130; Wolff 1974: 12, 17-19; Irvine 1995: 497-498. For different views on the meaning of this expression, see Jeremias 1983: 30-31.

106 On the meaning of פקד as "to punish", see Wolff 1974: 17-18; Irvine 1995: 497-498. McComiskey (1993), rejecting this view, suggested that it is a prophetic irony.

2.1.4. Historical Picture of Jehu's Rise as Reflected in the OJN

The literary-critical analysis of the OJN shows its legendary character. The narrative is probably based on historical events, but the historical authenticity of the details cannot be verified. Caution is thus necessary when discussing the historicity of the main events, such as the murders of the two kings (2 Kgs 9:17-29), the murder of Jezebel (2 Kgs 9:30-35), the murder of the "sons of Ahab" (2 Kgs 10:1-11), and the extermination of the Baal cult (2 Kgs 10:18-27).

Bearing the aforementioned limits in mind, I would like to present a picture of Jehu's coup d'état according to the OJN. Jehu, from the family of Nimshi, was a high officer of Joram, king of Israel. He participated in the war against Hazael of Aram-Damascus at Ramoth-Gilead. Joram and Ahaziah, king of Judah, were killed by Hazael (2.2.6.2.) and Jehu took advantage of the situation, rebelled, and annihilated the descendants of the Omride Dynasty.

2.2. The Inscription from Tel Dan

The Tel Dan Inscription consists of three basalt fragments, which will be designated as Fragments A, B1, and B2 in the present study. All fragments were discovered outside the outer city-gate in Area A, located on the southern side of the site.

Scholars concluded that Hazael, King of Aram-Damascus, composed the text on the stela in the second half of the ninth century BCE, in which he described his killing of two kings, Joram of Israel and Ahaziah of Judah. This inscription helps to reconstruct a history of Aram and Israel at the time of its composition.

2.2.1. Archaeological Context of Fragment A

The date of the Tel Dan Inscription has been disputed because the fragmentary text does not relate its author's name. For this reason, it is significant to review the archaeological context of each fragment. Some of the ambiguity of the archaeological context of Fragment A, as described by the original publisher,[107] has been removed by the excavator's recent publications (Biran 1999; 2002). According to Biran (2002:6), Fragment A was discovered in the foundation level of a wall (W5018) standing on the southeast corner of the city's piazza. He suggested that Structure A, which was superimposed by walls, including W5018, went out of use

---

107   Halpern 1994: 68-69; Cryer 1994: 5; Thompson 1995: 237; Noll 1998: 4-8, 19-20; Athas 2003: 6-13.

before the Assyrian conquest.[108] If so, the reuse of Fragment A in W5018 as building material can be dated between the first half of the eighth century BCE and 733/2 BCE.[109] The composition of Fragment A can be dated securely before the first half of the eighth century BCE.

2.2.2. Archaeological Context of Fragment B

In 1994, Fragment B1 was found "in the debris 0.80 m above the level of the pavement".[110] The debris is attributed to Tiglath-pileser III's 733/732 BCE military campaign to northern Israel.

Ten days after the discovery of Fragment B1, Fragment B2 was discovered; it had been reused as a pavement stone. According to the published architectural plan (Biran 2002, Fig. 1.18 and 17, Fig. 1.24), this pavement (Pvmnt5201) seems more recent than the other pavement (Pvmnt5301) dated between the end of the ninth and the beginning of the eighth centuries BCE (Biran and Naveh 1995: 5). Hence, Fragment B2 is possibly contemporaneous with the construction of the wall (W5108) and dated between the early eighth century and 733/732 BCE.

In light of the above observations, we may conclude that all three fragments of the Tel Dan Inscription were found in the same stratum. The inscription was possibly smashed in the early eighth century BCE, and two of its fragments were reused as building components immediately thereafter.

2.2.3. Physical Join of Fragments A and B

The physical join of Fragments B1 and B2 of the Tel Dan Inscription has been unanimously accepted. Most scholars also believe that Fragments A and B (B1+B2) are joinable below the surface of line 5, with Fragment A positioned to

---

108 In Biran's new plan (2002: 12, Fig. 1.18), a line of small stones is depicted at the eastern side of W5018. The construction of the line, possibly a wall, resembles those of other walls of small stones in the same plan. The difference in stone size between W5018 and other walls in this plan possibly shows two distinct phases of construction after Structure A's use. Yet, the chronological relation between the two phases is not clear.

109 The pottery from Structure A is dated to the eighth century BCE. Cf. Arie 2008. Athas (2003: 12) dated both the construction of Structure A and reuse of Fragment A to the early eighth century BCE.

110 Biran and Naveh 1995: 2. The exact locations of the Fragment B1 and B2 are marked in Biran 2002: 12, Fig. 1.18. The location of Fragment B marked by Athas (2003: 7, Fig. 2.2.) seems to be inaccurate.

the right of Fragment B.[111] This potential connection, however, has caused controversy.[112]

The join of Fragments A and B was questioned mainly for physical reasons.[113] Athas (2003: 175-182), examining the fragments first hand, supposed that Fragment A was located in the upper part of the original stela, while Fragment B was in the lower part, and that the locations of each fragment decided the shapes of, sizes of, and spaces between the letters in each fragment. His hypothesis is based on the following three pieces of evidence. (1) The alignment of letters in Fragment A slopes down to the left as the line goes down, while that in Fragment B is much more linear. (2) The letters in Fragment B are neater in shape. (3) The spaces between letters as well as lines in Fragment B are much smaller than those in Fragment A.

On the basis of his observations, Athas (2003: 27-30, 74-77) explained that the scribe positioned himself at the bottom edge of the inscription when he chalked the inscription onto the stone, and that his arm was stretched forward in order to write the upper portions of the original text. In consequence, "with this posture and the lack of marked lines to keep the text level, the text naturally sloped downwards to the left" (Athas, *op. cit.*, 29). On the other hand, the scribe would not have had his arm outstretched very far and would have "had good control over his hand while writing" the lower part of the inscription (See Athas, *op. cit.*, 32, Fig. 3.5.). Thus, observing the slants of each stela and the neatness of letters in Fragment B, he concluded that Fragment A belongs to the upper part while Fragment B belongs to the lower part of the inscription.[114] This is confirmed by the fact, according to Athas (*op. cit.*, 77), that many of the letters in Fragment B "almost encroach on the letters of the next line as though there was only a short space still available on the written surface and the scribe needed to put as much writing as possible in the last few lines".[115]

Athas's argument seems logical; yet, it is based on four highly conjectural hypotheses, which cannot be verified. (1) Two persons, i.e., scribe and engraver, made the inscription. (2) The scribe was right-handed. (3) The scribe did not correct his draft after he finished chalking. (4) The scribe did not move from the lower edge in order to write the upper section more comfortably.[116]

---

111 Biran and Naveh 1995: 11.
112 Cryer 1995: 224-227; Thompson 1995: 238-239; Schniedewind 1996: 77; Galil 2001b. A short
     review of the objections against this join is found in Athas 2003: 178-180.
113 Biran and Naveh 1995: 11; Lemaire 1998: 3.
114 As Athas himself admitted (*op. cit.*, 76), a weakness of this comparison is that the statistics it
     yields are not as significant as those of Fragment A, because Fragment B is much smaller.
115 Staszak (2009) accepted Athas's reconstruction of Fragments.
116 Cf. also Kottsieper 2007: 106-107.

On April 4, 2006, I had an opportunity to examine the Tel Dan Inscription at the Israel Museum in Jerusalem.[117] After careful observation of the physical join of the fragments, I arrived at the conclusion that Fragments A and B can and should be joined, as the publishers suggested. However, I found that the surfaces of Fragments A and B are not precisely flat, and that the two fragments were joined so that the upper side of Fragment A was slanted forward somewhat more than Fragment B. This slight "shear" might have happened either when the fragments were connected or later during the exhibition. This condition influenced the alignment of the joined inscription's lines, as well as Athas's analysis of the physical join of the fragments.

2.2.4. Restoration of Text

The restoration of the letters of the Tel Dan Inscription is necessary due to the inscription's fragmentary nature. Letters will be restored first by epigraphical analysis of other letters in the same inscription.

The restoration of the text is as follows:

.1   [XXXXXXXX]תשר.ע[XXXXXX]וגזר[XXXXX]

.2   [XXXXX].אבי.יסק[XXXXX]תלחמה.בא[פק].

.3   וישכב.אבי.יהך.אל[XXXX]ה.ויעל.מלכי[ש]

.4   ראל.קדם.בארק.אבי[Xוי]המלך.הדד[.]א[ית.]

.5   אנה.ויהך.הדד.קדמי[.ו]אפק.מן.שבע[XXX]

.6   י.מלכי.ואקתל.מל[כ][.]תק[פן.אסרי.א[לפי.ר]

.7   כב.ואלפי.פרש.[וקתלת.אית.יו][רם.בר.[אחאב]

.8   מלך.ישראל.וקתל[ת.אית.אחז][יהו.בר].רם.מל[

.9   ד.ביתדוד.ואשם.[ ].

.10 ית.ארק.הם.לל[ ]

.11 אחרן.ולה] מ[

.12 לד.על.יש[ראל.[ ]

.13 מצר.על] [

---

117   I am indebted to Ms. Michal Dayagi-Mendels, the curator of the Israel Museum and Mr. Eran Arie, for providing me an opportunity to examine the Tel Dan Stela at first hand. They kindly removed the showcase that covered the inscription so that I could examine the inscription closely.

2.2.4.1. Notes on the Restoration

Line 1

The restoration of *taw* and *sin/šin* in the middle of the line, as suggested by some scholars, seems plausible.[118] No space for a word divider was found between these two characters.[119]

Line 2

The restoration of the letters before *aleph* in Line 2 of Fragment A has been disputed. Schniedewind (1996: 77) originally read אל before *aleph*, and later (Schniedewind and Zuckerman 2001) restored ברקאל based on computer imaging. Athas (2003: 44-45) suggested a scar there, which once may have been a letter. I could not find any letters restorable on that part of the line, although a vertical line was clearly seen, about 5 cm to the right of the *aleph* letter. This vertical line could be a part of *gimel*, *waw*, *samekh*, *qof*, or *resh*.

A remnant of a letter can be seen at the end of this line. The restoration of *beth*, *yodh*, *lamed*, or *šin* for the letter was suggested (Athas 2003: 81-82). According to my observation, neither *yodh*, *lamed*, nor *šin* can be restored here, because there is a line extending upwards at the upper point of this broken letter. This line is not completely horizontal but leans slightly to the left. The letters which might fit this remnant are *beth* and *pe*. Comparing with the *beth* just two letters before, the curving point of this letter is located too high to form a *beth*. For this reason, I would restore *pe* for this broken character.[120]

Line 4

There is a hole between *aleph* and *beth* in the middle of line 4 on Fragment A. The publishers (Biran and Naveh 1993: 87, n. 6) regarded it as natural, and believed it must have existed already at the time of the inscription of the letters *aleph* and *beth*. In their opinion, the relatively large space between these two letters is due to this natural hole. In opposition to this, Athas (2003: 57) regarded this hole to have been formed when the inscription was ruined, and restored *lamed* between *aleph* and *beth* in this line.[121]

It seems that the damage on the *aleph* and *beth* letters, both next to the hole, supports Athas's view that the hole was made after the inscription of letters. However, the line itself seems to be more a scar than a letter.

---

118 Tropper 1993: 401; Schniedewind 1996: 79; Wesselius 1999: 173-174; Athas 2003: 194-195. *mem* was restored in the *editio princeps* instead of *sin/šin*.

119 *Contra* Wesselius 1999: 174-175.

120 *Contra* Lemaire 1998: 4; Irvine 2005: 342, n. 8.

121 Athas stated that *lamed* "fits perfectly" for the missing letter. In all other occurrences of *lamed* after *aleph* in Fragment A (Lines 3, 4, 7 and 8), however, the *lamed*'s left stroke protrudes upward above any strokes of *aleph*.

Line 6
Athas (2003: 62-63), instead of *nun*, restored *waw* at the end of this line on Fragment A; yet, this restoration is improbable. If it is a *waw*, its right horizontal line must protrude higher up, to the same level as the left horizontal line.[122] *nun* seems fine, as noticed in *editio princeps*.

The first letter of Fragment B is broken, and the publishers suggested restoring *'ayin*. Na'aman (1997c: 118, n. 22) restored *resh* here but admitted that this restoration is based on a contextual assumption. According to my observation of the inscription, *resh* is less likely because the remnant of this character forms a curve. *pe* and *qof* are alternative candidates for this sign. I suggest restoring *pe*.

Line 7
With Schniedewind (1996: 80) and Lemaire (1998: 10), I restore ‏וי‏ instead of ‏יהו‏, for the beginning of the name of the Israelite king in this line.

Line 8
It seems that there is no space for the publishers' restoration of the name ‏יהורם‏ "Jehoram" in the end of line 8. Here, I follow Na'aman's hypothetical restoration (1997c: 114) of the name of the king ‏רם‏ "Ram" as a short form of "Jehoram".

Line 11
Puech (1994: 218-220) and Schniedewind (1996: 81) read *pe* at the end of this line after *he*. As Schniedewind suggested, this letter can be a *beth*, *pe*, or *resh*. However, the angle formed by the two remaining lines possibly excludes *beth* and *pe*.

2.2.5. Translation of the Text

1.   [..........] you will rule over [..........] and cut [...................]
2.   [......] my father went up [........] in his fighting at A[phek?...]
3.   my father slept. He went to his [......] And the king of Israel entered
4.   formerly? in the land of my father[. And] Hadad made me myself king.
5.   And Hadad went before me, I went out from the seven [...]
6.   of my kingdom, and I slew [migh]ty kin[g]s, who harnessed thou[sands of cha-]
7.   riots and thousands of horsemen. [I killed Jo]ram son of [Ahab]
8.   king of Israel, and [I] killed [Ahaz]iahu son of [Ram kin-]
9.   g of the House of David. And I set [...............................]
10.   their land into [...]
11.   other [...ru]
12.   led over Is[rael...]
13.   siege upon [..]

---

122 Compare with *waw* in lines 1, 3, 5, 7, and 8.

2.2.5.1. Notes on the Translation

Line 1

The word תשר is supposed to be a verb or a part of a verb (Athas 2003: 194-195).[123] Its possible root is שרד (meaning "to rule, to reign") or שרר ("to be firmly closed, to become firm"). The first option is preferred in the context of a commemorative text, which the king dedicated to a cult place. It would be the second person, masculine, singular, and imperfect pe'al form of the verb שרר, and its meaning would be "you will rule over". The following word might be restored as על ("over"), which will make sense with the preceding verb שרר.

Line 3

Kottsieper's translation (2007: 110-111) of the word תלחמתה as "to ally" cannot be excluded, but I follow most scholars and translate it "in his fighting" on contextual ground.

Line 4

The interpretation of קדם in the beginning of line 4 is in dispute. Most scholars followed *editio princeps* and interpreted it as the temporal adverb "formerly".[124] However, קדם as an adverb does not fit the immediate context and it is odd that the author repeatedly mentions the Israelite aggression between his predecessor's death and his coronation (Lemaire 1994: 88; 1998: 5 and Na'aman 1995a: 389; 2000: 97).[125] Lemaire (*loc. cit.*) and Na'aman (*loc. cit.*) regarded קדם here as a verb that specifies the preceding verb ויעל, and translated it "to advance". Although attractive, this interpretation is not well-established, since קדם as a verb does not occur in Old Aramaic inscriptions (Irvine 2005: 343-344).[126] Irvine (*loc. cit.*) suggested identifying the enemy in line 2 not with a king of Israel, but with Shalmaneser III, who fought against Hadadezer during the 850s and 840s BCE. This proposal does not fit the context; the extant Tel Dan Inscription describes the Damascene conflict with Israel and Judah. Since no crucial solution for the interpretation of קדם in line 4 has been proposed, I would leave the translation of *editio princeps* with due caution.

---

123 *Contra* Kottsieper 2007: 112, n. 30.

124 See also Naveh 1999: 119.

125 Kottsieper (2007: 113-114) regarded this word as presenting a geographical name.

126 Lipiński (2000: 373-374, n. 152), from the grammatical point of view, rejected the view of considering קדם as a verb.

Line 6

The publishers restored the text in the middle of line 6 as מל[כן.שב[ען "[seve]nty kin[gs]".[127] The character ʿ*ayin* is not certain and therefore the restoration of the second word is in dispute. Lemaire (1998: 4) and Lipiński (2000: 378) restored *pe* instead of ʿ*ayin*, and read מל[כן.תק[פן "mighty/powerful kings".[128] Dion (1999: 148) restored *beth*, and read מל[כן.רברב[ן "great kings"; yet, the space is too narrow for this restoration.[129] Lemaire and Lipiński's restoration seems most reasonable for the following two reasons: (1) *pe* best fits here epigraphically (2.2.4.1.); and (2) the context includes the author's aggrandisement of his killing of the kings.

2.2.6. Historical Analysis

On the basis of the text restored above, two major issues for examining the historical picture of Jehu's rise will be evaluated: (1) the author of the Tel Dan Inscription; and (2) the historical background for the killing of Joram and Ahaziah.

2.2.6.1. Author of the Tel Dan Inscription

The name of the author did not survive anywhere in the extant fragments of the Tel Dan Inscription. The publishers identified him with Hazael and many scholars have accepted this identification.[130] This hypothetical identification is based primarily on the mention of two kings and their deaths. One is the king of Israel, whose name ends with "-ram" (רם), and the other is the king of the House of David, whose name ends with "-iahu" (יהו). According to the biblical chronology, the only combination of kings' names with those endings is Joram of Israel and Ahaziah of Judah. Indeed, these two kings are mentioned in the Book of Kings as having fought against the Aramaeans (2 Kgs 8:28). The mention of Joram of Israel and Ahaziah of Judah in the Tel Dan Inscription conforms well to the biblical description.[131]

---

127 Suriano (2007: 167) supported this restoration.

128 This restoration is accepted also by Naʾaman (2000: 100) who, in his previous publications (1995a: 389, n. 29; 1997: 113, 118, n, 22), restored *resh* here and read מל[כן.אד[רן "mighty kings".

129 Naʾaman 2000: 100, n. 26. The same terminology appears in the inscription of Bar-Rakib. See *KAI* 1: 216, lines 10, 13-14.

130 Athas (2003: 255-265) and Galil (2001b) proposed Bar-Hadad II, son of Hazael. Wesselius (1999; 2001) identified the author with Jehu. Cf. Becking 1999; Hafthorsson 2006: 62-63.

131 Cf. 2.1.2.2.2.1.

The identification of the author with Hazael is supported by the archaeological context in which the fragments of the Tel Dan Inscription were unearthed, as well as the palaeography of the inscription.[132]

2.2.6.2. Historical Background of the Killing of Joram and Ahaziah

Identification of the author of the Tel Dan Inscription with Hazael produces a contradiction between the texts of the Tel Dan Inscription and the Book of Kings. In 2 Kgs 9:24, 27, Jehu claims to have murdered the two kings Joram and Ahaziah. The author of the Tel Dan Inscription also boasts about the killing of the two kings. In what follows, various views on this contradiction will be outlined, and then a possible solution will be suggested.

Some scholars have endeavoured to reconcile the text of the Tel Dan Inscription with the biblical narrative in 2 Kgs 9. Biran and Naveh (1995: 18) have suggested that Hazael may have regarded Jehu as his agent who killed the two kings. Likewise, Schniedewind (1996: 83-85) regarded the text in 1 Kgs 19:15-18 as an implication of collusion between Jehu and Hazael,[133] and cited a parallel case in contemporary Assyrian inscriptions. Although it is well-known that Assyrian kings, in numerous texts, took credit for the military campaigns commanded by their officers and for achievements accomplished without their direct participation, Schniedewind's theory, based on an inaccurate reading of Shalmaneser III's inscription, is not well-established.[134] Yamada (1995: 618-621) compared the verb קתל in lines 6, 8 (and probably also in line 7) with the Akkadian verb *dâku* in the Assyrian royal inscriptions and interpreted the former as "to strike, defeat", rather than "to kill". In his opinion, Hazael defeated Joram and Ahaziah at

---

132 From the palaeographical point of view, the text of the Tel Dan Inscription is most comparable to the Zakkur Inscription, which is dated to the end of the ninth or to the beginning of the eighth century BCE (3.2.5.). It must be noted, however, that the palaeography cannot provide any decisive clues for dating the composition of the inscription. The corpus of available Old Aramaic texts is quite small, and the characters on the texts are diverse in region and time (Kaufman 1986; Cryer 1994: 6-7, n. 8). Cf. Puech 1994: 230-233. Here is a list of dates of the Tel Dan Inscription on the palaeographical analysis. Halpern (1994: 68): tenth-seventh centuries BCE; Knauf, de Pury, and Römer (1994: 61): from the end of the tenth to the beginning of the eighth century BCE; Schniedewind (1996: 78): 825 BCE ± 75 years; Biran and Naveh (1993: 87): the ninth century BCE; Noll (1998: 7): 850 BCE ± 50 years; Margalit (1994: 20), Lemaire (1994: 89-90), and Demsky (1995: 30): the second half of the ninth century BCE; Tropper (1993: 398-401; 1994: 487-489): between 840 and 825 BCE; Dion (1999: 146-148): 820-790 BCE; Cryer (1994: 8-9; 1996): the eighth century BCE; Lemche and Thompson (1994: 7) and (Lemche 1995: 101): the end of the eighth century BCE; Athas (2003: 94-174, esp. 136, 164) *ca.* 800 BCE±20 years.

133 Also Kottsieper 1998: 488-492; 2007: 125-126; Dion 1999: 152-153. For the criticism of using the passage for the historical reconstruction of the murders of Joram and Ahaziah, see 3.4.1.

134 Na'aman 2006: 160-162.

Ramoth-Gilead, and later Jehu killed the two kings.[135] However, this theory cannot be substantiated, because the Akkadian verb *dâku* is hardly a comparable example useful in determining the meaning of קתל in Aramaic (Na'aman 1997c: 118, n. 21).

These approaches in harmonising the biblical narrative and the Tel Dan Inscription were criticised by Na'aman (1997c: 115-116; 2000: 101-104; 2006: 160-162). In his opinion, it is inconceivable that Hazael in his inscription described an event in which he had not taken part. The aftermath of Jehu's coup also does not fit the hypothetical alliance between Hazael and Jehu. In the year 841 BCE, Hazael fought against Assyria, and despite the great devastation caused in his land, he did not submit. Jehu, on the other hand, submitted and paid taxes to Assyria in the same year. Hence, Damascus and Israel had different attitudes toward Assyria, and this contradicts the assumption that Hazael and Jehu were allies. That the rivalry prevailed between the two kingdoms is confirmed by Hazael's invasion and conquest of a large part of the Israelite territory (Chapters 3 and 4).[136]

Since the harmonisation approaches are invalid, the historical authenticity of the two sources must be examined. The following two criteria will be applied for their evaluation: (1) the date of the source; (2) the genre and nature of the source. The Tel Dan Inscription was evidently composed during Hazael's reign, whereas the OJN originated in the early years of the Jehuite Dynasty, but was redacted later (2.1.2.1.). The prophetic stories in the Book of Kings are novelistic in character, and its genre does not require the exact presentation of the chain of events. Furthermore, these stories were transmitted for many years by oral tradition and assembled in writing only later. It must also be taken into account that considerable changes could occur when oral tradition is edited into written story, as has been ethnographically observed (Nielsen 1954; Lord 1960; Culley 1976; Long 1976). Therefore, the use of prophetic stories as historical sources requires critical and cautionary perusal, even more so when their descriptions contradict those of contemporary sources.

Na'aman (2000: 101-104), placing priority on the description in the Tel Dan Inscription, suggested that it was Hazael who killed the two kings at Ramoth-Gilead, but Jehu extirpated the rest of the Omride Dynasty and then took power.

Lipiński (2000: 379-380) likewise suggested that the description in 2 Kgs 9 is based on a prophetic tradition that attributes the extirpation of the House of Ahab to Jehu.[137] He ascribed 2 Kgs 8:28, which states that "the Aramaeans struck Jehoram (ויכו ארמים את־יורם)", to the "annals of the kings of Judah". Hence, the

---

135 See also Dion 1997: 195.

136 Ishida (1977: 180-181) suggested that Hazael conquered the Israelite territory in revenge for Jehu's betrayal to Assyria.

137 1 Kgs 19:16-17; 2 Kgs 9:1-6, 10b-14a.

hiph'il form of the verb נכה in 8:28, which in the context of a battle means "to kill", shows that Ahaziah was killed at Ramoth-Gilead.

The approach of Na'aman and Lipiński is methodologically correct. The Tel Dan Inscription is a primary source, whereas the JN is a secondary source. Hence, the former is prioritised as a historical source. Based on the assumption that Hazael, as described in the Tel Dan Inscription, was the real slayer of the two kings, we can now conclude that the OJN distorts the historical picture. As an independent narrative, originating not long after the two kings were killed (2.1.2.1.), the OJN could have been composed intentionally to supplant Jehu as the real murderer. If so, why did the author of the narrative invent such a story and attribute the killing to Jehu?

It is well known that all the denunciations of the Omride kings[138] and the prophecies about the coming fall of the House of Ahab[139] were written by the Dtr or later scribes. However, one can easily imagine that the prosperity of the Omride Dynasty was established, to some extent, at the expense of the people in the Northern Kingdom.[140] The expense must have been increased by the repeated military conflicts with the Assyrians during Ahab's reign. It is thus natural to postulate that there were people who were dissatisfied with the Omride Dynasty. One of the aims of the OJN was probably to appeal to such people. If this hypothesis is correct, one would expect an element in the OJN, which emphasises Jehu's killing of Joram, to be in line with the people's will. There are some elements in the OJN that probably attest to the author's intention to present Jehu as a true murderer. (1) Jehu himself killed Joram with his bare hands (9:24). (2) Although wounded, Joram, the king of Israel himself, came out of Jezreel expressly to be killed (9:21-24). (3) Jehu heralded somewhat theatrically the murder in front of the people (10:9). Does this show the author's attempt to conceal that Joram never came back to Jezreel after the battle against Hazael at Ramoth-Gilead? As Lipiński suggested, 2 Kgs 9:15 (as well as 8:29) also looks like an attempt to conceal this. The fictional feature of the OJN thus comes to the foreground. The story apparently stresses Jehu's religious devotion to YHWH more than his legitimacy to the throne. The kings of the House of Ahab had devoted themselves to the Baal cult and therefore had to be killed. This assumption can explain why the author of the OJN emphasises that Jehu himself killed Joram.

2 Kgs 10:9 illuminates the hidden polemic that may have been one of the primary motivations to compose the OJN. It reads: "Then, in the morning, when he (Jehu) went out, he stood and said to all the people, 'You are innocent. It was I who conspired against my master and killed him; but who struck down all these

---

138 1 Kgs 16:25-26, 30-33; 18:18; 21:25.

139 1 Kgs 20:42; 21:19-24, 29; 22:53-54; 2 Kgs 1:16; 3:2-3.

140 For the prosperous period of the Omride Dynasty, see Timm 1982. The prosperity during the Omrides is well-attested in archaeological findings (Finkelstein 2000).

(seventy princes of the House of Ahab)?' " Jehu, declaring the people's inno-
cence,[141] claimed before the people that he himself killed Joram, but not Ahab's
descendants.[142] It seems to me that this passage well presents the author's two
conflicting aims: (1) to lessen the bloodguilt of Jehu; (2) to depict Jehu as the true
murderer of Joram. That the author made such an effort to put the two *prima facie*
contradictory speeches into Jehu's mouth may show the significance of the two
issues in composing the OJN.

There may have been another reason to attribute the murders of Joram and
Ahaziah to Jehu at the court of the Jehuite Dynasty. During the early years of the
dynasty, Israel was under the Aramaean hegemony (Cf. 2 Kgs 10:32-33; 13:3;
Chapters 3 and 4). Jehu's successors would have had hostile feelings toward the
Aramaeans even after it was delivered from their yoke. Therefore, neither Jehu
nor his descendants would have attributed the murder of the apostatised kings of
the House of Ahab to Hazael. Hence, in the OJN, Jehu was depicted as a hero
who killed the apostatised king and swept the Baal cult from Israel.

In sum, the historical information derived from the Tel Dan Inscription
brings to light the relation between the deaths of Joram and Ahaziah and Jehu's
rise to power. After Hazael's army killed Joram and Ahaziah at Ramoth-Gilead,
Jehu launched a coup d'état and killed the rest of the House of Ahab at Jezreel.

2.3. Jehu in the Inscriptions of Shalmaneser III

Four inscriptions of Shalmaneser III refer to Jehu and his tribute soon after the
latter's rebellion: (1) Paper Squeeze (*III R*, 5, no. 6 = *RIMA* 3, A.0.102.8, 1"-27");
(2) Marble Tablet from Ashur (*RIMA* 3, A.0.102.10, iii 45b - iv 15a); (3) Kurbail
Statue Inscription (*RIMA* 3, A.0.102.12, 21-30a); and (4) Inscription on a Royal
Statue from Calah (*RIMA* 3, A.0.102.16, 122'b-137'a). These four inscriptions are
important for understanding Israel's political relation with Assyria soon after
Jehu's rebellion. Since the four texts are quite similar to each other, only one of
them (Paper Squeeze *III R*, 5, no. 6) will be presented below, and the variants will
be indicated in the footnotes.

---

141 The excavations at Tel Jezreel revealed a small domestic area inside the enclosure (Ussishkin and
     Woodhead 1994; Naʾaman 2008: 207). "All the people (כל העם)" mentioned in the passage may
     be an author's exaggeration.
142 It seems to me that Jehu's speech compares the gravity of each crime: the people = innocent <
     Jehu = usurper = minor crime < the representatives of Samaria = murderers of seventy princes
     = major crime.

2.3.1. Texts

2.3.1.1. Paper Squeeze III R, 5, no. 6 (A.0.102.8, 1"-27")

Translation

(1") In my eighteenth *palû* I crossed the Euphrates for the sixteenth time. Hazael of Damascus trusted in the massed body of his troops (and) mustered massive troops. (5") Mount Saniru, peak of the mountain, which is facing Mt Lebanon, he fortified. I fought with him (and) inflicted a defeat.[143] 16,000[144] of his soldiers (10") I put to the sword, 1,121 of his chariots (and) 470 of his cavalry together with his military camp I took away from him. To save (15") his life he ran away (but) I pursued him. In Damascus, his royal city, I confined him. His gardens I cut down.[145] To Mount Hauran I marched. Cities without number I razed, destroyed (and) (20") burnt with fire. Booty without number I carried off. To Mount Ba'li-ra'si, which is facing the sea,[146] I marched. My royal image I erected there. At that time,[147] (25") tribute from the land Tyre,[148] land Sidon[149] (and) from Jehu son of Omri I received.[150]

Jehu appears in these texts as "son of Omri", who paid tribute to Shalmaneser III at Ba'li-ra'si after the latter marched to Damascus and Mt Hauran. In the following sections, three important issues for Jehu's rise will be examined; (1) the location of Ba'li-ra'si; (2) Shalmaneser III's route from Mt Hauran to Ba'li-ra'si; and (3) the significance of Jehu's filiation as "son of Omri".

2.3.1.1.1. The Location of Ba'li-ra'si

The place where Jehu paid tribute to Shalmaneser III is called Ba'li-ra'si (KUR-*e* KUR *ba-'-li-ra-'-si*). Several identifications have been proposed for this toponym: (1) the promontory at the mouth of Nahr el-Kelb, north of Beirut, where six

---

143 This sentence is missing in the Marble Tablet from Ashur and in the Inscription on a Royal Statue from Calah.

144 16,020 in the Marble Tablet; the number is illegible in the Calah Inscription.

145 This part is restored according to the Marble Tablet. The same sentence possibly appears also in the Calah Inscription: "(and) his sheaves I burnt".

146 In the Marble Tablet and in the Calah Inscription, the phrase "facing the land Tyre" follows here.

147 This phrase is missing in the Marble Tablet and possibly also in the Calah Inscription.

148 In the Marble Tablet and in the Calah Inscription, this sentence reads "tribute from Ba'li-manzēri of Tyre".

149 "Land Sidon" is missing in the Marble Tablet and possibly also in the Calah Inscription.

150 In the Marble Tablet follows the sentence: "On my return Mt Lebanon I verily ascended (and) my royal image with the image of Tiglath-pileser, a strong king who preceded me, I erected". In the Calah Inscription, a word "a prince" might replace "a strong king" in this sentence.

Assyrian rock reliefs were engraved;[151] (2) Mt Carmel, which is famous as the location of the confrontation between Elijah and the priests of Baal (1 Kgs 18);[152] (3) Rosh-haniqra (Rās en-Nāqūra), situated at the modern Israeli-Lebanese border;[153] and (4) the region of Reshba'l east of Qamqa't and north of Mt Lebanon.[154]

Tyre was an island until Alexander built the dyke in 332 BCE.[155] Ba'li-ra'si is a name of a mountain (KUR-*e* = *šadê*) that both faced the sea and the land of Tyre.[156] It was located on the coast, in a place from where Tyre would be visible. It was therefore identified with either Mt Carmel or Rosh-haniqra, both of which are not very far from Tyre, although such a royal image is yet to be found in the region.[157]

2.3.1.2. Shalmaneser's Itinerary from Mt Hauran to Ba'li-ra'si

Due to the brevity of the text, it is difficult to trace the route of Shalmaneser's campaign from Mt Hauran to Ba'li-ra'si. Darb el-Hawarneh[158] and the Jezreel Valley[159] are two possible candidates. I suggest that Shalmaneser III marched through Darb el-Hawarneh, since this route was the easiest way to travel from Damascus to the Mediterranean coast, and which stretched across northern

---

151 Hommel 1885: 612, n. 3; Winckler 1909: 16; Weißbach 1922: 23-24; Katzenstein 1997: 176-178. However, the Nahr el-Kelb seems too far from Tyre (more than eighty kilometres) and Israel.

152 Olmstead 1921: 372, n. 58; Malamat 1964: 259, n. 32; 1965a: 86-87; 1965b: 372; Dussaud 1952: 385; Aharoni 1965a: 61-62; 1970: 6-7; Astour 1971: 384-386; Ikeda 1977: 196; Miller and Hayes 1986: 287; Galil 2001b: 37.

153 Malamat 1965b: 87; 1965b: 372; Lipiński 1969: 165, n. 31; 1971a: 84-85; 1979: 87, n. 123; 2004: 1-6. Cf. also Pitard 1987: 148, n. 4; Cogan and Tadmor 1988: 121, n. 11; Reinhold 1989: 175; Kuan 1995: 55, n. 174.

154 Elayi 1981: 331-341. Her argument is based on the inversion of *b'l* and *rš* in West Semitic (*op. cit.*, 334-336). The inland location of Reshba'l, however, does not seem to fit the description *ša pūt tam-ti ša pu-ut* KUR *ṣur-ri*.

155 See Katzenstein 1997: [9].

156 A principal meaning of *ša pūt* is "opposite". See *AHw* II: 884-885. There is an ambiguity in the logogram for the word *pūtu* (SAG). It might be taken either as *pūtu* or as *rēšu*. Cf. *CAD* "R": 282-283, where SAG is interpreted as "top end, front end". The description of Shalmaneser III's twentieth year campaign (839 BCE) to Que (A.0.102.10, Col. iv 30-33; A.0.102.16, 148'-150') uses similar phrasing: II *ṣalam šarrūtīya ēpuš tanatti kiššūtīya ina libbi alṭur ištēn ina rēš*(SAG) *ālānīšu šanû ina qanni ālānīšu ina pūt*(SAG) *tâmdi azqup* "I made two royal images of myself, inscribed thereon 'the praise for my power', placed one in the nearest of his cities and the other in the remotest of his cities, facing the sea" (Yamada 2000a: 200).

157 Dion 1997: 197; Yamada 2000a: 191-192. Mt Carmel is some fifty kilometres from Tyre, while Rosh-haniqra is about twenty kilometres from Tyre.

158 Lipiński 1971b: 90; Oded 1971: 193. See Lissovsky and Na'aman 2003: 306-307 with earlier literature.

159 Astour 1971: 384; Green 1979: 36 with n. 16.

Transjordan, crossed the Jordan River south of the Sea of Galilee, and continued westward through the Lower Galilee to the coast of Akko (Oded 1971:191).

2.3.1.3. Jehu, Son of Omri

"Jehu, son of Humri" (^{m}iu-$\acute{u}$-a $m\bar{a}r$ (DUMU) hu-um-ri-i) was one of the tribute bearers in Shalmaneser III's inscriptions and is generally identified with the biblical Jehu.[160] Na'aman (1997d: 19-20) and Zadok (1997: 20) suggested that the theophorous element IA should be read iu, which is equivalent to *yaw/ *$y\hat{o}$ in the Northern Israelite Hebrew of that time, and that ^{m}iu-$\acute{u}$-a represents biblical yhw' (equivalent to Jehu).[161]

The designation of Jehu as "son of Omri" in the Assyrian inscriptions has drawn scholars' attention, since it contradicts the biblical narrative, which refers to Jehu as "son of Jehoshaphat, son of Nimshi" (2 Kgs 9:2, 14).[162] Schneider (1996: 100-107) suggested that this designation should be interpreted literally as "son" or "descendant", meaning that Jehu biologically belonged to the Omride Dynasty.[163] Considering the designation of the Northern Kingdom or the kings of Israel in other places in the Assyrian royal inscriptions, however, it is unnecessary to assume that the designation reflects Jehu's actual filiation. This term has been interpreted sometimes as designating Jehu as the king of KUR $B\bar{\imath}t$ $Humri(a)$, that is, "the house of Omri", the term employed as the designation of the Kingdom of Israel in some Assyrian inscriptions (Eph'al 1991: 37, nn. 6-7).[164] The Assyrians may not have been accurate in designating foreign rulers and may have employed

---

160 McCarter (1974: 5-6) identified the tribute bearer as J(eh)oram, son of Ahab (2 Kgs 3:1-2). According to him, ^{m}ia-$\acute{u}$-a or ^{m}ia-a-$\acute{u}$ is the hypocoristic form of the theophoric element Yaw, and can stand for J(eh)oram as well as for Jehu. Weippert (1978: 113-118) suggested that ^{m}ia-$\acute{u}$-a or ^{m}ia-a-$\acute{u}$ is not a hypocoristicon, rather it linguistically represents the name of Jehu. In his opinion, the theophoric element in this name is ia and not ia-$\acute{u}$ nor ia-a, as McCarter suggested. See also Galil 2001b: 37, n. 31.

161 Halpern (1987: 81-85) assumed the original form as *$Yah\hat{u}wa$', whose last a' is a hypocoristic affix.

162 The Black Obelisk ($RIMA$ 3, A.0.102.88, line 1) also names Jehu as DUMU ^{m}hu-mu-ri.

163 Na'aman (1997c: 116; 1998: 236-238) suggested that the Assyrians intentionally designated Jehu as the legitimate successor of the Omride Dynasty, who, in contrast to his predecessors, took a pro-Assyrian policy.

164 This view was suggested by Ungnad (1906: cols. 224-226). The designation $B\bar{\imath}t$ $Humri(a)$ is attested in two royal inscriptions: Tiglath-pileser III (See Tadmor 1994: 296) and Sargon II (See Winckler 1889, vol. 1, 148, line 32 = Fuchs 1994: 261). KUR hu-um-ri-i is attested in Adad-nērārī III's Nimrud Slab (4.2.3.2.3. = $RIMA$ 3, A.0.104.8, line 12). See also Parpola 1970: 82-83. For the mention of KUR sir-$\ddot{\imath}$-la-a-a (= Israel or Jezreel?) in the Kurkh Monolith, see Yamada 2000a: 193, n. 402.

the same designation, even though the dynasty has changed.[165] Without further evidence, "Jehu, son of Humri" should be interpreted as designating Jehu as the king of the Northern Kingdom.

2.3.1.4. Background for Jehu's Rebellion in Light of Assyrian Inscriptions

It is worth noting that both Jehu's coup d'état and Shalmaneser III's military campaign to the Syro-Palestinian region took place in the same year – 841 BCE. This may show that Jehu's rebellion was related to the impending Assyrian thrust. It may have been, as Na'aman (1991: 82-83) suggested, that the battle between Joram and Hazael broke out because of the former's refusal to participate in the anti-Assyrian coalition led by the latter.[166] After Hazael killed Joram and Ahaziah and withdrew from Ramoth-Gilead to prepare for the approaching Assyrian attack, Jehu took advantage of this opportunity and usurped the Israelite throne.

2.3.2. Shalmaneser III's Campaign in 841 BCE and Jehu's Rise

Shortly after Jehu's accession to the throne (841 BCE), Shalmaneser III and his army came to Syria-Palestine. The Assyrian troops devastated the land of Damascus and then marched southward to Hauran. Passing through Lower Galilee, possibly by the Darb el-Hawarneh route, Shalmaneser arrived at Ba'li-ra'si on the Mediterranean, not far from Tyre. Jehu paid tribute there to the Assyrian king and became an Assyrian vassal.

2.4. The Mesha Inscription and Jehu's Rise

The Mesha Inscription was discovered in 1868 at Dhiban (ancient Dibon) in Transjordan. It was broken by Bedouins after its discovery; yet, most of the text has been well reconstructed, based on the paper squeeze made before the smash of the Inscription. The restored text consists of thirty-four lines, but a few lines at the bottom have not been obtained.

---

165 It is notable, however, that Ahab was designated in Shalmaneser III's inscriptions as ^{m}a-ḫa-ab-bu KUR sir-'i-la-a-a (RIMA 3, A.0.102.2, lines 90-91). For a possibility that the Assyrians began to call Israel Bīt Ḫumri already in the time of the Omride Dynasty, see Ishida 1969: 136, n. 4.

166 Na'aman (1991: 82-83) suggested that one of the motives behind Jehu's rebellion was the elimination of the anti-Assyrian party in both Israel and Judah. Yet, the motive of Jehu's rebellion cannot be explained by this hypothesis. Joram was not an enemy of Assyria at the time of Jehu's rebellion.

The Inscription can be classified as a commemorative inscription,[167] composed for the dedication of the cult place that Mesha built in Qeriho. It commemorates the king's deeds and dedicates the victories to the god Chemosh. The text divides into two main parts: (1) Mesha's victory over Israel and the restoration/conquest of its Transjordanian territory; and (2) Mesha's building activity. Mesha refers to the fall of the Omride Dynasty in line 7 of the Inscription as follows:

וארא.בה.ובבתה וישראל.אבד.אבד.עלם.

"I looked down upon him and his house, and Israel utterly perished forever."

The expression ב- ראה is an ellipsis for the meaning "to see (the fall of)..." A similar expression can be found in the Hebrew Bible.[168] "Him" and "his house" here mean Omri's son and the house of Omri, namely Israel. Mesha does not refer to the person who caused this event. Yet, the lack of the reference is natural because it was not his own achievement. It shows that the Dynasty ended during Omri's "son's" reign, which can mean one of the sons of Ahab, as the word "son" can be interpreted as a descendant of the Omrides.[169] Mesha's rebellion against Israel can thus be dated to the time of Joram of Israel, son of Ahab.[170] Hence, the Mesha Inscription indirectly corroborates Jehu's coup d'état in the time of Joram.

2.5. Synthesis

In 841 BCE, Joram of Israel and Ahaziah of Judah went to fight against Hazael of Aram-Damascus at Ramoth-Gilead. Joram and Ahaziah were killed in the battle. Jehu, the high official of the Israelite army, went to Jezreel from Ramoth-Gilead and murdered the other members of the Omride Dynasty. Soon after this event, Shalmaneser III led his army into southern Syria-Palestine. He destroyed the area around Damascus and Hauran, and then passed through Darb el-Hawarneh to reach the Mediterranean. Jehu, in contrast to the Omride kings, immediately went to this Assyrian king and paid tribute.

---

167 Drinkard 1989: 131-151; Na'aman 2001b: 12, esp. n. 8. Cf. Miller 1974: 9-18.
168 Ob 12; Ps 22:18; 37:34; 54:9; 59:11; 112:8; 118:7; Mic 7:10.
169 Cf. Gen 31:28, 43; 32:1; Ex 34:7; Pr 13:22.
170 Miller 1974: 15, n. 9; Davis 1891: 181-182.

3. The Rise of Hazael and the Aramaean Expansion

The available sources for the rise of Hazael and the Aramaean expansion during his rule include these four types: (1) Assyrian inscriptions; (2) Aramaic inscriptions; (3) biblical narrative; and (4) archaeological evidence from the Syro-Palestinian sites.

3.1. The Assyrian Sources

Some Assyrian royal inscriptions mention Hazael as Shalmaneser III's enemy. These inscriptions describe the Assyrian military campaigns during Shalmaneser's eighteenth regnal year (841 BCE) and twenty-first and twenty-second regnal years (838–837 BCE).[1] The campaign during the eighteenth regnal year is described in six annalistic texts, four of which are identical to those mentioned in the previous chapter (2.3.).[2] The campaign during the twenty-first and twenty-second regnal years is described in three inscriptions: (1) a stone fragment from Ashur (*RIMA* 3, A.0.102.13, Rev., lines 4'b-11'); (2) the Black Obelisk (*RIMA* 3, A.0.102.14, lines 102b-104a); and (3) a royal statue from Calah (*RIMA* 3, A.0.102.16, lines 152'-162'a). Furthermore, two summary inscriptions mention Hazael: (4) a royal statue from Ashur (*RIMA* 3, A.0.102.40, i, line 25 – ii, line 1) and (5) a stela in the Walters Art Gallery (*RIMA* 3, A.0.102.9, Right side, line 1'-15').[3] A booty inscription on a stone tablet from Ashur (*RIMA* 3, A.0.102.92, lines 1-8) also refers to Hazael.

---

1   I follow Reade (1978: 251-260) and Yamada (2000a: 59-67), who suggested that the campaigns during the twenty-first and the twenty-second regnal years are conflated into one single campaign in Shalmaneser III's annals. See also Yamada 2000a: 205-206.

2   A stone fragment from Ashur (A.0.102.13, lines 9'b-10') also mentions the campaign during the eighteenth regnal year. It is quite fragmentary and only the beginning of the account is readable: "[In] my eighteenth *palû*". The Bull Inscription (*RIMA* 3, A.0.102.8, lines 1"-13") is equivalent to Squeeze *III R*, 5, no. 6 of the British Museum (*RIMA* 3, A.0.102.8, lines 1"-13").

3   For the classification of this inscription as a summary inscription, see Yamada 2000a:42-43.

3.1.1. Hazael as Usurper

The inscription on a royal statue from Ashur (*RIMA* 3, A.0.102.40, i, line 25 – ii, line 6) refers to the change of rulers in Damascus during the mid-ninth century BCE.

3.1.1.1. The Inscription on a Royal Statue from Ashur (*RIMA* 3, A.0.102.40, i, line 14 – ii, line 1)

(i, 14) On Adad-idri of Damascus with twelve kings, his helpers, I inflicted a defeat. 29,000 of his powerful fighters I laid down like rushes. The remainder of his army, into (i, 20) the Orontes River I laid out. To save their lives, they ran away. (i, 25) Adad-idri passed away (and) Hazael, son of nobody, took the throne. He mustered his massive troops (and) moved against me to wage war. I fought with him (and) inflicted a defeat. I took away the wall of his camp. To save his life he ran away. I pursued (him) as far as Damascus, his royal city. (ii, 1) [His] gardens [I cut down].

This inscription summarises four historical events which occurred in 853–841 BCE.[4] These events can be summarised as follows: (1) the battle with Adad-idri and his allies in 853 BCE (i, 14-24); (2) the death of Adad-idri (i, 25); (3) the rise of Hazael (i, 26-27a); and (4) the battle with Hazael in 841 BCE (i, 27b – ii, 1). Although the exact dates cannot be established, Adad-idri's death and the rise of Hazael must have occurred between 845 and 841 BCE.[5] 2 Kgs 8:28-29, 9:14-15, and the Tel Dan Inscription suggest that Hazael fought Joram, the predecessor of Jehu, who usurped the former's throne in 841 BCE. Hence, Hazael's usurpation must have occurred earlier than 841 BCE. Since a usurper must establish his position in the kingdom at the first stage of his usurpation, it would take time before he could organise a military campaign abroad. Therefore, Hazael's usurpation can be dated some time before that of Jehu, a few years before the battle of Ramoth-Gilead (*ca.* 843 BCE).[6]

In this text, Hazael is called *mār lā mammāna*, "son of nobody", the term which generally refers to a usurper or an upstart.[7] The view that Hazael was a usurper may be supported by Assyrian inscriptions from Tiglath-pileser III's reign,

4 See Yamada 2000a: 188-195.
5 Adad-idri is described as leader of the anti-Assyrian coalition during Shalmaneser's fourteenth regnal year (845 BCE) campaign (*RIMA* 3, A.0.102.6, iii, lines 24-27; A.0.102.8, lines 44'b-45'; A.0.102.10, Col. iii, lines 14-18). See Yamada 2000a: 179-183.
6 Galil 2007: 82.
7 Seux 1980-83: 152. In his opinion, this term is not a pejorative appellation. On the other hand, Oded (1992: 69-75) suggested that the term is one of stigmatisation. For the usage of this term in the Neo-Assyrian texts, see Stith 2008: 52-53.

which refer to Damascus as "Bīt Hazaili".[8] Here, Damascus is designated by the name of Hazael: "Bīt Hazaili" = "house of Hazael". By using the form of "Bīt X", Assyrians designated the kingdoms by the name of its legendary or actual founder.[9] Also, a biblical anecdote about the change of the throne in Damascus in 2 Kgs 8:7-15 may possibly support the view that Hazael was not the nominated royal heir (see 3.4.2.). Consequently, Hazael would have not been the first in line of succession to the throne, although he was a member of the royal family.[10] If this is the case, it is plausible that the other coalition members were required, according to the ancient Near Eastern practice, to remain loyal to Adad-idri's line of succession and oppose Hazael, the usurper.[11] This hypothesis conforms well to the account of the campaign of Shalmaneser's eighteenth regnal year (841 BCE), which describes how Hazael, without allies, confronted the Assyrian army. This change of political situation in Syria probably offered Shalmaneser III the opportunity to conduct a military campaign in Syria in 841 BCE (Yamada 2000a: 190).

3.1.2. Shalmaneser III's Campaign during His Eighteenth Regnal Year (841 BCE)

In 841 BCE, Shalmaneser III launched a military campaign to Syria-Palestine. The Assyrian army probably took the route through the Beqaʿ Valley, located between the Lebanon and the Anti-Lebanon Ranges, as in the later campaign of the twenty-first *palû* (838–837 BCE).[12] Shalmaneser encountered the Aramaean army led by Hazael[13] at Mt Sanir, identified with the Anti-Lebanon Range that lies east of Mt Lebanon.[14] The Assyrian army inflicted defeat upon the Aramaean army; as a result, Hazael fled to Damascus. The Assyrian army confined Hazael in Damascus and cut down the orchards.[15] Then Shalmaneser took the road southward and destroyed the towns of Hauran (KUR-*e* KUR *Ha-ú-ra-ni*),[16] possibly the modern

---

8   Tadmor 1994 (Summ. 9, Rev., line 3; Summ. 4, line 7'). Naʾaman 1995a: 387.

9   Ungnad 1906: 224-226. See also Naʾaman 1995a: 385, n. 19 for literature.

10   This issue will be discussed below (3.2.1.).

11   Esarhaddon's succession treaty (Parpola and Watanabe 1988) and the Sefire Inscription (*KAI* 1: 224, lines 9-14) include stipulations that obligate the signatory monarchs to oppose any illegitimate claimant to the throne of the author (Stith 2008: 59).

12   On this route and its alternative, see Yamada 2000a: 191 with n. 390 for earlier literature.

13   *RIMA* 3, A.0.102.8, lines 5"-13"; A.0.102.10, Col. iii, line 49 – iv, line 1; A.0.102.12, lines 22-25; A.0.102.16, lines 124'-128'; A.0.102.40, Col. i, lines 29-31.

14   See Aharoni 1965a: 295; Ikeda 1978: 36-37.

15   *RIMA* 3, A.0.102.8, lines 14"-17"; A.0.102.10, Col. iv, lines 1-4; A.0.102.12, lines 25-26; A.0.102.16, lines 129'-130'; A.0.102.40, Col. i, line 32 – ii, line 1. For the custom of cutting trees in Assyrian warfare, see Cole 1997; Wright 2008: 443.

16   *RIMA* 3, A.0.102.8, lines 17"-21"; A.0.102.10, Col. iv, lines 4-7; A.0.102.12, lines 26-28; A.0.102.16, lines 130'-132'.

Jebel ed-Druz, in the Suweida area,[17] and proceeded westward, to the Mediterranean. He erected a stela at Ba'li-ra'si (KUR-*e* KUR *ba-'-li-ra-'-si*), and received tribute from Tyre, Sidon, and Israel (2.3.1.1.).[18]

3.1.3. Shalmaneser III's Campaign in His Twenty-First and Twenty-Second Regnal Years (838–837 BCE)

Three years after the 841 campaign, Shalmaneser III conducted another military expedition to Syria (838–837 BCE). There are long and short versions that describe this campaign; the longer version covers the shorter and will be cited here.

3.1.3.1. The Inscription on a Royal Statue from Calah (*RIMA* 3, A.0.102.16, 152'-162'a)[19]

(152') [In] my [twenty-first pa]llû [I crossed] the Euphrates [for the twenty-first time]. [Trib]ute from all the kings [of the land Hatti] I received. From [the land Hatti(?)] I moved. The stretching road of the Leba[non] I took. Mt Saniru I cro[ssed]. To the cities (155') [of] Hazael of Damascus (K[UR] imērīšu) I went down. The cities […] became afraid 20 and to the difficult mountain they took. Ya[…], […], Danabu, Malaha, the fortified cities, I conquered by [tunnel, battering]-rams, and towers. I massacred. I plundered them. The [town]s I destroyed (and) set them on fire. Ba'il (160') of the land of [. . .]ra seized my feet. I received his tribute. My royal image, in the temple in Laruba, his fortified city, I erected and received the tribute of the people of Tyre, Sidon (and) Byblos. I went as far as the land/mountain of Muṣuruna.

Some scholars have suggested that Shalmaneser might have conducted two separate campaigns in 838–837 BCE, but conflated the descriptions of the two campaigns into one.[21] However, no solid reasons for two separate campaigns have

---

17   It must be distinguished between Mt Hauran (KUR-*e* KUR *Ha-ú-ra-ni*) in the inscriptions of Shalmaneser III and the province Haurīna (URU/KUR *Ha-ú-ri-i-na*). The latter appears in the later lists of provinces and has been identified with Ḥawwārīn between Qaryetên and Ṣadād, about ninety kilometres west of Palmyra. See Eph'al 1984: 149, n. 514 with earlier literature. For the identification of Mt Hauran with Jebel ed-Druz, see Aharoni 1979: 37; Dussaud 1927: 323-324.

18   *RIMA* 3, A.0.102.8, lines 22"-27"; A.0.102.10, Col. iv, lines 7-12; A.0.102.12, lines 28-30; A.0.102.16, lines 132'-135'.

19   Hulin's copy of this inscription was published by Yamada (2000b: 77-85, esp. 80). The inscription on a stone fragment from Ashur (*RIMA* 3, A.0.102.13, Rev. lines 4'b-11') is fragmentary and most of the text must be restored by the text in A.0.102.16, lines 152'-162'a.

20   Cf. GAG §101f; CAD "G" garāru B, 49.

21   Reade 1978: 254; Kuan 1995: 21, 64; Yamada 2000a: 206; Younger 2005: 262.

been adduced; hence, the itinerary and the chronological order of events of this campaign will be reconstructed according to the order in the text.

Shalmaneser did not encounter opposition when he headed toward Damascus.[22] He probably took the Beqaʿ Valley route, as the itinerary suggests. Then, he conquered four fortified cities of Hazael, but only two names survived in the extant text: Malaha and Danabu.[23] The conquest of these cities was apparently a significant event during these years as two pieces of evidence show. First, the conquest of the four cities is mentioned in the short text of the Black Obelisk (RIMA 3, A.0.102.14, 103). Second, Malaha and Danabu are also described in the entries of the Eponym Chronicles for 838 and 837 BCE.

Several identifications have been suggested for the city of Malaha: (1) Al-maliha, several kilometres east of Damascus; (2) Safiyet-Melah, seventeen kilometres east of Salhad;[24] and (3) Hazor in the Huleh Valley.[25] Nonetheless, the exact location of Malaha cannot be determined because many toponyms with the root mlḥ are known throughout the region (Lemaire 1991a: 100-101).[26] It was probably located in the Hauran region, where many mlḥ-toponyms are preserved.[27]

Danabu has been identified with Ṣednaya, located about twenty kilometres north of Damascus and known as Danaba/Danoba in the classical sources.[28] Another possible candidate is Daniba/Dhouneibe in the Bashan, located eighteen kilometres east of Naveh, between Sheikh Meskin and Ezraʿa.[29] Lipiński (2000:352) dismissed both identifications and suggested that ad-Dunaybah, a settlement located fifteen kilometres north of modern Irbid, may preserve the ancient name Danabu, while near-by Tell Abila may be the actual site of ancient Danabu. Parpola and Porter (2001: 8, Map 8) located it at modern Ḍunaiba in the Beqaʿ Valley. Evidently, the location of Danabu cannot be determined with certainty.

---

22   RIMA 3, A.0.102.16, line 154'.

23   RIMA 3, A.0.102.16, lines 155'-159'.

24   Sader 1987: 266.

25   Lipiński (2000: 350-351) identified Malaha with Hazor; yet, the change of the city-name from the traditional form Ha-ṣu-ra to Malaha seems unlikely. Hazor was spelled as Ha-ṣú-ra, Ha-ṣú-ra-a, and Ha-ṣu-ra-yu in the Mari documents from the eighteenth century BCE. For example, see ARM VI, 78, Rev. lines 14, 15. Later, the Amarna Letters from the mid-fourteenth century BCE also mentions the city as Ha-ṣu-ri. EA (El-Amarna Letters) 148:41; 227:3, 21; 228:4, 15, 23; 364:18. The Hebrew Bible preserves the name חצור Ḥāṣôr.

26   See also Galil 2001b: 38, n. 35. The major difficulty is that almost no systematic archaeological survey in the region south and southeast of Damascus has been conducted.

27   Dussaud 1927: 366; Sader 1987: 266.

28   Kraeling 1918: 80; Honigmann 1938: 116; Pitard 1987: 150; Lemaire 1991a: 101. Cf. Sader 1987: 266. See Lipiński 2000: 352, n. 26; Yamada 2000a: 208, n. 446; Galil 2001b: 38, n. 35 with earlier literature. Olmstead (1921: 374, n. 62) located Danabu in the vicinity of ʿAzaz or Aleppo. Cf. Yamada 2000a: 208, n. 446.

29   Dussaud 1927: 332; Aḥituv 1984: 89; Lemaire 1991a: 101. Cf. Sader 1987: 266.

Shalmaneser does not mention Damascus during this campaign and obviously failed to conquer it.[30] After mentioning Hazael's four cities, Shalmaneser relates that a ruler named Ba'il submitted to him and he received his tribute and erected his royal image in Ba'il's city.[31] The name of Ba'il's country is illegible (⸢KUR⸣ Z[I]/G[I]-x-[r]a-a). Most scholars have sought his country in the Phoenician region because the name Ba'il includes the theophorous element "Ba'al", a characteristic divine element of Phoenician names.[32] Based on this consideration, two candidates have been suggested: Tyre and Ṣimirra. The reading of Ba'il's country as Tyre (Ṣurrāya)[33] is difficult, as pointed out by Yamada (2000b: 80).[34] Another candidate, Ṣimirra (Lipiński 1999: 242), likewise faces difficulties. Na'aman (2002b: 205) dismissed this reading for the following three reasons. (1) Its location does not agree with Shalmaneser's itinerary; it must be sought to the east of the Anti-Lebanon. (2) Ṣimirra is always written with the ṢI sign and not with the ZI (= ṢÍ) sign. (3) Ṣimirra appears in the Assyrian inscriptions with the determinative URU (city) and not with KUR (land).[35] Instead, he tentatively restored the land name as Geshur ([KU]R G[i⁽ʳ⁾-šu(r)-r]a-a), which appears in the Hebrew Bible as a small Aramaean kingdom located in the southern part of the Golan Heights to east of the Sea of Galilee.[36] Based on this restoration, he identified Laruba, Ba'il's fortified city, with 'En Gev, on the eastern shore of the Sea of Galilee, where a massive casemate wall was uncovered.[37] The identification of Ba'il's country with Geshur is inconclusive as Geshur is never attested in extrabiblical sources, except for in an emended cuneiform text from the Amarna period (EA 256, line 23),[38] and the extensive excavation at the site of 'En Gev has

---

30   Miller and Hayes (1986: 285-287) suggested that Hazael already submitted himself to Assyria in 841 BCE. In Galil's (2001b: 38) view, Shalmaneser III intentionally avoided conquering Damascus in order to preserve the balance of power in the Syro-Palestinian region.

31   *RIMA* 3, A.0.102.16, lines 159'-161'.

32   Benz 1972: 234.

33   The ruler of Tyre in the year 841 BCE was Ba'li-manzēri (A.0.102.10, Col. iv, line 10). A fortified city called *Ma-ru-ba* has been attested in the territory of Sidon at the time of Esarhaddon. Borger 1956: 49, Nin. A, iii 15. For details, see Yamada 2000a: 209, n. 450. If *La-ru-ba*, described in the text as a fortified city of Ba'il, was a scribal error for *Ma-ru-ba* (the two graphemes are similar), Ba'li would have been Ba'li-manzēri of Tyre. For this possibility, see Yamada 2000a: 208-209; 2000b: 80.

34   See also Grayson *RIMA* 3: 79.

35   Na'aman pointed out an exceptional case, in which the Assyrian text refers to Ṣimirra with the determinative KUR after it became an Assyrian province. At least two more such cases exist: Balawat texts 126, line 25 (KUR *Ṣi-mir-ra*), see Parker 1963: 98; and Sargon's inscription (KUR *Ṣi-mir-ra*), see Winckler 1889, vol. 1, 102, line 33.

36   2 Sam 3:3; 13:37-38; 14:23, 32; 15:8.

37   Na'aman 2002b: 206 with earlier literature.

38   Mazar (1961: 20) emended *ga-ri* to *ga-<šu>-ri*.

not revealed any Assyrian royal image (Tsukimoto, Hasegawa, and Onozuka 2009; Tsukimoto and Kuwabara *forthcoming*).

Shalmaneser's itinerary ends with a place called Muṣuruna, which is the furthest place he reached in his campaign.[39] The toponym Muṣri/Muṣur/Muṣuri in Assyrian texts, which is usually identified with Egypt,[40] does not fit the context of this campaign (Garelli 1971: 37-42). Disappearance of Muṣuruna in the shorter version of this campaign may suggest that the later Assyrian scribe regarded this achievement as marginal.

The itinerary suggests locating Muṣuruna on the Phoenician coast: Shalmaneser reached this place after he received the tribute of the men of Tyre, Sidon, and Byblos. Na'aman (2002a: 207) tentatively identified this Muṣuruna with the ridge of Nahr el-Kelb, about ten kilometres north of Beirut. A relief of a royal image, engraved at the river's mouth, may possibly represent Shalmaneser III.[41] In addition, the location of the ridge of Nahr el-Kelb fits nicely with the geographical context described in the text. Hence, Muṣuruna can be identified with Nahr el-Kelb.

3.1.4. Assyria and Syria-Palestine after the Campaign of 838–837 BCE

The Assyrian hegemony in Syria-Palestine, which Shalmaneser III achieved by the campaigns in 841 and 838–837 BCE, did not last long. During the later years of Shalmaneser's reign and the beginning of his son's, Šamšī-Adad V (826–820 BCE), Assyria suffered from internal revolts. Shalmaneser's last campaign to the Syro-Palestinian region (to Unqi) was in 829 BCE. From this year until 805 BCE, for more than twenty years, Assyria did not conduct campaigns to Syria. During this power vacuum, Hazael established his hegemony over the entire Syro-Palestinian region.

3.2. The Aramaic Sources

Several Aramaic sources pertaining to Hazael are available: (1) the Tel Dan Inscription; (2) the Arslan-Tash Inscription; (3) the Nimrud Inscription; (4) the Samos and Eretria Inscriptions; (5) the Zakkur Inscription; and (6) the Tell Deir

---

39 *RIMA* 3, A.0.102.16, line 162'.

40 Miṣr in modern Arabic and Miṣrāyim in the Hebrew Bible. For example, scholars discussed whether KUR *Mu-uṣ-ra-a-a*, mentioned in the Kurkh Monolith of Shalmaneser III (*RIMA* 3, A.0.102.2, Col. ii, line 92) as one of the members of an anti-Assyrian coalition, can be identified as Egypt. See Lipiński 2000: 204-205; Yamada 2000a: 157-158 with nn. 281 and 282 with earlier literature.

41 Weißbach 1922: 23-25.

'Alla Inscription. Since the Tel Dan Inscription was already discussed in detail (Chapter 2), I would like to open the discussion with the Arslan-Tash Inscription.

3.2.1. The Arslan-Tash Inscription

In 1928, an Aramaic inscription dedicated to Hazael was discovered. It was found in a building next to an Assyrian palace at Arslan-Tash (ancient Hadattu), located between Tel Ahmar in Syria and Urfa in modern Turkey. Three pieces of a broken ivory plaque bear an inscription and were published in 1931.[42] It was read as follows:

... זת.ח.[...].בר.עמא.למראן.חזאל.בשנת ...

Later, Puech (1981: 545-550) rejected the arrangement of the pieces and proposed a different reconstruction of the text:

[...].זי.ק.[רב.עמא.למראן.חזאל.בשנת.]אח[זת.ח.]מתˀ]

Translation

[... which] the troops [o]ffered to our Lord, Hazael, in the year of the [cap]ture of Ha[math?].

Most scholars followed Puech's decipherment, albeit with slight modifications.[43] Various opinions concerning two elements in the text were proposed: the meaning of the word עמא and the restoration of the toponym at the end of the inscription. Puech translated עמא as a noun, "troops", whereas Lipiński (1994: 93) interpreted it as a city name 'Imma, located on "strategic crossroads, where a sanctuary of Hadad was certainly not out of place".[44] Bron and Lemaire (1989), Röllig (*KAI* 2: 282; 1974: 39), and Naʾaman (1995a: 382) construed it as a personal name. Considering the absence of a preposition, such as מן "from", before עמא, it is preferable to construe the word as a personal name. 'Amma could have been either a vassal king of Hazael or an official in his court.

It is generally assumed that the end of the inscription "ח[...]" is a toponym, which has been diversely restored: (1) Hauran (Puech 1981); (2) Hamath/ Hadrach/Hazor (Bron and Lemaire 1989); (3) Hazaz (Bron and Lemaire 1989; Lipiński 2000: 388-389); and (4) Haleb (Lipiński 1994: 93). Although none of these restorations is decisive,[45] it is tempting to restore Ha[math] here in light of the Zakkur Inscription (Naʾaman 1996: 177, n. 3).[46]

---

42 Thureau-Dangin *et al.* 1931.

43 For example, Bron and Lemaire 1989: 37; Naʾaman 1995a: 382.

44 He read the word before עמא as [ה]דד and interpreted it as the name of person who sent the plaque.

45 Mazar (1962: 112, 114) suggested that this ivory plaque, which was discovered in Arslan-Tash, is sufficient evidence to testify that Hazael ruled over northern Syria. Yet, the find site of this

The Arslan-Tash Inscription was dedicated to Hazael on the occasion of a remarkable achievement. This is why that the penultimate word was restored as אח[זת] "[cap]ture of"; yet, the restoration is highly speculative. If this restoration is correct, Hazael probably conquered a certain city, and the dedication was made on that occasion. At any rate, such or a similar remarkable achievement of Hazael could be dated to the period after Shalmaneser III stopped campaigning to Syria-Palestine (after 837 BCE).

3.2.2. The Nimrud Inscription

Mallowan (1966: 598) published an Aramaic inscription on a fragment of ivory found during the excavations of 1960–63 at Fort Shalmaneser in Nimrud, ancient Kalhu. The text reads:

למר[אן חזאל...]

Millard suggested that the inscription might have been a parallel text of the Arslan-Tash Inscription.[47]

3.2.3. The Samos Inscription

An Aramaic inscription on bronze horse trappings was published by Kyrieleis and Röllig in 1988.[48] It was unearthed in debris dating to the early sixth century BCE at the Heraion (temple of Hera) in Samos. The iconographical style of four naked goddesses, which lie in the centre of the inscription, indicates its northern Syrian origin. Kyrieleis and Röllig read the text as follows:

זי נתן הדר למראן חזאל מן עמק בשן תערה מראן נהר

Translation

   (This is) what HDR gave our Lord Hazael of the Valley of Bashan. "Forehead-cover" of our lofty Lord.

Röllig (Kyrieleis and Röllig 1988: 70-71) suggested that this text is identical with that of the Eretria Inscription, a damaged bronze blinker with an Aramaic inscription found at Eretria in Greece (Charbonnet 1986: 117-156, Pls. 33-41). This view has been accepted by scholars.

---

plaque does not help to identify the place name; it was most probably brought there by the Assyrians as booty (Pitard 1987: 153-156; Hafthorsson 2006: 42-43).

46   Cf. Puech 1981: 549.

47   Millard's comment is mentioned in Mallowan 1966: 598. Cf. Röllig 1974: 48; Puech 1981: 546; Pitard 1987: 156; Eph'al and Naveh 1989: 197; Bron and Lemaire 1989: 37; Hafthorsson 2006: 43.

48   Kyrieleis and Röllig 1988.

Two critical studies of this text were published by Eph'al and Naveh (1989) and by Bron and Lemaire (1989). They restored the text as follows:

זי נתן הדד למראן חזאל מן עמק בשנת עדה מראן נהר.

Despite the identical restoration, Eph'al and Naveh and Bron and Lemaire translated the text differently. The former translated it: "That which Hadad gave our lord Hazael from 'Umq in the year that our lord crossed the river." The latter rendered it: "That which Hadad from 'Umq, gave our lord Hazael in the year that our lord crossed the river." The two translations differ in the following three issues: (1) the identification of Hadad; (2) the location of עמק ('Umq); and (3) the identification of the river (נהר) Hazael crossed.

Bron and Lemaire (1989: 42-43) construed Hadad as the king of עמק, who paid tribute to Hazael at that time,[49] whereas Eph'al and Naveh (1989: 194) interpreted Hadad as the name of the major Damascene god.[50] The latters' view is corroborated by the study of Amadasi-Guzzo (1996: 331-334) who compared the use of the verb נתן in the Samos Inscriptions with those of other Aramaic inscriptions from various places and periods. She reached the conclusion that Hadad must have been a name of a divinity who bestowed this object upon Hazael.

Both scholars identified עמק in the inscriptions with 'Umqi/Patina, which is attested in some inscriptions from the first millennium BCE.[51] This kingdom, also called Unqi/Pattin, was a Neo-Hittite kingdom located in the neighbourhood of modern Antakya and is mentioned as עמק in the Zakkur Inscription.[52] Eph'al and Naveh (1989: 194-195) suggested that עמק is the origin of the object dedicated to Hazael, while Bron and Lemaire (1989: 42-43) regarded it as the origin of Hadad, Hazael's tributary. Hafthorsson (2006: 48-49) suggested that Hazael originally came from 'Umqi/Patina and later usurped the Damascene throne.[53] However, no source supports the view that the Eretria and Samos Inscriptions refer to the

---

49 Kyrieleis and Röllig (1988: 63-64) suggested that the person here was the king who offered this object to Hazael, although they read the name as הדר "HDR".

50 They also suggested the inscription as being made in this city, because "in Old Aramaic Hadad should first of all be considered as a divine name." This view was accepted by Lipiński (1994: 92; 2000: 388) and Dion (1995: 484). Lipiński (2000: 388, n. 222) found it difficult to assume an Aramaean ruler in 'Umq between the reigns of Sasi (ca. 830 BCE) and Tutamuwa (ca. 740 BCE), both bearing Hittite names.

51 Also Lipiński 1994: 92; 2000: 388; Dion 1997: 201-202; Hafthorsson 2006: 48.

52 KAI 1: 202, A. line 6. On the Assyrian references to the kingdom of Unqi/Pattina, see Parpola 1970: 158 (Hattina); 368 (Unqi); Hawkins 1972–75a: 160-162 (Hattin); 1974: 81-83; Klengel 1992: 194-201.

53 Pitard (1994: 221), because of the popularity of the name Hazael at that time, even doubted the identification of Hazael in the inscriptions with Hazael of Aram-Damascus. Assyrian inscriptions refer to at least eleven different Hazaels (Zadok 1977: 86; Baker 2000: 467-469). Even so, considering the title of our Hazael מראן "our lord", Hazael of Aram-Damascus, whom Shalmaneser III could not subjugate, and whose son led the army of Syrian states against Zakkur of Hamath, is the best candidate.

homeland of Hazael. Following Eph'al and Naveh, I interpret עמק as the provenance of the object, which was brought to Hazael either as tribute or as booty.[54]

Interpreting נהר as indicating the Orontes River cannot be excluded due to its proximity to 'Umqi/Patina.[55] In the Assyrian texts, the word *nāru* "river" often appears without any qualification and must be interpreted according to the context. Similarly, נהר in the Hebrew Bible refers either to the Jordan (Num 22:5; Jos 24:14, 15) or to the Euphrates (Jos 24:2, 3; 2 Sam 10:16; 1 Kgs 5:1, 4; 14:15; Isa 7:20). Nonetheless, the significance of crossing the Euphrates is self-evident, when considering the unremitting mention of the Euphrates crossing in Shalmaneser III's inscriptions. Yamada (1998) explained that the reference to the Euphrates crossing was so significant that it was even manipulatively counted in the later inscriptions of Shalmaneser III. Likewise, it is possible that crossing the Euphrates could have been one of the greatest achievements of the Aramaean king.[56] To commemorate this outstanding deed, it is likely that court officials or vassal kings offered prestigious objects to Hazael. Hazael's crossing of the Euphrates must be dated after Shalmaneser III stopped crossing the Euphrates, specifically after 829 BCE, his campaign to Unqi.[57] More precisely, it would have been after 826 BCE when the Eponym Chronicles no longer mention Assyrian military campaigns.[58] Thus, the campaign of Hazael beyond the Euphrates can be dated between 826 BCE and 805 BCE, when Adad-nērārī III resumed the campaign to the west of the Euphrates.

3.2.4. The Zakkur Inscription

At the beginning of the twentieth century, Pognon (1907–08) published an Aramaic inscription engraved on fragments of a basalt stela. The original location of the inscription was not mentioned by Pognon; later, Dussaud (1922) located it at Tell Afis, some forty-five kilometres southwest of Aleppo. The author of the stela

---

54   Amadasi-Guzzo 1996: 337.

55   Eph'al and Naveh 1989: 196; Bron and Lemaire 1989: 40; Lemaire 1991a: 101-106; Lipiński 1994: 92; Na'aman 1995a: 391; Amadasi-Guzzo 1996: 334; Dion 1997: 202; Bordreuil 1998: 56-57; Lipiński 2000: 389; Hafthorsson 2006: 49.

56   Bron and Lemaire (1989: 37, 41, 43) suggested the possibility of using it for chronological reference. Cf. Eph'al and Naveh 1989: 195, n. 16. Harrak (1992: 67-73) and Dion (1995: 484, n. 11) rejected this possibility.

57   Eph'al and Naveh (1989: 198) and Dion (1995: 486) dated it between 830–806 BCE, whereas Bron and Lemaire (1989: 43) dated it between 810–805 BCE, to the end of Hazael's reign.

58   Only the revolts are mentioned during this period. Lemaire (1991a: 104) tentatively dated it to around 810–809 BCE.

is Zakkur, [59] king of Lu'ash and Hamath, who composed and dedicated the inscription to the gods Ba'al-shamayin and El-wer in the early eighth century BCE. The inscription describes the siege of Hadrach, the city of Zakkur, by a coalition of Syrian kingdoms, which was led by Bar-Hadad, son of Hazael. The siege suddenly ended and Zakkur expressed his thanks to Ba'al-shamayin.

The siege took place either at the end of the ninth or at the beginning of the eighth century BCE.[60] Assuming that Bar-Hadad inherited the hegemony from his father, the inscription reflects the Damascene hegemony over the Syrian kingdoms at Hazael's time.[61]

At least eight kingdoms are named as members of the coalition led by Bar-Hadad: Arpad (= Bar-gush), Que, 'Umq, Gurgum, Sam'al, Melid, and another two kingdoms whose names do not survive.[62] In addition to these eight named kingdoms, a specific number of other participants is mentioned in the text.[63] Israel apparently did not participate in this coalition, which might indicate that it had thrown off the Damascene yoke by that time.

3.2.5. The Deir 'Alla Inscription

In 1967, a heavily damaged inscription was unearthed by the Dutch expedition at Tell Deir 'Alla in the eastern Jordan Valley (Hoftijzer and van der Kooij 1976).[64] The text has been considered as evidence of an Aramaean control in Transjordan

---

59   The name of the king was long read as Zakir. However, the Assyrian transcription in the Anta-
      kya Stela, referring to the same king as ᵐZakkuri, established the reading Zakkur. See Donbaz
      1990: 6-7, line 4.

60   For the date of this event, see 4.2.3.

61   Lemaire 1991a: 104; 1993: 150*.

62   Gibson (1975: 14) and Lemaire (1993: 151*) restored Kummuh and Carchemish here. Yet,
      Na'aman (1991: 84-86) and Lipiński (2000: 302-303) questioned the restoration of Kummuh be-
      cause this kingdom did not participate in the struggle against Assyria in the ninth through eighth
      centuries BCE. See Hawkins 1974: 79-80; 1983: 338-340 with early literature. Lipiński (*op. cit.*,
      303) suggested restoring Tabal and Kittik.

63   Some scholars restored "sixteen" in lines 4-5 for the number of kings (Dupont-Sommer 1949:
      46-48; Gibson 1975: 8; Reinhold 1989: 251, 253; Lemaire 1993: 151*; Dion 1997: 140, n. 15),
      whereas others read "seventeen" (Friedrich 1966: 83; Lipiński 1971b: 398, n. 34; Sader 1987:
      208). For the discussion, see *KAI* 2: 207-208. Seven or eight more kingdoms are to be expected
      in the continuance of the inscription if sixteen or seventeen kings, in total, are mentioned here.
      Actually, line 8 refers to "seven kin(gs)" as Lemaire suggested (*op. cit.*, 151*). Cf. Gibson 1975: 8,
      14; Delsman 1985. Lemaire (*op. cit.*, 151*) read אמר, instead of the general reading [ה]מו, in the
      beginning of line 9 and restored "seven kin(gs) of Amurru" in lines 8-9. However, the number
      "seven" in the text might be a typological number.

64   Tell Deir 'Alla is commonly identified with biblical Succoth. See MacDonald 2000: 144 for
      earlier literature. For bibliography, see Aufrecht 1986; Lemaire 1991c: 55-57. For identification
      of Tell Deir 'Alla with Penuel, see MacDonald, *op. cit.*, 148-149.

during the eighth century BCE[65] because of the following three reasons: (1) linguistic affinity of the text to Aramaic; (2) the location of the site; and (3) the date of the inscription.

Gilead was under Aramaean hegemony after Hazael's invasion, possibly *ca.* 825 BCE,[66] until Bar-Hadad's submission to Adad-nērārī III in 796 BCE. From 796 BCE until the reign of Rezin (*ca.* 750 BCE), however, relations between the Aramaeans and the inhabitants of Transjordan remain unknown.[67] The language of the Deir ʿAlla Inscription might help us to establish these undetermined relations.

Despite its similarities to Aramaic, the language of the text cannot be defined as Aramaic proper due to some features which are foreign to Aramaic but common in the Canaanite languages. It seems that the text of the Deir ʿAlla Inscription retains archaic features of a Proto-Northwest Semitic language (McCarter 1991: 90-95).[68] Hence, this inscription alone cannot be evidence for Aramaic influence at that time.

However, an Aramaic inscription (זי שרעא) was discovered on a jar from the same stratum (IX).[69] Combined with the inscription, the Deir ʿAlla Inscriptions

---

65   This dating is based on the archaeological context that is corroborated by 14C dating (880-770 BCE). See Ibrahim and van der Kooij 1991: 27-28; Lipiński 1994: 104-106. See also Lemaire 1991c: 34-35, nn. 3-6 with earlier literature.

66   For the dating, see 3.1.4. The date of Hazael's expansion in Transjordan might have been earlier than 825 BCE. Cf. Naʾaman 1995b: 107 (*ca.* 835 BCE). Yet, it is not clear whether Hazael conquered Gilead in 841 BCE immediately after the battle at Ramoth-Gilead described in the Book of Kings.

67   Largely depending on the biblical source (2 Kgs 15:29), Lemaire (1985b: 272-273; 1991c: 36-41) suggested that Gilead and the middle Jordan Valley on the Transjordan side was controlled by the Aramaeans of Damascus between *ca.* 835 and *ca.* 750 BCE and by the Israelites before the annexation of Gilead by Tiglath-pileser III in *ca.* 733 BCE. See also Halpern 1987: 121; Hübner 1992: 42.

68   The language of the inscription has features peculiar to Aramaic (Hoftijzer and van der Kooij 1976: 300; McCarter 1991: 87-89), which led some scholars to define this language as a dialect of Aramaic (Hoftijzer and van der Kooij, *op. cit.*, 300-302; Caquot and Lemaire 1977; Fitzmyer 1978; McCarter 1980; Kaufman 1980; Levine 1981; Pardee 1991: 105). On the other hand, it has other features that are customarily regarded as distinctively Canaanite (McCarter 1991: 89-90), which led some scholars to categorise it as Canaanite (Naveh 1979: 133-136; Greenfield 1980: 248-252; Hackett 1984a: 109-124; 1984b: 57-65). Since no clear dichotomy exists between Aramaic and Canaanite, the categorisation of the language of these texts is only a matter of relativity. Lemaire (1985b; 1985c: 38), to explain its archaic linguistic features, suggested that the texts might have been copied from an older Aramaic text (also Wolters 1988).

69   Hoftijzer and van der Kooij 1976: 15, 167, 267, Pls. 19-22; Lemaire 1985c: 273; Ephʿal and Naveh 1993; Lipiński 1994: 107. Whether the Aramaeans "controlled" this region is not clear. Cf. Levine 1985: 327-28. Wolters's suggestion (1988) to ascribe the Aramaic influence in the region to the Aramaean population deported after the Assyrian annexation of Damascus in 732 BCE must be rejected, because the date of the strata M/IX predates 732 BCE (most probably 880–770 BCE by C14). Cf. Dion 1997: 200, n. 127.

possibly show the Aramaic cultural influence in the region during the first half of the eighth century BCE.[70]

3.2.6. The Damascene Hegemony under Hazael and Bar-Hadad

The Aramaic sources discussed above supply valuable information on Hazael's military activities outside his kingdom. Hazael was probably the son of Adad-idri, but not the crown prince nominated by his father. His military expansion was directed both southward and northward. The Tel Dan Inscription attests to Hazael's wars with Israel and Judah, which was followed by his territorial expansion into Israel. The Deir 'Alla Inscriptions demonstrate an Aramaic cultural influence in Transjordan around 800 BCE. The Arslan-Tash Inscription, and perhaps also the Nimrud Inscription attest to Hazael's expansion northward, beyond the Damascene territory. In addition, the Samos and Eretria Inscriptions indicate that Hazael crossed the Euphrates eastward, to northern Mesopotamia. The combination of these inscriptions shows Hazael's territorial expansion in the Syro-Palestinian region, by which he achieved hegemony over the north Syrian kingdoms in the late ninth century BCE. The Zakkur Inscription shows the Damascene leading role in Syria-Palestine in the time of Bar-Hadad, Hazael's son.

3.3. Archaeological Data

The Tel Dan Inscription indicates that the Aramaean expansion under Hazael occasionally entailed military conflicts with the local regimes. These conflicts would have resulted frequently in the destruction of the assaulted cities and fortresses. The destruction layers of sites in the territory of the Northern Kingdom reflect the disastrous results of Hazael's conquests and are important witnesses for evaluating the extent of Hazael's military activities.

The dates of archaeological strata are critical for relating destruction strata to Hazael's invasion. There is an on-going controversy among archaeologists about the dates of strata at the major sites in the Northern Kingdom and I will review it in the following section.

3.3.1. The Low Chronology and Its Validity

At the outset, I will outline the Low Chronology perspective. In a series of articles, Finkelstein (1995; 1996; 1999; 2000; 2005) suggested lowering both the dates of

---

70   Eph'al and Naveh 1993; Na'aman 1995b: 107.

the strata formerly dated to the time of the United Monarchy as well as those hitherto attributed to the Omride Dynasty. In short, this "Low Chronology" hypothesis lowers all the dates of the Iron Age strata until the early eighth century BCE, by fifty to eighty years.

The "conventional" dating of Megiddo VA-IVB to the tenth century, along with Strata X-VII at Hazor and Stratum VIII at Gezer, was proposed by Yadin (1972a: 147-164). It relies, according to Finkelstein, principally upon 1 Kgs 9:15, which mentions Solomon's building activities at Hazor, Gezer, and Megiddo.[71] Finkelstein (1999: 57-58) criticised Yadin's uncritical use of the biblical description for establishing the date, and emphasised that the archaeological strata must be dated independently of the historical sources. Finkelstein's claim that the relationship between text and archaeology must be sought only thereafter is methodologically correct.

One of the pillars of Finkelstein's Low Chronology is the synchronisms between the strata at Megiddo and Jezreel. Zimhoni (1992; 1997) demonstrated that the pottery assemblage from the Jezreel enclosure is contemporary with that from Stratum VA-IVB at Megiddo. On the basis of the biblical text (1 Kgs 21; 2 Kgs 9-10), Finkelstein dated the Jezreel enclosure, which is contemporary with Megiddo VA-IVB, to the first half of the ninth century BCE (Finkelstein 2005: 36-37; Finkelstein and Piasetzky 2010: 381). Accordingly, he dated Megiddo VA-IVB to the same period. Further, he associated six architectural features found at the five major Israelite sites (Samaria, Jezreel, Hazor, Gezer, and Megiddo) with the building activities of the Omrides (1999: 121-122).[72] According to Finkelstein, some of these strata were destroyed by Hazael in the second half of the ninth century BCE.

Although accepted even by his main opponent (Mazar 2007: 147), Finkelstein's date of the enclosure has not escaped criticism. Zarzeki-Peleg (1997), while dating Megiddo VA-IVB to the tenth century BCE, argued that the Jezreel enclosure is later than Megiddo VA-IVB, since three types of pottery from the floors of the Jezreel enclosure do not appear in Stratum VA-IVB at Megiddo.[73]

---

71 Finkelstein (2000: 133, n. 20) suggested interpreting the description of Solomon's building activity in 1 Kgs 9:15 against the background of the Omride construction activities or those by the Jehuhites in the early eighth century BCE.

72 Hafthorsson (2006: 188-189) attributed the architecture of *bīt-hilāni* to typical Aramaean architecture. The same feature is described as the typical Omride architecture by Finkelstein (2000: 122). Cf. Takata 2005.

73 Finkelstein (1999: 56) questioned Zarzeki-Peleg's claim because she used the pottery assemblage from the previous Megiddo excavations (see 6.6.8.), which is an unreliable source for discussing the dates. Instead, he suggested using, for the comparative study only, the safe and clean assemblage from the previous and renewed excavations of the site. The results of the recent excavations at Megiddo, however, did not yet shed more light on the dating of Megiddo VA-IVB (Finkelstein, Ussishkin, and Halpern 2006b: 854).

Recently, Franklin (2008), based on its architectural comparison, dated the Jezreel enclosure to the eighth century BCE.

Finkelstein's Low Chronology was opposed by other scholars, above all by Mazar (1997) and Ben-Tor (Ben-Tor and Ben-Ami 1998; Ben-Tor 2000).[74] Mazar (2005: 19; 2007: 147-148) pointed out the similarity in pottery between the Jezreel enclosure and the construction fills below it, which possibly shows that the same pottery assemblage was continuously used throughout most of the tenth and ninth centuries BCE.

A natural-scientific method was recently brought into this chronological debate. Radiocarbon dating (^{14}C dating) is a method of determining the date of carbonaceous materials using the rate of decay of ^{14}C. By this method, one can ascertain the age of the death of an organic sample up to about 60,000 years. This method, despite its range of error, has lately developed and contributed much to establishing the absolute dating of the Iron Age strata.[75] It supplies chronological data that is independent of both subjective archaeological interpretations and historical considerations.

Gilboa and Sharon (2001) demonstrated the validity of radiocarbon dating of the Iron Age strata in Palestine. Using samples from Iron Age strata at Tel Dor, their radiocarbon dating resulted in lowering the conventional chronology by some seventy-five years, which may support Finkelstein's Low Chronology. The radiometric dating of other sites such as Megiddo (Carmi and Segal 2000; Boaretto 2006) and Tel Hadar (Finkelstein and Piasetzky 2003a: 774-775) is argued as supporting the Low Chronology.[76] These scholars also claimed that the accumulated results of radiocarbon dating of various sites in Israel favour the Low Chronology (Boaretto et al. 2005; Sharon et al. 2007; Finkelstein and Piasetzky 2009; 2010).[77] Nevertheless, scholarly concensus is yet to be achieved; there are scholars who used the same or additional samples and concluded that the results show rather the probability of the conventional chronology (Mazar and Ramsey 2008; van der Plicht, Bruins, and Nijboer 2009).[78] Thus, the Low

---

74 See also Bunimovitz and Faust 2001.

75 For the recent development of this dating method, see Levy and Higham 2005: 9-13; Ramsey 2005.

76 See also Piasetzky and Finkelstein 2005; Finkelstein and Piasetzky 2006a; 2006b.

77 The study of Gilboa, Sharon, and Zorn (2004: 51-53) did not reach an exclusive conclusion, but at least, they showed that the conventional chronology is less likely than the Low Chronology. In addition, the studies of Egyptian "mass produced" stamp seals of the Egyptian twenty-first Dynasty reached a conclusion favourable to the Low Chronology (Münger 2003; 2005; Gilboa, Sharon, and Zorn 2004).

78 For instance, although the 14C date from Tel Rehov was construed by some scholars as supporting the conventional chronology (Mazar and Carmi 2001; Bruins, van der Plicht, and Mazar 2003; Mazar et al. 2005; van der Plicht and Bruins 2005; cf. also Holden 2003), it was demonstrated that the same data could be interpreted alternatively as being supportive of Low Chronology (Finkelstein 2004; Finkelstein and Piasetzky 2003a; 2003b; 2003c; Gilboa and Sharon 2003:

Chronology theory on the whole is far from warranted, and we should be cautious when discussing the chronology of the relevant strata.

The main focus of this on-going chronological issue is on the transition between the Iron Age IB and the Iron Age IIA, for which recent radiometric analyses, especially the dating of the destruction layer of Megiddo VI, disclose results unfavourable to the Low Chronology (Mazar and Ramsey 2010; Finkelstein and Piasetzky 2010a; 2010b; 2011; Mazar 2011). On the other hand, a wide scholarly consensus seems to be emerging concerning the date of the transition between the Iron Age IIA and the Iron Age IIB. Based on the ceramic evidence from Tel Jezreel and Tel Rehov, Mazar (2003a: 174; 2003b: 158-159; 2005; 2007: 148-149; 2008: 98-99) recently suggested a "modified conventional chronology (MCC)" and dated the destruction of Megiddo VA-IVB, along with other contemporary strata in the north, to the latter half of the ninth century BCE (840–830 BCE). He also raised the possibility that devastation of these strata was brought about by Hazael.[79] Dating the IAIIA/IIB transition to 840/830 has been accepted by scholars (Ben-Shlomo, Shai, and Maeir 2004: 2; Herzog and Singer-Avitz 2004),[80] if not unanimously (Zarzecki-Peleg 2005a).

To conclude, support for Finkelstein's Low Chronology, used for dating the destruction level of Megiddo VA-IVB and other contemporary strata in the north to the latter half of the ninth century BCE, has increased considerably, and the best candidate for these destructions is Hazael of Aram-Damascus, although due caution is necessary for applying this date to all the sites, since there might be some regional differences (Finkelstein and Piasetzky 2009).[81] Likewise, we should be careful in dealing with the date of the destruction layer without radiometric analysis, since it might be influenced by the historical consideration.

3.3.2. Archaeological Evidence for Hazael's Campaigns

The following strata in northern Palestine are contemporaneous with Megiddo VA-IVB; Dan IVB; Hazor IX; Jezreel enclosure; Yoqne'am XIV; Ta'anach IIB (Finkelstein 1998); Tell el-Hammah lower (Cahill 2006; Finkelstein and Piasetzky 2007); Jebel 'Adatir Stratum III; 'En Gev Stratum IV in Area A and Stratum III* in Areas B-C; Beth-Shean Lower V (Mazar's S-1a and S-1b) and P-9; Tel Rehov

---

60; Gilboa, Sharon, and Zorn 2004: 42, n. 14; Piasetzky and Finkelstein 2005; Sharon, Gilboa, and Boaretto 2007). Cf. also Mazar 2003b: 160, n. 30.

79   Cf. Mazar 2003b: 160, n. 35.

80   Mazar (2008: 99) provides a list of the scholars who support the MCC.

81   Finkelstein and Piasetzky (2009: 270-271) suggested that the destruction layer of Beth-Shemesh Stratum 3 can be dated to the early eighth century BCE, which means the Iron Age IIA/IIB transition occurred in that period at this site. For attributing Beth-Shemesh Stratum 3 to the Iron IIA/IIB transitional period, see Bunimovitz and Lederman 2009: 136; 2011: 45; Mazar 2011: 107.

IV; Tel ʿAmal III; and Tel Gezer VIII.[82] Following Naʾaman (1997b: 126-127), Finkelstein dated the destruction of these strata to *ca.* 830 BCE. On the basis of radiocarbon dating, the destruction layers of two of these sites, Hazor IX and Tell el-Hammah lower, were dated to *ca.* 830–800 BCE and ascribed to Hazael's military campaigns (Finkelstein and Piasetzky 2007; 2009: 268). The other sites were only partly discussed in connection with Hazael's invasion and will thus be analysed in the following sections. The sites in Transjordan are excluded from the discussion, since the archaeological information from the region is limited (Hindawi 2007).

3.3.2.1. Jebel ʿAdatir

An Iron Age site on top of the mountain (Jebel ʿAdatir / Har ʿAdir; 1,008 m above the sea level), located close to Sasa in the Upper Galilee, was excavated in 1975–76 (Vitto and Davis 1976). A monumental casemate wall was unearthed, and fill was found inside the casemate rooms, under the room floor (Stratum III). In Stratum II, the inner wall collapsed, and a casemate room (or a tower) was discovered at the corner. Most of the walls continued to be used in Stratum I. According to the report, no destruction layer was detected. The excavators dated these strata from the late-eleventh to the ninth centuries BCE. Observing the appearance of a small high-necked jar from Stratum II, however, Ilan (1999: 182-184) equated Stratum II to Dan IVA and Hazor X-IX, and Stratum III to Dan IVB and Hazor X. If so, Stratum III can be re-dated to the first half of the ninth century BCE by the Low Chronology perspective and to the tenth to ninth centuries BCE by the MCC perspective. Finkelstein (2000: 124-125; Finkelstein and Naʾaman 2005: 183) connected this casemate fortress at Jebel ʿAdatir to the Omride architecture. This fortress, together with that at Tel Harashim (Ben-Ami 2004) near Peqiʿin, could be construed as one of the fortresses of the Northern Kingdom (Ben-Ami, *op. cit.*, 207; Finkelstein and Naʾaman, *op. cit.*, 183).

3.3.2.2. Tel Kinrot (Tell el-ʿOrēme)

Tel Kinrot is located on a hill overlooking the Sea of Galilee from the north. The site is generally identified with Kinneret/Kinrot mentioned in the Bible (Jos 19:35; Fritz and Münger 2002: 2-4; Pakkala, Münger, and Zangenberg 2004: 8-11). The city reached its zenith during Stratum V, when it was fortified possibly by the Aramaeans (Pakkala, Münger, and Zangenberg, *op. cit.*, 19-20). In the following

---

82   Oded (1971: 196) ascribed Hazor VII-IX and Tell Abu-Hawam III to the time of the Aramaean campaigns.

period (Stratum IV), the site was sparsely inhabited. The excavators defined Stratum III as an "intermezzo", since only a watchtower has been discovered on the upper mound (Pakkala, Münger, and Zangenberg, *op. cit.*, 24). The time span between Strata IV and II is wide and Stratum III can be attributed either to the Omrides or to Hazael and his successors (Knauf 2000: 223, n. 19).[83]

3.3.2.3. Tel Bethsaida

Tel Bethsaida (et-Tell), one of the largest sites north of the Sea of Galilee, has been excavated since 1987 by Arav (Arav 1995; 1999; 2004; 2009). He attributed Strata VI-IV to the Iron Age II and dated them according to the conventional chronology (Stratum VI = *ca.* 950–*ca.* 850 BCE; Stratum V = *ca.* 850–732 BCE; Stratum IV = Assyrian and Babylonian occupation).[84] Large-scale architecture, such as a city wall, a city gate, and *bīt-hilāni* palace, unearthed at the site, were dated to Stratum VI.[85] Radiocarbon dating of the destruction of the Stratum VI granary is *ca.* 850 BCE (Boaretto *et al.* 2005: 49; Sharon *et al.* 2007: 44; Arav 2009: 71).[86] Following the destruction, the city reached its zenith in Stratum V by reusing and expanding the architecture of Stratum VI. The gate in Stratum V is architecturally similar to those at Megiddo, Dan, and Lachish (Arav 1999: 26). The city of Stratum V was destroyed by Tiglath-pileser III in 732 BCE.

The identity of the destroyer of Level 6b is open to discussions. It might have been connected either to the Aram-Israel conflict prior to Hazael's reign (Tel Dan Inscription lines 3-4),[87] or to the Damascene attack against the independent Geshurite kingdom in an attempt to establish sovereignty over the latter.[88] The destruction of Stratum VI (Level 6a) was possibly brought by Shalmaneser III's campaign in 838–837 BCE. After the destruction, Hazael extensively re-fortified the city (Stratum V).

---

83   It is noteworthy that Stratum III shows no signs of destruction.

84   Arav 2009: 3. For his earlier dating of the strata (Levels 6-4), see Arav 1995: 6; 1999: 14-15. He (2004: 14) divided both Levels 6 and 5 into substrata, namely 6a and 6b (*ibid.*, 7) and 5a and 5b. A destruction layer was detected between 6a and 6b but only in the city gate area (*ibid.*, 11).

85   On the *bīt-hilāni* palace at Bethsaida, see Arav and Bernett 1997; 2000.

86   Finkelstein (2000: 125), from the Low Chronology perspective, suggested dating Stratum VI (former Level 6), together with Dan IVA and Hazor VIII, to the late ninth century, and related the massive architecture of this stratum to the expansion of Aram-Damascus under Hazael. On the other hand, Arav (2004) ascribed Level 6a to Hazael's time.

87   See 2.2.5.1.

88   Cf. Na'aman 2002b: 206.

3.3.2.4. Tel ʿEn Gev

Tel ʿEn Gev is situated on the eastern shore of the Sea of Galilee. On the basis of Mazar's excavations, Finkelstein (2000: 124) suggested that the casemate fort at Tel ʿEn Gev (Stratum IV in Area A and Stratum III* in Areas B-C) was built by the Omrides.[89] During the years 1990–2004, a Japanese Expedition conducted eight seasons of excavations on the acropolis at ʿEn Gev (Tsukimoto, Hasegawa, and Onozuka 2009).[90] Two Iron Age II strata were detected on the acropolis: the casemate complex and the lower tripartite pillared buildings (Stratum V); and the upper pillared buildings (Stratum IV). The lower part of the casemate rooms was filled with grey soil (0.70 – 0.80 m thick) that contained almost no pottery shards. This soil was possibly filled in at the time of the construction of the casemate wall and the lower pillared buildings, so that the wall could function as a retaining wall for the building complex on the acropolis. The inner side of the casemate wall was also filled with constructional fill, which apparently functioned in the same manner. This architectural feature is similar to that of the Jezreel enclosure (Ussishkin 2000: 253-254). No floor was detected on the horizontal surface of this constructional fill, but the casemate rooms were paved with flagstones at the bottom. No clear mark of destruction has been detected on the acropolis area except for the burnt soil on the floor of the southernmost pillared building. The acropolis was deserted in the latter half of the eighth century, possibly when Tiglath-pileser III attacked this region.

According to the conventional chronology, Stratum V dates to the tenth century BCE, and Stratum IV dates to the ninth-eighth centuries BCE.[91] In accordance with the recent chronological perspective, the date of Stratum V will be modified to the mid-tenth to *ca.* 840/830 BCE (Iron IIA), possibly including also the Iron IIA/IIB transitional phase.[92] The pottery from Stratum IV (Iron IIB) dates to the eighth century BCE.

In spite of some ambiguity about the dates of the strata, the results of the excavations clearly show the continuation of the material culture of the site throughout the Iron Age II. Some architectural change did occur between Strata V and IV, such as the layout of the lower and upper pillared buildings, but the casemate wall was used continually during these periods. The lack of destruction layer between Strata V and IV indicates that the city escaped the enemy's assaults.

---

89 Tel ʿEn Gev was first excavated by Mazar and others in 1961 (Mazar *et al.* 1964).

90 For the excavations by the Japanese Expedition, see also Kochavi 1991; 1993a; 1993b; 1994; 1996: 192-193; Kochavi *et al.* 1992; Sugimoto 1999; Miyazaki and Paz 2005; Kochavi and Tsukimoto 2008; Hasegawa and Paz 2009. The renewed excavation of the acropolis by Sugimoto was conducted between 2008 and 2010 (Sugimoto 2010).

91 Sugimoto 1999.

92 Whether there is a gap between Strata V and IV or part of pottery from Stratum V should be dated to the Iron IIA/B transition is a matter of further research.

This suggests that the site was out of the target of Hazael's violent attack. Furthermore, there is no evidence that the Kingdom of Israel ruled the eastern side of the Sea of Galilee in the ninth century BCE. This region had a close relationship with Syria during the Iron Age, as demonstrated by the Aramaic inscriptions from Tel 'En Gev, Tel Hadar, and Tel Bethsaida. Thus, I suggest ascribing Stratum V at Tel 'En Gev to the Aramaeans.[93] The destruction layer found at the lower city (Stratum III by Mazar) could be related either to the campaign of Adad-nērārī III in 796 BCE, or that of Joash of Israel in the early eighth century BCE. Soon thereafter, the city was renovated by either Bar-Hadad, son of Hazael, or by his successor (Hadiānu), and continued to be an Aramaean fortified city until Tiglath-pileser III's invasion (Strata IV). This reconstruction is tentative and requires further investigation using the new data from the recent excavations.

3.3.2.5. Tel Soreg

Tel Soreg is a small site on the western fringe of the Golan Heights, about four kilometres east of Tel 'En Gev. An Iron Age casemate wall was discovered during the excavations (Kochavi 1989: 6-9; 1991: 181; 1996: 189; Kochavi *et al.* 1992: 33). The excavators dated this defence system to the ninth-eighth centuries BCE and its destruction to the ninth century BCE. Considering its proximity to Tel 'En Gev, Tel Soreg might have served as an Aramaean fortress. The destruction can be attributed either to the Assyrian invasions of 838–837 BCE or 796 BCE, or to Joash of Israel in the early eighth century BCE.

3.3.2.6. Tel Beth-Shean

Tel Beth-Shean is a major site in the Beth-Shean Valley, located near the place where two ancient roads meet. One road traverses the Jezreel and Harod Valleys towards the east, and the other runs along the Jordan Valley from north to south. The site was first excavated by the University of Pennsylvania between 1921 and 1933.[94] Then, it was excavated by Mazar between 1989 and 1996. Mazar (2006: 173) correlated the strata S-1a, S-1b, and P-9 of the new excavation with Lower V of the older.[95] These strata were dated by him to the Iron IIA (tenth to mid-ninth centuries BCE), and the pottery assemblage is equivalent to that of Tel Rehov VI-

---

93   This region is traditionally connected with the Geshurites; yet, whether the kingdom of the Geshurites existed cannot be verified. For the concise history of the kingdom of Geshur, see Ma'oz 1992; Na'aman 2002b: 205-207.

94   See Mazar 2006: 6-7 for literature.

95   For the two phases of the Level V at Tel Beth-Shean, see James 1966: 30-45; 140-148.

IV.[96] Mazar (*op. cit.*, 381-382) dated the end of P-10 to P-9 and S-1a and S-1b to *ca.* 840 BCE; no evidence of destruction was detected.

3.3.2.7. Tel Rehov

Tel Rehov, situated about six kilometres west of the Jordan River, is a lare tell in the Beth-Shean Valley. The excavations were launched in 1997 and uncovered an Iron II city. Mazar (2003a; 2003b), the director of the Rehov excavation, dated the destruction of Stratum IV to *ca.* 840–830 BCE and related it to Hazael's invasion in this region. On the basis of radiocarbon dating, Mazar (Mazar *et al.* 2005: 243-244; Mazar 2011: 107) later dated this destruction to 877–840 BCE, which was basically confirmed by Finkelstein and Piasetzky (2007: 270; 2009: 267-270), who ascribed the destruction of Stratum IV to a conflict between Aram-Damascus and Israel under the Omride Dynasty (*ca.* 875–850 BCE). Hence, Tel Rehov might not have been destroyed by Hazael.[97]

3.3.2.8. Tel 'Amal

Tel 'Amal is located near Kibbutz Nir David, about five kilometres west of Beth-Shean. In the 1960s, the site was excavated by the Musée d'archéologie méditerranéenne (Levy and Edelstein 1972). At niveau III, all the houses were destroyed by conflagration.[98] The excavators dated this stratum to the second half of the tenth century.[99] Mazar (Mazar *et al.* 2005) recently suggested the similarity of pottery assemblage between Tel 'Amal III-IV and Rehov VI-IV. Considering this, the conflagration was possibly a result of Hazael's attack on the site in the second half of the ninth century BCE, or slightly earlier than that.

3.3.2.9. Tel Gezer

Tel Gezer is located on the northern boundary of Shephelah. The tell overlooks the road (the Valley of Ayalon) that leads to the highlands north of Jerusalem as well as the coastal highway, making it an important strategic centre in the Northern Kingdom. The site was first excavated by Macalister in 1902–05 and 1905–07;

---

96   Mazar 2006: 202-203.
97   It may be tempting to connect a massive solid wall newly built in Stratum III (Mazar 2003b: 157-158) to Hazael's construction; yet, no epigraphical evidence for the Aramaean occupation has been found.
98   Levy and Edelstein 1972: 328.
99   Levy and Edelstein 1972: 342.

thereafter, several excavations were carried out at the site in the 1930s, 60s, and 80–90s by Rowe, Wright, and Dever.[100]

Finkelstein (2002: 284-287) re-examined the Iron Age II (VIII-VI) strata at Gezer from the Low Chronology perspective. He dated the end of Stratum VIII, which shows signs of destruction, mainly near the gate, to the second half of the ninth century.[101] He ascribed this destruction, albeit with reservations, to Hazael's military campaign.[102] Radiocarbon dating is required to check the date of the destruction and the identification of the destroyer.

3.3.2.10. Tell eṣ-Ṣāfi

Tell eṣ-Ṣāfi, located in the Shephelah, is identified with Philistine Gath (Rainey 1975; Schniedewind 1998; Ehrlich 2002). The excavators uncovered a vast destruction layer which they dated to the end of the ninth or beginning of the eighth century BCE (Boas and Maeir 1998; Maier 2001; 2003; Maeir and Ehrlich 2001). They unearthed a deep trench and identified it as a dry siege moat that was cut by the Aramaean army, when Hazael besieged the city (Maeir and Ehrlich 2001: 30-31; Maeir 2003: 244-246; 2004: 323-325). Their dating of the destruction is also supported by radiocarbon dating (Maeir, Ackermann, and Bruins 2006; Sharon *et al.* 2007).[103]

3.3.3. Hazael's Conquests and Building Activities in Southern Levant

Archaeological data sheds new light on Hazael's conquests and building activities in the territory of the Kingdom of Israel, although the dating of each destruction layer must be checked by further radiocarbon analyses. First, a series of destruction levels of Iron Age II sites in northern Palestine is dated to the latter half of the ninth century BCE. These destructions reflect Hazael's military expansion into the territory of the Northern Kingdom. In the north of Israel, Hazael conquered cities such as Hazor. In the Beth-Shean and Jezreel Valleys, he probably conquered Tell el-Hammah, Tel 'Amal, Jezreel, Ta'anach, and Megiddo. In the northern Shephelah, he might have captured Gezer. He also conquered the Philistine city of Gath and utterly destroyed it. Second, there are indications that Hazael rebuilt or reinforced the captured cities and fortresses. He possibly rebuilt Dan

---

100   For publications, see Dever 1993: 506.

101   For the criticism, see Dever 2003, esp. 267-270.

102   See also Na'aman 1997b: 127. Cf. Master 2001: 119, n. 9.

103   Ussishkin (2009) suggested that the trench may not be a "siege trench". For the counterargument, see Maeir and Gur-Arieh 2011, esp. 238-241.

and Hazor. The site of Jezreel, on the other hand, was left in ruins. At Dan, Hazael erected his stela (Stratum IVA). Likewise, Hazael might have refortified Hazor (Stratum VIII).[104] The sites on the eastern side of the Sea of Galilee, such as Bethsaida and Tel 'En Gev, were formerly in Aramaean hands. Hazael fortified Bethsaida, probably after the Assyrian withdrawal from Syria-Palestine. The massive fortifications and monumental buildings at the site show their prosperity under Hazael.

3.4. The Biblical Source

Various biblical texts mention the name of Hazael: 1 Kgs 19:15-17; 2 Kgs 8:7-15; 8:28-29; 9:14-15; 10:32-33; 12:18-19; 13:3, 22-25.[105] The historicity of the description in 2 Kgs 8:28-29; 9:14-15 was addressed in Chapter 2 (2.1.2.2.2.). 2 Kgs 10:32-33 describes Hazael's invasion of the territory of the Kingdom of Israel. These verses refer to the reigns of Jehu and Joahaz and will be discussed in the next chapter. The other passages will be analysed in the following sections.

3.4.1. The Anointment of Hazael, Jehu, and Elisha by Elijah (1 Kgs 19:15-18)

This passage is included within the story of Elijah's flight from Jezebel to Mt Horeb, where he encountered YHWH (19:1-18).[106] In v. 17, YHWH orders Elijah to anoint Hazael, Jehu, and Elisha: "And him who escapes from the sword of Hazael shall Jehu slay; and him who escapes from the sword of Jehu shall Elisha slay." These verses have been cited by some scholars as evidence for the conspiracy between Hazael and Jehu.[107] However, the assumption that these verses are a literary unit reflecting the time of Hazael's hegemony over Israel (Steck 1968: 92; Cogan 2001: 457) must be reconsidered. The passage includes a later interpolation, namely vv. 15b-17 (Fohrer 1957: 19-22, 36-39, 42, 44; Hentschel 1977: 56-60; Sekine 1977: 63-66; Otto 2001: 184-185, n. 161; Lehnart 2003: 252-253).[108] It is

---

104 Finkelstein 1999: 61.

105 Am 1:4, which also mentions Hazael, will be discussed in 6.1.4.3.

106 1 Kgs 19:3-18 is generally regarded, particularly in the recent studies, as an entity inserted by a post-Dtr editor. Cf. von Nordheim 1992: 152; Long 1984: 197-198. For the earlier literature, see Otto 2001: 184-186, n. 161; Lehnart 2003: 240-241, n. 185. 1 Kgs 19:15-18 is not well integrated into the Dtr history, as pointed out by Wellhausen (1899: 280-281). See also Montgomery 1951: 325; Cogan and Tadmor 1988: 92.

107 See, for example, Schniedewind 1996: 83-85. Cf. 2.2.6.2.

108 The range of this interpolation is in dispute (Fohrer: vv. 15aβ-18; Hentschel and Lehnart: vv. 15b-17; Sekine: vv. 15aβ-17; Otto vv. 15-16, 18). Otto (2001: 184-185, n. 161) assumed that v. 17 is older prose which derives from the time of Hazael, Jehu, and Elisha. Würthwein regarded

obvious that Hazael, Jehu, and Elisha were not contemporaneous with Elijah. Moreover, YHWH's order to anoint these three persons (vv. 15b-16) is not ful-filled: Hazael was not anointed by Elijah (2 Kgs 8:7-15); it was Elisha's disciple who anointed Jehu (2 Kgs 9:1-10); Elijah did not anoint Elisha (1 Kgs 19:19-21; 2 Kgs 2:1-18). It is clear that these verses are a result of a scribe's efforts to associ-ate these individuals with Elijah's authority. Finally, the reference to the incidents that took place during the Jehuite Dynasty (v. 17), such as Hazael's attack on Israel and Jehu's elimination of Baal's worshippers and the House of Omri, is a *vaticinium ex eventu*.[109] To summarise, 1 Kgs 19:17, which is an attempt to connect Hazael, Jehu, and Elisha with Elijah, represents a late theological interpretation of the history of Israel during the early Jehuite Dynasty. The attempt might have been made already during the Jehuite Dynasty, but the verse cannot be regarded as evidence for the conspiracy between the Damascene and Samarian kings.

3.4.2. Throne Change in Damascus (2 Kgs 8:7-15)

The story describes the meeting between Hazael and Elisha in Damascus. Hazael was sent by Ben-Hadad, the king of Damascus, to Elisha, who visited Damascus, to ask the man of God whether he would recover from illness. Elisha replied in an enigmatic way: "Go, say to him,[110] 'You shall certainly recover'; but the LORD has shown me that he shall certainly die" (v. 10). Then, Elisha[111] burst into tears (v. 11) because Hazael would distress the people of Israel in the future (v. 12). At the end of this story, Ben-Hadad dies and Hazael becomes king of Damascus.[112]

The story relates how Hazael, not having been the designated royal heir, rose on the throne of Damascus (vv. 14-15).[113] Despite its fictional features,[114] the historical nucleus of this story may be confirmed by the Assyrian source which

---

(1984: 231-232) vv. 15-18 as a secondary interpolation. Otto (*loc. cit.*) ascribed vv. 15-16, 18 to the second post-Dtr editor ("BE2" = "Zweite nachdeuteronomistische Bearbeitung im Bereich der Elia-Erzählungen"). McKenzie (1991: 81-87) regarded Chapters 17-19 as a post-Dtr interpolation.

109 Cf. Campbell and O'Brien 2000: 397. Cf. Blum 1997: 287-288, 290-291.

110 *Qere* לֹא is a later attempt to avoid giving the impression that the prophet Elisha instigated Hazael to lie. Cf. Montgomery 1951: 393; Gray 1977: 530-531; Cogan and Tadmor 1988: 90.

111 For the view that the subject here is Hazael and not Elisha, see Cogan and Tadmor 1988: 90. See also Montgomery 1951: 393-394 with earlier literature.

112 The cause of the death of Ben-Hadad is not clear. See Montgomery 1951: 394; Cogan and Tadmor 1988: 91. This verse does not signify that Hazael murdered the king. Gray 1977: 532. *Contra* Würthwein 1984: 320.

113 Cf. Galil 2007: 89.

114 Most commentators regarded the description of the gift from Ben-Hadad to Elisha in v. 9b as fictional due to the exaggerated number of camels (Montgomery 1951: 392; Gray 1977: 530; Würthwein 1984: 318; Cogan and Tadmor 1988: 90).

attests to Hazael's illegitimacy in occupying the Damascene throne (3.1.1.).[115] Thus, it is plausible that this piece of information, together with the historical setting of the account, retains historical memory of Hazael's rise.[116]

Another main theme of the account is found in vv. 11-12, which describes the prophet's weeping over Israel's impending misfortune. By this description, great emphasis is placed on Elisha's sympathy toward the people of Israel, who would be suffering from Hazael's hegemony.[117] This emphasis helps in dating the anecdote to the time of the Jehuite Dynasty,[118] either under the Aramaean hegemony or immediately thereafter.[119] People in the Northern Kingdom might have asked themselves why Elisha, despite his meeting with Hazael, did not remove Israel's oppression under the Damascene hegemony. The answer is provided in v. 13b: YHWH "allowed" Hazael to ascend to the Damascene throne. In other words, vivid memory of Hazael's invasion of Israel forms the backbone of this anecdote.[120] To sum up, 2 Kgs 8:7-15 testifies to two historical points: Hazael was a usurper;[121] Hazael invaded Israel and caused a dire plight.

---

115 Montgomery 1951: 392; Gray 1977: 470.

116 Most commentators (Montgomery 1951: 392; Gray 1977: 470; Cogan and Tadmor 1988: 90) interpreted vv. 10-12 together with v. 15 that the prophet was involved in Hazael's usurpation, whether directly or indirectly. Cf. 1 Kgs 15:17.

117 Elisha operates as a man of God in this story, unlike 1 Kgs 19:15b-17. In 1 Kgs 19:15b-17, Elijah was sent by YHWH to anoint Hazael, and yet Elisha's role in the story is restrictive; he does not anoint Hazael as the king of Damascus. The anecdote in 2 Kgs 8:7-15 does not reflect the concept that foreign kings served as tools of YHWH in the history of Israel; it merely exhibits the change on the throne in Damascus.

118 Cf. Gressmann 1921: 304; Stith 2008: 48-49. McKenzie (1991: 95-100) regarded 2 Kgs 3:4-8:15 as post-Dtr additions.

119 White (1997: 42) suggested that 8:7-15 was added to the OJN during the reign of either Joahaz or Jeroboam II, in order to provide another piece of prophetic authorisation to Jehu's coup.

120 Vv. 12b-13a appears to be a secondary interpolation, probably influenced, in terms of phraseology, by the descriptions of the foreign nations' attack on Israel in Am 1:13 (Ammon) and Isa 13:16 (Babylonia). Cf. Cogan 1983: 755-757; Na'aman 1995c: 38-39. Cf. 2 Kgs 15:16.

121 Neither the Assyrian text nor the Book of Kings prove Hazael murdered Adad-idri (as in Assyrian text) or Ben-Hadad (as in the Book of Kings), as many scholars have suggested. The earliest citation of this view is found in Josephus (*Antiquities* IX 92) who stated: "he killed him by suffocation". For earlier literature, see Na'aman 1995a:387, n. 24. The expression for "to pass away" *šadāšu ēmid* (*RIMA* 3, A.0.102.40, Col. i, line 25), employed in the description of Adad-idri's demise, does not necessarily imply a violent death (Kottsieper 1998: 485-486). See Lemaire 1991a: 95-96, n. 40 for earlier literature. Lemaire (*op. cit.*, 95-96) demonstrated the ambiguity of the description in 2 Kgs 8:15 as evidence for Ben-Hadad's murder by Hazael. See also Na'aman, *op. cit.*, 387-388; Dion 1999: 153-154.

3.4.3. Hazael's Attack on Gath (2 Kgs 12:18-19)

These verses tersely report Hazael's conquest of Philistine Gath and his march toward Jerusalem in the time of Jehoash, king of Judah (v. 18). Jehoash avoided the attack by paying heavy tribute to Hazael (v. 19).

This short account apparently reflects a genuine historical memory. (1) Only four Philistine kingdoms (Gaza, Ashkelon, Ashdod, and Ekron) are mentioned both in the Assyrian royal inscriptions of the eighth-seventh centuries BCE and in the biblical prophecy of the eighth to fifth centuries BCE (Jer 25:20; Am 1:6-8; Zeph 2:4; Zech 9:5-6). The name of Gath is missing from these sources except in the annals of Sargon II, which refers to Gath as a secondary city in the territory of Ashdod.[122] (2) The on-going excavation at Tell eṣ-Ṣāfi (3.3.2.10.), identified with biblical Gath, detected a destruction layer dating to the late ninth-early eighth century BCE.

3.4.4. Decline of Israel under Joahaz (2 Kgs 13:3-7)

2 Kgs 13:1-8 describes Joahaz's reign as the lowest ebb in the history of Israel. Vv. 1-2 and 8-9 are inserted in the Dtr formula for the Israelite king, which will be examined in the next chapter.[123] To this formula, vv. 3-7 adds further information, which can be summarised as follows: (1) Hazael and his son Ben-Hadad subjugated Israel (v. 3); (2) a "saviour" delivered the Israelite people from the Aramaean hegemony (v. 5); (3) the Israelite army was depleted by the Aramaeans (v. 7).

Vv. 3-7 are not a literary unit and the majority of scholars regard vv. 4-6 as secondary.[124] Dietrich (1972: 34, n. 51) ascribed vv. 4-6 to the DtrN, and Würthwein (1984: 361) suggested that these verses were added to explain why Israel did not come to an end despite the catastrophic situation under the Aramaean hegemony. Similar explanation can be found in 2 Kgs 13:23 (Joash) and 14:26-27 (Jeroboam II), all of which can be attributed to the same late hand.[125]

Hoffmann (1980: 114-118) surmised a single Dtr composition of vv. 3-6 due to the similarity between vv. 3-5 and Jgs 3:7-11 both in phraseology and in plot.[126] He suggested that the similarity is derived from the same author who composed both verses in the typical structure of the Book of Judges ("Richterrahmen"), a

---

122 Fuchs 1994: 134, line 250; 220, line 104. Cf. Na'aman 2002b: 202.

123 Würthwein 1984: 360; Cogan and Tadmor 1988: 144.

124 For example, Montgomery 1951: 433; Gray 1977: 594-596; Briend 1981: 42-45. See Long (1991: 164) for more literature.

125 Dietrich 1972: 34.

126 Hoffmann 1980: 114. The phraseology ויחר אף ה' ב(בני)ישראל is found also in: Num 25:3; 32:13; Jos 7:1; Jgs 2:14; 2:20; 10:7. Cf. Ps 106:40.

formula of "infidelity – oppression – repentance – liberation". [127] However, Briend (1981:42-45) demonstrated the late date of the phraseology in vv. 4-6. Hence, it is not necessary to connect this passage directly to the structure of the Book of Judges.

The general situation of Israel as described in v. 3 conforms to the historical reality: Israel was subjugated by Hazael and his son Ben-Hadad. Hence, it is logical to assume that the author, using a similar phraseology to that in the Book of Judges, composed v. 3 by consulting an old source, most probably the Chronicles of the Kings of Israel.[128]

In 2 Kgs 13:7, the number of the reduced Israelite army in the time of Joahaz are enumerated: 50 horses for a chariot (פרשים),[129] 10 chariots, and 10,000 foot soldiers.[130] These numbers are displayed here as concrete data to show the decline of Israel under the Aramaean oppression. Some scholars assume that the verse was derived from an ancient source and belongs to the Dtr history,[131] and some suppose that it was inserted at a later date.[132] Since numbers in the ancient historiography are often subject to manipulation for the author's purpose, the authenticity of these numbers must be re-evaluated in light of recent research on numbers in the ancient Near Eastern literature.[133]

Two contemporary extra-biblical sources have been cited for the evaluation of the numbers of Joahaz's army. Shalmaneser III's Kurkh Monolith (RIMA 3, A.0.102.2: Col. ii, 91-92) describes his encounter with Syrian allied forces at Qarqar in 853 BCE. Ahab of Israel was one of the three biggest allies in the coalition, and his military force described was 2,000 chariots and 10,000 troops. These numbers are debated among scholars.[134] De Odorico (1995: 103-107) suggested

---

127   For this reason, Hoffmann (1980: 116-118) suggested that vv. 3-5 are not directly derived from a source and recognised no historical information or reflexion of older tradition in vv. 3-6.

128   Cf. 2 Kgs 13:22.

129   Whether פרשים here means "team of horses/horses for a chariot" or "horsemen/charioteers" is not clear. Gray 1977: 596. See HAL III: 919 for literature.

130   Cogan and Tadmor (1988: 143) suggested emending עשרת "ten" to אלפים "two thousands" in v. 7. They also suggested that " 'ten thousand' sets in contrast the depleted chariot and cavalry forces and the relatively larger infantry." However, the emendation of the text based on speculation must be avoided because there is no comparable source for the numbers of the Israelite army at that time.

131   For example, Montgomery 1951: 433.

132   Würthwein 1984: 361. Gordon and Rendsburg (1997: 240) suggested that this verse may be taken out of the peace treaty.

133   Jepsen (1941–44: 159) suggested that this verse originally followed v. 22, because it has the conjunction כי in the beginning of the sentence. Also, Gray 1977: 596. Another suggestion is that this verse is an expansion of v. 3 as an editorial interpolation (Montgomery 1951: 434). In this case, v. 22 might originally have followed v. 7 (Gray, op. cit., 596). The Lucianic recension puts v. 23 after v. 7.

134   See for example, Elat 1975; Galil 2002: 43-46.

that the numbers in this text, particularly those of the first three, including Ahab's army, were deliberately exaggerated in order to multiply the total numbers of the enemy forces. The numbers of the first three contingents are extremely high compared with the others, which may show the possibility that the author multiplied the numbers to reach an adequate total of the enemy troops. Therefore, these numbers should not be taken at face value.[135]

The Tel Dan Inscription (lines 6-7) also refers to the chariots and horsemen (פרשים) of the Israelite and Judahite armies. In the text, the author claimed that he slew "thou[sands of cha]riots and thousands of horsemen". One should bear in mind, however, that these numbers are exaggerated to aggrandise the author's victory. In sum, the reliability of the numbers of these sources is questionable, and we should not expect that the comparison of the numbers of Joahaz's army with those in the ancient Near Eastern literature will shed light on the logic behind the concrete numbers in 2 Kgs 13:7.

The most comparable numbers of the Israelite army in v. 7 can be found in other places in the Hebrew Bible, especially in the Dtr history. 1 Kgs 5:6 and 10:26 state that Solomon had 12,000 פרשים and 1,400 chariots. As for foot soldiers, Jgs 20:4 gives 400,000 and 1 Sam 15:4 numbers 200,000, excluding those from Judah. Compared with these numbers, the numbers of the army in 2 Kgs 13:7 are indeed small. The result of the comparison shows that the numbers of Joahaz's army are not directly derived from a credible source. The Dtr might have an older source that possibly mentions concrete numbers of Joahaz's army. However, to emphasise Joahaz's military weakness, he could have intentionally described small numbers as compared to the quantity of the Israelite army at the peak of its power. Therefore, the numbers of the Israelite army in 2 Kgs 13:7 cannot be regarded as reliable.[136]

3.4.5. Historical Information in the Description of the Relationship between Israel and Aram under Joahaz and Joash (2 Kgs 13:22-25)

Vv. 22-25 are located within the framework of Joash's reign (13:10-13 and 14:15-16). The first verse (v. 22), using similar phraseology as 2 Kgs 13:3, reminds the reader of the Aramaean yoke in the time of Joahaz. This similarity led Gray (1977: 600) to place this verse either between vv. 3 and 7 or after v. 7, assuming that v. 22, 24-25 are from the Book of the Chronicles of Israel.[137]

---

135 The emendations of the numbers of the Israelite army in the Kurkh Monolith inscription were suggested by some scholars. See Na'aman 1976: 97-102; Katzenstein 1997: 168.

136 More detailed discussion will be found in Hasegawa 2010a.

137 V. 22 contradicts the statement given in v. 5, according to which Israel was relieved of the Aramaean oppression in the days of Joahaz. Cf. Cogan and Tadmor 1988: 150.

In the Lucianic recension, a lengthy addition follows v. 22: "and Hazael took the Philistine (ἀλλόφυλον) from his hand, from the sea of the West to Aphek". Indicating the geographical impossibility of the transcription, Rahlfs (1911: 289) suggested that this verse is a secondary expansion that was partly based on the mistranslation of ים הערבה as ים המערב "western sea".[138] Schenker (2004: 113-115), on the other hand, accepted its originality and discussed the dissonance of this Lucianic addition for the political-historical situation at that time.[139] To solve this problem, he suggested that the Philistines were, in reality, under Israelite domination until the time of Joahaz and obtained their independence after Hazael's conquests. However, there is no evidence for this theory that does not conform to the relations between Israel and Philisitine emerging from the biblical and extra-biblical sources. Be that as it may, this additional information can hardly serve as a historical source for describing the political relations on the eve of Hazael's conquest.[140] Richelle (2010a; 2010b), on the other hand, identified the "sea" here with the Dead Sea and located Aphek on the eastern side of the Sea of Galilee, and suggested that Ἀζαὴλ τὸν ἀλλόφυλον should be construed as "Hazael of Aram". Consequently, he equated the geographical extent delineated here with that in 2 Kgs 10:33. This information, employing the two toponyms in 2 Kgs 13:17 (Aphek) and 14:25 (the Sea of the Arabah), seems to be ideological rather than historical.[141]

It appears that v. 23 was composed by a post-Exilic editor to explain the reason for Joash's reversal of the power balance between Israel and Damascus.[142] The covenant with Abraham, Isaac, and Jacob appears for the first time after the Exile (Briend 1981: 45-47). The context of the present text (vv. 22, 24-25) creates an impression that the cause of the power shift in the time of Joash and Ben-Hadad was the throne-changes in both kingdoms. Hence, the intention of the later editor was to ascribe this power shift to the grace of YHWH.[143]

The descriptions of Hazael's death and the subsequent enthronement of Ben-Hadad reported in v. 24 provide historically authentic information. It is worth noting that the description of the throne-change in Damascus employs a verb מות (cf. 2 Kgs 8:10, 15), which is different from those in the concluding statements of the kings of Israel and Judah (שכב). It may suggest that the author deliberately employed a different verb for the description of the Damascene throne change, since Ben-Hadad is a foreign king.

---

138 Cf. Šanda 1912: 157-158; Montgomery 1951: 438.
139 Stade and Schwally (1904: 245) accepted this addition as original.
140 Cogan and Tadmor 1988: 149.
141 I would like to discuss this issue elsewhere in detail.
142 The thematic similarity between this verse, v. 4, and 2 Kgs 14:26-27 is notable. See Long 1991: 163-164.
143 Cf. Würthwein 1984: 369.

V. 25a depicts Joash's fighting against Ben-Hadad and the retaking of the cities lost during Joahaz's time.[144] It should be emphasised that the victory over Aram mentioned in v. 25 also fulfils the magical omen in vv. 14-19.[145] According to 2 Kgs 13:14-19, Elisha predicts the three defeats of the Aramaeans. Most commentators accept the unity of this anecdote, except for the specific mention of Aphek as the place of the Israelite victory (v. 17).[146] Yet, the contextual difference between v. 17 and v. 18 seems unnatural and thus negates the unity (Würthwein 1984:365-366).[147] In vv. 15-17, Elisha transfers his supernatural power to the king of Israel, thereby enabling him to defeat the Aramaeans.[148] Despite the declaration of total victory in v. 17, the king of Israel was ordered to shoot again towards the ground (vv. 18-19). Thus, vv. 18-19 function as a correction of the total victory over Aram declared in v. 17. It seems that a late editor, who read v. 25b and learned that Joash did not completely defeat Aram, interpolated vv. 18-19 as a corrective to the original anecdote (vv. 14-17).[149] Whether the Dtr, when composing v. 25, knew the exact number of Joash's victories over Aram (three times) remains unknown. "Three times" can also be a rhetorical emphasis to show that Joash's victory was sufficient to throw off the Aramaean yoke. Likewise, whether Joash regained all the territories lost to Aram or only a part of them is unknown.[150]

In short, 2 Kgs 13:22-25 present the following information. (1) Israel was subjugated to Hazael in the reign of Joahaz. (2) Ben-Hadad succeeded Hazael. (3) Joash defeated the Aramaeans in the days of Ben-Hadad and recovered some cities which had been lost to the Aramaeans during Joahaz's time.

3.4.6. Hazael and Israel in the Book of Kings

This chapter discussed Hazael's rise to power and his domination over Israel during the second half of the ninth century BCE. 2 Kgs 8:7-15 attests to Hazael's usurpation of the Damascene throne from Adad-idri (Ben-Hadad). Short descrip-

---

144 Long (1991: 167) pointed out the exact diction, in which the author brings Israel and Aram in "familial relation": son regains from son what father had lost to father.

145 It should be noted that this anecdote, as 1 Kgs 20, originally preserved no name of the king of Israel and belonged to the legendary story of the prophet. Cf. Wellhausen 1899: 288-289; Würthwein 1984: 364.

146 Montgomery 1951: 435; Gray 1977: 598; Cogan and Tadmor 1988: 148. Hentschel (1985: 60-61) discerned two layers in this text and regarded "at Aphek" as secondary. Würthwein (1984: 364), on the other hand, included "at Aphek" in the original text.

147 Also Fritz 1998: 72.

148 Cf. 2 Kgs 2:1-15, where Elijah transfers his supernatural power to Elisha.

149 Würthwein (1984: 366) regarded v. 15b as a secondary interpolation.

150 Cf. Chapter 4.

tions derived from a chronistic source reflect the overall chain of events during Hazael's reign, which roughly corresponds to the combined reigns of Jehu and Joahaz (2 Kgs 13:3). 2 Kgs 12:18-19 shows the extent of Hazael's military campaigns in the south. Hazael attacked Gath and received tribute from Jehoash, the king of Judah. His campaigns brought about a dire plight to Israel, which possibly formed the background of the prophetic stories in 2 Kgs 8:7-15 and 1 Kgs 19:15-18. As a result, Joahaz's military power considerably decreased (2 Kgs 13:7). The military power gained by the Omrides in the first half of the ninth century BCE gradually dissolved. The Aramaean dominance under Hazael seemed to have continued until the early days of Joash, king of Israel (2 Kgs 13:22). After Hazael's death, Ben-Hadad ascended the throne of Damascus (2 Kgs 13:24). Joash regained power, threw off the Aramaean yoke, and conquered some of the captured territories (2 Kgs 13:25).

3.5. Synthesis

Four kinds of sources, each supplementing the other, contribute to the historical picture of the rise and dominance of Hazael. His usurpation of the throne ended the alliance between Israel and Aram-Damascus and thus inaugurated a hostile era. Under Hazael, Damascus became a dominant power in Syria-Palestine. Especially after the Assyrian withdrawal from the region in 829 BCE, Hazael deeply invaded the territory of the Northern Kingdom, eventually subjugating it.

4. The Reigns of Jehu and Joahaz (841–798 BCE)

Only a handful of direct sources for the reigns of Jehu and Joahaz are available; some of them were already discussed in Chapter 3. The Book of Kings provides us with general information concerning these two kings. The Assyrian and Aramaic (Zakkur) inscriptions illuminate the political developments, while the Mesha Inscription describes how the Israelite territory in Transjordan was captured by the Moabites.

4.1. The Biblical Source

The biblical texts that briefly describe the reigns of Jehu and Joahaz are (1) 2 Kgs 10:28-29; (2) 10:32-33; (3) 10:34-36; and (4) 13:1-9.

4.1.1. Dtr's Evaluation of Jehu's Religious Policy (2 Kgs 10:29)

2 Kgs 10:29 does not belong to the original Jehu Narrative (cf. Chapter 2). It was added to summarise and evaluate Jehu's reign from a Dtr viewpoint. Since the biblical description of Jehu's reign lacks the usual opening formula, v. 29 serves as an expanded concluding formula. Vv. 29, 34-36, together with 10:30-33, constitute the summary description of Jehu's reign. Vv. 29-31 are the Dtr's judgment on Jehu's religious policy, and vv. 32-33 describes Hazael's invasion of the Northern Kingdom.

2 Kgs 10:29 accuses Jehu of maintaining the cult of the golden calf in Bethel and Dan. The Tel Dan Inscription, however, suggests that Dan belonged to the Aramaeans during the early Jehuite Dynasty. Recent analysis of the pottery from Stratum IVA at Tel Dan suggests that the city was rebuilt during the late ninth century BCE after a gap of occupation (Arie 2008: 33-38). Since the Tel Dan Inscription is dated to the same period, it was most certainly Hazael who built Dan in the late ninth century BCE, between the Assyrian withdrawal from the region in 829 BCE and Hazael's death. It could probably be dated between 830-820 BCE, which still falls within Jehu's reign. If this had been the case, the mention of Dan in the religious evaluation in 2 Kgs 10:29 indicates that the Dtr did not know that Dan had belonged to the Aramaeans during Jehu's reign and used

a schematic judgment formula in order to emphasise Jehu's sins (Hoffmann 1980: 115-116, 118).[1] It is clear that 2 Kgs 10:29 does not reflect historical reality.

4.1.2. The Extent of Hazael's Invasion (2 Kgs 10:32-33)

2 Kgs 10:32-33 delineates the geographical extent of Hazael's invasion of Transjordan. If the geographical information in v. 33 is correct, Hazael conquered the entire Transjordanian areas as far as the Arnon River. Certain parts of these verses might have been based on a source. V. 32 begins with an expression "in those days" (בימים ההם) which might refer to an archival source.[2] On the other hand, the double mention of Gilead in v. 33 may suggest that part of this verse is a late addition.[3] Thus, a reconstruction of the original text is necessary in order to discuss the historical authenticity of these verses. Kittel (1900: 242) and Würth-wein (1984: 343) ascribed v. 33aβ-b (הגדי והראובני והמנשי מערער אשר על־נחל ארנן והגלעד והבשן) to a later editor, who "(was) perhaps motivated by such texts as Num 32 and Deut 3:12-13 – felt compelled to specify what he called 'the whole land of Gilead' according to tribal boundaries" (Barré 1988: 22-23).[4] Fol-lowing this view, Na'aman (2001b: 37) pointed out the literary relationship be-tween the extent of David's conquest in 2 Sam and the geographical extent of Gilead in this segment of v. 33.[5] It indicates that v. 33aβ-b was added to v. 33 in order to show that all the territory held by Israel since David's days was lost to Hazael. Only v. 33aα ("from the Jordan eastward, all the land of Gilead") was based on an ancient source.

It is unlikely that this short note is Dtr's invention, although the source for the composition of vv. 32-33 is unknown. We may assume that an ancient source

---

1   It is notable that the exemplification of religious sin in Bethel and Dan appears only here except for the description of Jeroboam I (1 Kgs 12:29) who introduced the cult. It may show Dtr's em-phasis on Jehu's sin and imperfection, possibly in contrast to that of Josiah, although Jehu did expel, as Josiah did, the Baal cult from Israel. 2 Kgs 13:6, which mentions the existence of Asherah in Samaria, is also schematic but it belongs to a secondary interpolation. See 3.4.4. Cf. 1 Kgs 16:33; 18:19).

2   Montgomery 1934; 1951: 33-37.

3   Stade (1885: 279) suggested that v. 33 is later than v. 32a, and vv. 33a and 33b do not consist of the same layer. Otto (2001: 53) ascribed all vv. 28-36 to the Dtr.

4   Benzinger (1899: 155) regarded the second mention of Gilead (מערער אשר על־נחל ארנן והגלעד והבשן) as original, whereas the first mention (כל־ארץ הגלעד) as a gloss because it is a general de-scription of Transjordan. Šanda (1912: 119-120), while ascribing v. 32b (ויכם חזאל בכל־גבול ישראל) to the Dtr (Rj), regarded כל־ארץ הגלעד as a later addition. He assumed that v. 32b was composed on the information in 2 Kgs 13:3 by the Dtr. Montgomery (1951: 412) and Gray (1977: 563) ascribed כל־ארץ הגלעד הגדי והראובני והמנשי to a secondary editor. Cf. also Na'aman 1995b: 109; 2001b:37; Barré 1988: 22-23.

5   2 Sam 24:5-6.

was available to the Dtr for composing v. 33, to which he added v. 32. Ben-Zvi (1990: 100-105) suggested that 2 Kgs 10:32 as well as 2 Kgs 15:37 are based on prophetic sources, which might have contained "a more frightening and detailed description" of the punishment of the kings who were seen to be relatively good in the eyes of YHWH.[6] Assuming that this hypothesis is correct, the expression "החל" might have been employed here to "moderate the severity of the divine stroke" upon Jehu, the "good" king.

Whereas the Aramaeans conquered Gilead, it was Mesha who conquered the southernmost part of the Israelite territory in Transjordan. As related in the Mesha Inscription, during the early Omride period Israel held some cities in the Mishor, north of the Arnon River, such as Medeba, Ataroth, and Yahaz.[7] Under Jehu, Mesha conquered all the territory up to Nebo on the Transjordanian plateau and built/rebuilt some cities in the area (lines 11-31).

4.1.3. Dtr's Final Assessment of Jehu's Reign (2 Kgs 10:34-36)

According to the concluding verses on his reign, Jehu was buried in Samaria (v. 35), Joahaz his son ascended the throne (v. 35) and reigned for twenty-eight years (v. 36).[8] It should be noted that v. 36 is not a schematic description of the length of the Israelite king's reign (והימים אשר מלך יהוא על־ישראל עשרים־ושמנה שנה בשמרון).[9] The author might have had a full scheme for Jehu, which he excluded due to the interpolation of the prophetic narrative and historical notes (Steuernagel 1912: 343).[10]

---

6   2 Kgs 15:37 describes the reign of Jotham. V. 34 reads: "he did what was right in the eyes of YHWH".

7   On the historical background of the Israelite expansion in Transjordan during the Omride Dynasty, see Na'aman 2001b: 34-35.

8   The phrase "in Samaria" in v. 36 is out of position and thus may be a gloss. See Thenius 1873: 330; Benzinger 1899: 155; Kittel 1900: 243; Stade and Schwally 1904: 234; Montgomery 1951: 416; Cogan and Tadmor 1988: 117.

9   A schematic description of an Israelite king's reign is put into an opening formula specific to the king. It has a synchronism with the contemporary Judahite king, the names of the king and his father, his capital, and the length of the reign in this order.

10 See also Würthwein 1984: 343. Cf. 1 Kgs 2:11 (David); 1 Kgs 14:20 (Jeroboam I). See also Long 1991: 127.

4.1.4. Dtr's Assessment of Joahaz's Reign (2 Kgs 13:1-2, 8-9)

In 2 Kgs 13:1-2, 8-9, the Dtr gives a negative judgement on Joahaz, represented by the usual expression for the king of Israel "the sin of Jeroboam" (חטאות ירבעם) (v. 2).[11]

4.1.5. The "Saviour" of Israel (2 Kgs 13:5)

2 Kgs 13:5 refers to a "saviour" (מושיע) sent by YHWH to deliver Israel from the Aramaean yoke. Some scholars regarded him as a historical figure and proposed several identifications: Elisha, Adad-nērārī III, Joash, Jeroboam II, and Zakkur.[12] However, vv. 4-6 is a secondary interpolation and thus should be excluded from the historical discussion.[13] It is likely that a later author employed this expression without having a specific character in mind, or at least did not intend that the "saviour" would be identified with a specific character.[14]

The secondary origin of v. 5 is also corroborated by its contents. There is a marked discrepancy between vv. 3-5 and v. 22. V. 3 states that Israel was subjugated by the Aramaeans "all the days" (כל-הימים); and v. 22 states that Hazael, king of Aram, oppressed Israel "all the days of Joahaz" (כל ימי יהואחז). And yet in v. 5, YHWH sends a deliverer during the reign of Joahaz. This inconsistency indicates the secondary origin of v. 5.[15] Israel was not delivered from the Aramaean yoke during Joahaz's days.[16] It was during Joash's reign that the Israelite kingdom regained its independence.

4.1.6. Joahaz's "might" (2 Kgs 13:8)

Joahaz's "might" (גבורתו) is mentioned in the concluding formula in v. 8. A king's "might" is mentioned in other concluding formulae when a battle or a rebellion is

---

11   This expression appears twelve times in the Bible, all of which are found in the Book of Kings. 1 Kgs 14:16; 15:30; 16:31; 2 Kgs 3:3; 10:31; 13:2, 6; 15:9, 18, 24, 28; 17:22. Cf. Debus 1967.

12   For the literature, see Gray 1977: 594-595; Briend 1981: 41-42; Cogan and Tadmor 1988: 143.

13   See 3.4.4.

14   Similar plot and phraseology appear in the Book of Judges (Jgs 3:9, 15; cf. also 2:18). The stories follow a basic plot: (1) the sinning Israelites; (2) YHWH becomes enraged and hands them over to foreign kings; (3) Israel returns to YHWH; (4) YHWH provides a means of reconciliation through a saviour and Israelites are able finally to enjoy peace. See Gray 1977: 591-592; Hoffmann 1980: 114-116; Würthwein 1984; Hentchel 1985: 58; Long 1991: 116.

15   The verb לחץ "to oppress" in 2 Kgs 13:4, 22 is often used in the Hebrew Bible, particularly in the Book of Judges, for oppressions of Israelite people by foreign nations. Ex 3:9; Jgs 1:34; 2:18; 4:3; 6:9; 10:22; 1 Sam 10:18; Am 6:14.

16   Joahaz might have refused to take part in the siege of Hadrach. See 4.3.

described in the previous part of the king's history.[17] Thus, Joahaz's "might" may refer to the Aramaean oppression which would inevitably entail military operations (2 Kgs 13:3, 7, 22).[18]

4.2. The Assyrian Sources

The only direct Assyrian source for Jehu's reign is Shalmaneser III's Black Obelisk that depicts his tribute. The available Assyrian sources provide no information on the reign of Joahaz. The Eponym Chronicles and Adad-nērārī III's inscriptions provide information on the resumed Assyrian military campaigns to Syria which began in 805 BCE. These sources will be analysed in the following sections in order to clarify the political situation in Syria-Palestine during Jehu's reign and the last days of Joahaz.

4.2.1. The Campaign of Shalmaneser III in 838–837 BCE

The last military campaign of Shalmaneser III to Syria-Palestine was in 838–837 BCE (Chapter 3). The descriptions of this campaign do not mention the Kingdom of Israel, whereas Hazael of Damascus is depicted as the sole Assyrian enemy.[19] It is thus likely that Jehu remained loyal to Assyria from 841 BCE until at least 838–837 BCE.

4.2.2. An Epigraph on the Black Obelisk (RIMA 3, A.0.102.88)

The epigraph on the so-called "Black Obelisk" (*RIMA* 3, A.0.102.88) relates the details of Jehu's tribute. The Obelisk has four sides, each of which has five rows of relief displaying various scenes to commemorate Shalmaneser III's deeds. Each row has a text above the relief, which describes the pictorial scene. According to the text, this inscription was most probably composed in 828 or 827 BCE, during the last years of Shalmaneser III, since the main text ends with the description of the event in 828 BCE.[20]

17　"Might" (גבורתו) is mentioned in the concluding formulae of the following kings: Asa (1 Kgs 15:23), Baasha (1 Kgs 16:5), Omri (1 Kgs 16:27), Jehoshaphat (1 Kgs 22:46), Jehu (2 Kgs 10:34), Joash (2 Kgs 13:12; 14:15), Jeroboam II (2 Kgs 14:28), and Hezekiah (2 Kgs 20:20).

18　Na'aman 2007: 107-108. *Contra* Montgomery 1951: 434; Würthwein 1984: 360.

19　*RIMA* 3, A.0.102.13, Rev. lines 4'b-11'; A.0.102.14, lines 102b-104a; A.0.102.16, lines 152'-162'a.

20　*RIMA* 3, A.0.102.14, lines 174b-190. Shalmaneser III reigned until 824 BCE.

The second panel from the top on the first side depicts Shalmaneser with his entourage and a man kneeling down before him. The text (*RIMA* 3, A.0.102.88) of the scene reads:

> The tribute of Jehu (*Iu-ú-a*), son of Omri (*Hu-um-ri-i*): silver, gold, a gold bowl, a gold tureen, gold vessels, gold buckets, tin, the staffs of the king's hand (and) spears, I received from him.

The kneeling man is identified by the inscription as Jehu (ᵐ*iu-ú-a*),[21] paying his tribute to Shalmaneser in 841 BCE.[22] Keel and Uehlinger (1994) pointed out that the image might represent Jehu's delegate who brought the tribute to Assyria.[23]

The fact that only two vassal kingdoms (Gilzanu and Israel) are depicted on the Obelisk indicates that those two kingdoms were rendered as geographical merismus; they represent the whole area which Shalmaneser III subjugated.[24] Simultaneously, these kingdoms represent the virtual boundaries of Shalmaneser's Empire. Israel was on the south-western and Gilzanu the northeastern boundary.[25] They were selected due to their geographical locations on the borders of the newly established empire.[26]

The study by Keel and Uehlinger (1994: 406-414) clarified that the prostration of the man in front of an Assyrian king does not mean humiliation. Rather, it displays his voluntary obeisance, and as reward, his position in his local kingdom is assured by the Assyrian king. They pointed out that the Obelisk was made much later than 841 BCE and suggested that the panel does not necessarily depict the event in 841, but a certain time during Jehu's long vassalage. However, it is unlikely that Jehu continued paying tribute to Shalmaneser after Assyria stopped conducting military campaigns to the west. Hence, the description of both boundaries of Shalmaneser's hegemony encompasses the largest extent of this Assyrian king's realm and does not necessarily indicate Jehu's vassalage at the time of its composition (828–827 BCE).

---

21 For the reading of ᵐ*iu-ú-a*, see 2.3.1.3.

22 See above, 2.3.1.

23 Keel and Uehlinger 1994 with earlier literature (esp. 393, n. 8).

24 Cf. Porada 1983: 15-16; Lieberman 1985: 88; Marcus 1987: 87-88; Na'aman 1997d: 20.

25 Gilzanu is located in the vicinity of the Lake Urmia, which is in modern Azerbaijan. See Röllig 1957–71: 375; Keel and Uehlinger 1994: 400. For earlier literature, see Porada 1983: 15.

26 Keel and Uehlinger 1994: 402-406. *Contra* Green 1979: 38-39.

4.2.3. Adad-nērārī III and Syria-Palestine (805–802 BCE)

4.2.3.1. The Eponym Chronicles

In Assyria, dignitaries were appointed yearly as eponyms side by side with the kings and high officials. Those eponyms were registered in texts which can be divided into two classes: Eponym Lists and Eponym Chronicles.[27] The Eponym Lists register year by year the name of the eponym and his title. The Eponym Chronicles have an additional entry: an event that was regarded as important for Assyria.[28] From 840 BCE, the Eponym Chronicles continuously record events, usually designated by a place name[29] that designates the objective of the campaign.[30] Since the annals of Adad-nērārī III are missing, these entries are particularly important for reconstructing the chronology of his campaigns.

During the reigns of Jehu and Joahaz (841–798 BCE), Assyria was ruled by three successive kings, Shalmaneser III (858–824 BCE), Šamšī-Adad V (823–811 BCE), and Adad-nērārī III (810–783 BCE). According to the Eponym Chronicles, the Assyrian kings did not launch military campaigns to Syria-Palestine between 828–806 BCE (see 3.1.4.). In 805 BCE, Adad-nērārī III launched a series of campaigns to the areas west of the Euphrates. The entries in the Eponym Chronicles of the years 805 to 798 are as follows (Table 3):

Year (BCE)	Event Entry
805	to Arpad
804	to Hazazu
803	to Ba'li
802	to the "Sea"; plague
801	to Hubuškia
800	to Mannea
799	to Mannea
798	to Lušia

Table 3. The Eponym Chronicles between 805 and 798 BCE

The identifications of Ba'li (803) and the "Sea" (802) are the keys in establishing the directions of Adad-nērārī's military campaigns in those years.

---

27   Eponym Lists are lists of eponym names in chronological order. See Millard 1994: 4.

28   It should be noted that the extant Eponym Chronicles were subject to editiing after the events had been first recorded. As a result, different copies present some differences in names and events. In addition, there is an apparent tendency in the entries: the later events are described in detail in the entries (Millard 1994: 4).

29   In the tablet SU 52/18+18A+21+333+337, "in (ina)" is used instead of "to (ana)".

30   See also Kuan 1995: 7-18.

Ba'li appears in the entry of the Eponym Chronicles for 803 BCE as *a-na* URU *ba-'-li* (B1, 15').[31] Amurru,[32] Ba'albek,[33] Bala (Roman Abila),[34] Ba'li-ṣapuna,[35] Ba'li-ra'si, [36] and Ibleam [37] have been suggested for its identification. Since toponyms with the name Ba'al often appear on the Syrian and Phoenician coast, Ba'li is probably located in Syria (Millard 1973: 161-162).

Two possible identifications have been suggested for the identification of "the Sea" (*tâmtim*):[38] the Mediterranean[39] and the Persian Gulf.[40] Its identification with the Mediterranean is corroborated by the mention of Adad-nērārī's visit to Arvad in the Tell al-Rimah and Tell Sheikh Hammad Stelae (Millard and Tadmor 1973: 59; Weippert 1992: 50; Siddall 2011: 27-32).[41]

The 805 to 802 BCE entries in the Eponym Chronicles point to Adad-nērārī III's military advance into the west. In the first year (805) he conducted a campaign against Arpad, which is identified with Tell ar-Rif'at, thirty-five kilometres to the north of Aleppo.[42] In the following year, he led a campaign to Hazazu, identified with the region of modern 'Azaz, about fifteen kilometres northwest of Tell ar-Rif'at. [43] In 803 BCE Adad-nērārī passed through northern Syria and reached the Mediterranean coast. The campaign in 802 BCE may also have been directed to the same region.

---

31   Or *i-na* URU *b[a-]* (B10, r., line 1). For the earlier literature, see Lipiński 1971b: 84, n. 1-3; Elayi 1981: 331, n. 1.

32   Poebel 1943: 83.

33   Honigmann 1928: 327.

34   Cazelles 1969: 115, n. 15. He suggested this identification because its mention – before that of Damascus – fits his interpretation that the campaign against Damascus occurred in 803 BCE (*op. cit.*, 110-112).

35   Cazelles 1969: 115, n. 15; Millard and Tadmor 1973: 59.

36   Lipiński (1969: 165, n. 31; 1971b: 84-85; 1979: 87, n. 123) identified Ba'li with KUR-*e* KUR *ba-'-li-ra-'-si,* as attested in Shalmaneser III's inscription, which depicts the campaign of year 841 BCE (*RIMA* 3, A.0.102.8, lines 21"-23"; A.0.102.10, Col. iv., lines 7-10; A.0.102.12, lines 28-29; A.0.102.16, lines 132'-134').

37   Lipiński 2000: 396; 2004: 13-15.

38   The full text reads *ana muḫḫi tâmtim* "to the Sea".

39   Poebel 1943: 83; Page 1968: 147; Cody 1970: 329; Jepsen 1970: 359; Donner 1970: 57; Lemaire 1993: 149*.

40   Brinkman 1968: 217, n. 1359; Lipiński 1969: 169-170, n. 43; 1979: 91, n. 136.

41   My thanks go to Luis Robert Siddall, who kindly provided me a translation of the second fragment of the Sheikh Hammad Stela, which was on sale at an antique market (for the fragment of the Stela, see Radner 2002: 15, nn. 172-173; Siddall 2011: 27-32).

42   On the history and territory of Arpad, see Buccellati 1967: 53-56; Abu Taleb 1973: 147-157; Sader 1987: 99-152; Dion 1997: 113-136; Lipiński 2000: 195-219.

43   On the identification of Hazazu, see Hawkins 1972–75b: 240; Liverani 1992: 74 with nn. 346-347; Yamada 2000a: 106, n. 110, for earlier literature. Dion (1997: 114) located it at Jebel Sim'ān, which rises south of 'Azaz.

4.2.3.2. Adad-nērārī III's Inscriptions

The chronological framework of the events having been established, the details of Adad-nērārī III's campaigns as described in his summary inscriptions will be analysed.

4.2.3.2.1. The Saba'a Stela (A.0.104.6)

The Saba'a Stela was found in 1905 at Saba'a, south of Jebel Sinjar. The stela consists of thirty-three lines inscribed under the king's image and divine symbols. The poor condition of the stela renders deciphering of the text difficult.

The text can be divided into seven sections: (1) dedication (lines 1-5); (2) Adad-nērārī III's genealogy (lines 6-11a); (3) campaign to the land of Hatti "in the fifth year" (lines 11b-18a); (4) tribute from Mari' king of Damascus (lines 18b-20); (5) erection of the statue in Zabanni (lines 21-22); (6) introduction of Nergal-ēreš (lines 23-25); and (7) curses (lines 26-33).[44] Following is a translation of the campaign to the west (section 3):
Translation

> 11b-18a) In the fifth year <since> I sat on the throne in majesty, I mustered the land (and) the troops of wide Assyria, and I verily commanded to march to the land of Hatti. I crossed the Euphrates in its flood. The kings of extended [land of Hatti] who, in the time of Šamšī-Adad my father, became strong and organised their [army][45] — by the command of Aššur, ʿMardukʾ, Adad, Ištar, the gods, my support, the fearsome radiance overwhelmed them and they seized my foot. They brought tribute and t[ax] [...] (and) I received (it).

Adad-nērārī III launched his first campaign to the west in his "fifth year", namely 805 BCE.[46] The chronological designation does not indicate that all the land of

---

44 Publication: Unger, 1916; Donner 1970: 52-53 (lines 11-22); Tadmor 1973: 144-148; Weippert 1992: 44, n. 16 (lines 21-22); *RIMA* 3, A.0.104.6; Hasegawa 2008: 1-4; Siddall 2011: 34-40.

45 ʿik-ṣuʾ-[ru ÉRIN.ḪÁ.MEŠ]-šú-un. This restoration is only tentative. Compare ummāni-šú DUGUD-tú ik-ṣur-ma in the Babylonian Chronicle, (BM 21946, Obv. line 21: Wiseman 1956: 70; Grayson 1975: 100). Unger (1916: 10) and Donner (1970: 52) reconstructed si-d[ᵡ⁽ᵗ⁾-irᵗ⁽ᵗ⁾-ʾ]dᵗ⁽ᵗ⁾-šúᵗ⁽ᵗ⁾-un, which is less probable. Tadmor's reconstruction (1973:145) is ʿik²-luʾ² -[ú IGI.DU⁸]-šú-un "withheld their tribute" and was followed by Grayson in *RIMA* 3. However, Adad-nērārī III states, in the Pazarcık Stela (Obv. lines 7-10), that the rebellious kings caused him and his mother to cross the Euphrates. This reinforces the restoration of lines 14-15 of the Saba'a Stela, in which Adad-nērārī III considers an offensive action taken during his father's reign as a *casus belli* ("organised their [army]"), rather than only a "withholding [of] tribute".

46 I adopt Adad-nērārī III's chronology suggested by Poebel 1943: 74-79. Cf. Page 1968: 147, n. 27; Cazelles 1969: 108; Tadmor 1969: 46, n. 3; Lipiński 1969: 167, n. 37; Donner 1970: 56, n. 23; Cody 1970: 328-329; Grayson 1976: 140, n. 48; Shea 1978: 102-103; Millard 1994: 13; Yamada 2003: 75. For further discussion of this chronological issue, see Hasegawa 2008.

Hatti was conquered in this year. Compared with the Eponym Chronicles, it is apparent that the scribe brought together all the western campaigns of Adad-nērārī from 805 to 796 BCE, the year when the stela was probably engraved.[47] As a summary inscription, this stela summarises Adad-nērārī III's military achievements in the west up to 796 BCE.

4.2.3.2.2. The Tell al-Rimah Stela (A.0.104.7)

This stela was uncovered in 1967 inside the *cella* in a shrine at Tell al-Rimah located near the Jebel Sinjar. The king's image and divine symbols are located on the upper part of the stela and the text is inscribed below it.

The inscription consists of twenty-one lines, but the last nine lines (lines 13-21) were effaced.[48] The text can be divided into the following six sections: (1) dedication (lines 1-2); (2) Adad-nērārī III's genealogy (line 3); (3) campaign to the land of Hatti and the tribute from the kings in the region (lines 4-8); (4) campaign to the Great Sea and Mt Lebanon and tribute from the kings of Na'iri (lines 9-12); (5) addition of lands to Nergal-ēreš's governorship (lines 13-20); and (6) curse (line 21).[49] Following is a translation of the campaign to the Hatti land (section 3).
Translation

> 4-8) I verily mustered my chariots (and) camps. I verily commanded the march to the land Hatti. In one year I verily submitted the land Amurru (and) the land Hatti at my feet. I verily imposed upon them tribute of obligation for the future. He[sic!] received 2,000 talents of silver, 1,000 talents of copper, 2,000 talents of iron, 3,000 multicoloured clothing and linen — the tribute of Mari' of the land Damascus. He[sic!] received the tribute of Joash of the land Samaria, of the land Tyre, of the land Sidon.

> 9-12) I verily marched to the great sea of the setting sun. I verily erected the image of my lordship in the city of Arvad which in the middle of the sea. I verily ascended Mt Lebanon. I verily cut down 100 beams of strong cedar for the requirement of the palace and my temples.

This summary inscription assigns all the military achievements of Adad-nērārī III in the west to "one year" (line 4). The terminology of "one year" should be interpreted as the literary expression magnifying the king's deeds.[50] The stela commemorates and magnifies Adad-nērārī III's military achievements in the west.

---

47 Tadmor 1973: 147-148.

48 The effacement of these lines probably happened when Nergal-ēreš fell from power. On the date of Nergal-ēreš's fall from power, see 5.2.5.

49 Publication: Page 1968: 139-153; Donner, 1970: 50-51 (lines 1-12); Tadmor 1973: 141-144; Weippert 1992: 60-62; *RIMA* 3, A.0.104.7; Siddall 2011: 42-46.

50 See Tadmor 1973: 143; Younger 1990: 122. Similar examples in the Assyrian royal inscriptions can be found in Tadmor (*op. cit.*, 143, n. 16).

4.2.3.2.3. The Nimrud Slab (A.0.104.8)

This broken slab was found in 1854 by Loftus at a mound between the North West and South West Palaces at Calah. The text, although the lower part was missing, was squeezed by Norris and published in the first Rawlinson folio. Its importance is notable because this is the sole inscription discovered in the Assyrian homeland; all other inscriptions originated from the provinces.

The remaining text consists of twenty-four lines, which are divided into the following four sections: (1) Adad-nērārī III's name and epithets without his genealogy (lines 1-5a); (2) range of Adad-nērārī III's conquest described from east to west (lines 5b-14); (3) conquest of Damascus and tribute from Mariʾ king of Damascus (lines 15-21); (4) tax imposed on the Babylonian kings (lines 22-24).[51] Here is the translation of the part (section 2), depicting the range of Adad-nērārī's conquest in the west.

Translation

> 5b-14) The conqueror from the land Siluna, where the sun rises, the land Namri, the land Ellipi, the land Harhar, the land Araziaš, the land Mesu, the land Media, the land/mountain Gizilbunda in its totality, the land Munna, the land Parsua, the land Allabria, the land Abdadanu, the land Naʾiri to the border in totality, the land Andia, which is a distant place, BAD-hu, the mountain to the border in its totality, until the great sea where the sun rises. From the Euphrates, the land Hatti, the land Amurru in its totality, the land Tyre, the land Sidon, the land of (the house of) Omri, the land Edom, the land Philistia, until the great sea where the sun sets, to my feet I subjected. Tribute of obligation I imposed on them.

This inscription is a "summary inscription" that relates in great detail the western (lines 15-21) and southeastern (lines 21-24) frontiers of the king's conquest. To emphasise the extent of the conquest, the author uses merismus such as "from … until the great sea where the sun rises"; "from … until the great sea where the sun sets". This is followed by description of the events which happened at both extremities.

It is notable that the conquest of Babylonia is mentioned in the text. This campaign might be dated to 795–794 BCE, when the Eponym Chronicles refer to the campaign against Dēr.[52]

The tributaries in line 12 include Tyre, Sidon, Israel (KUR *humri*), Edom, and Philistia (Palastu). The first three are also mentioned in the Tell al-Rimah Stela (line 8) as tributaries, but Edom and Philistia are not mentioned in the other

---

51   Publication: *I R*, Pl. 35, no. 1; Tadmor 1973: 148-150; *RIMA* 3, A.0.104.8; Siddall 2011: 48-52.
52   See Millard 1970: 448; Tadmor 1973: 150. On Adad-nērārī III's possible campaign against Babylonia and its aftermath, see Brinkman 1968: 213-220.

Adad-nērārī III inscriptions.[53] The payment was made either in the years 803, 802, or 796 BCE.[54]

4.2.3.2.4. The Scheil Fragment (A.0.104.4)

This fragmentary stone slab was published by Scheil in 1917 (Scheil 1917: 159-160). Millard (Millard and Tadmor 1973: 60-61) attributed it to Adad-nērārī III's reign for two reasons.[55] (1) The name of the king's predecessor is Šamšī-[...]. (2) The name Ataršumki (line 5') is mentioned in other Adad-nērārī III's inscriptions (Antakya Stela and Sheikh Hammad Stela). The fragment is the middle part of a stela consisting of ten lines whose right side is also missing.[56]
Translation

> [...] they drew the yoke [...] who, in the time of Šamšī-[Adad (V) ...] the lords of the river Eup[hrates...] he heard [of ...]. Atarš[umki ...] he trusted in [...] and [came] to w[age battle ...] (and) I took away his camp. [...] the treasure of [his] pa[lace ... Ataršumki], son of Abirāmu[57] [...] fr[om ... his tribute] without number [I received ...].

This text describes Adad-nērārī III's campaign(s) against Arpad in years 805–804 BCE. Millard (Millard and Tadmor 1973: 61), associating the river mentioned in line 3' with that mentioned in the Sheikh Hammad Stela, identified it with the Euphrates. Grayson (RIMA 3, 206, footnote) identified it with the Orontes River since Ataršumki is mentioned in the Antakya Stela (lines 4-8a) in conjunction with that river. However, it is questionable whether these two inscriptions relate to the same event. The river mentioned in line 3' of the Sheikh Hammad Stela is certainly the Euphrates, which Adad-nērārī III claimed to have crossed (line 4). The "lords of the river" might have been the eight kings mentioned in the Pazarcık Stela (Obv. line 12), and possibly also in the Sheikh Hammad Stela (line 6).

The Scheil Fragment was probably written before the subjugation of Damascus in 796 BCE because of the detailed description of the campaign(s) against

---

53 At one time, *ana* KUR *hat-te-e* in the end of line 12 of the Saba'a Stela had been mistakenly regarded as *ana* KUR *pa-la-as-tu*. Tadmor (1969:47; 1973:145) rejected this transliteration and corrected it to *ana* KUR *hat-te-e*.

54 Thus, if one dates the tribute from the first three kingdoms to 803 BCE, that of the others would be dated to 802 or 796 BCE; if to 802 BCE, then the others to 796 BCE. Philistia was possibly under the Aramaean hegemony during the absence of Assyria from the region (2 Kgs 12:18).

55 Scheil ascribed the fragment to Shalmaneser III. Borger (1967: 451) suggested already in 1967 that the text belongs to Adad-nērārī III. Cf. Weippert 1992: 44.

56 Publication: Scheil 1917: 159-160; Millard and Tadmor1973: 60-61; RIMA 3, A.0.104.4; Siddall 2011: 32-34.

57 In this study, I follow the reading of Abirāmu suggested by Zadok 1997: 805; Mattila and Radner 1998: 12-14. The reading of Adramu, based on the reading "Hdrm" in line 2 of the Melqart Stela, is far from certain; see Lipiński 2000: 196-198, n. 12 with earlier literature.

Arpad. This event was counted as Adad-nērārī's major deed in the west during his first years and thus was described in detail.

4.2.3.2.5. The Sheikh Hammad Stela (A.0.104.5)

Two fragments of the Sheikh Hammad Stela (BM 131124) are known. One fragment was found in 1879 by Rassam at Tell Sheikh Hammad, (Assyrian Dūr-kat-limmu) in the region of the Habur River, where many Neo-Assyrian documents were unearthed.[58] The bust of the king is depicted on the left side with three divine symbols on the right. Only the right upper part of the stela remains. The other fragment was put on sale in 2000 with Christie's of New York.[59] This fragment forms the lower part of the original stela. The combined fragments consist of thirty-two lines. Millard and Tadmor noted the similarity in phrases and the relief's motifs to those of the Tell al-Rimah stela.[60]

The inscription begins with (1) Adad-nērārī III's genealogy (lines 1-2) and then describes (2) Adad-nērārī's campaign against Ataršumki the Arpadite (lines 3-10). The twenty-two lines in the lower fragment describe the construction of the temple of the god Sulmanu. The following translation of the first ten lines is highly conjectural due to the damaged condition of the text.[61]

Translation

> 3-10) [By the command of Aššur] I verily mustered my camp, and to the land Hatti [I verily ordered (them) to march.] I crossed the Euphrates in (its) flood (and) went down [to Paqarhu]buna.[62] Ataršumki, [son of Abirāmu the Arpadite and the eight king]s of the land of Hatti, who were with him. [I fought against them ... the te]rror of radiance of Aššur, [my lord], [overwhelmed them. In on]e⁽⁷⁾ year, the land Hatti[...] I s[ubdued].

The text commemorates the victory over Arpad as a major military achievement.[63] It indicates that the stela was probably erected soon after the campaign against Arpad in 805 BCE.[64]

---

58 Radner 2002.
59 Radner 2002: 15; Kühne and Radner 2008: 33-34.
60 Millard and Tadmor 1973: 58; *RIMA* 2: 296.
61 Publication: Millard and Tadmor 1973: 57-64, Pl. XXIX; *RIMA* 3, A.0.104.5; Siddall 2011: 27-32.
62 Paqarruhbuni is identified with Gaziantep, see also Yamada 2000a: 92-94.
63 Millard (1973: 162), conjecturing about the rest of the stela, stated that the text narrates only the victory over Arpad and her allies and the list of tribute from them. His conjecture is now confirmed by the second fragment, which narrates no military report but rather building activities (Siddall 2011: 27-32). Cf. Timm 1993: 71.
64 Radner (Kühne and Radner 2008: 33) dated the stela to 805 BCE.

4.2.3.2.6. The Pazarcık Stela (Obverse A.0.104.3)

The Pazarcık Stela was found during the construction of a dam in the Pazarcık area in Turkey. The stela is inscribed on two sides. The obverse was inscribed in the time of Adad-nērārī III and the reverse during Shalmaneser IV's reign.[65] The stela is almost intact but inferior in workmanship.

The obverse consists of twenty-three lines, which can be divided into the following five sections: (1) Adad-nērārī III's genealogy and mention of Semiramis[66] (lines 1-7a); (2) Adad-nērārī III and Semiramis's crossing of the Euphrates against nine anti-Assyrian kings at the time of Ušpilulume of Kummuh (lines 7b-10); (3) battle against Ušpilulume and his ally Ataršumki of Arpad at Paqarhubunu (lines 11-15a); (4) erection of the stela as the boundary stone between Kummuh and Gurgum (lines 15b-18); and (5) curses (lines 19-23).[67] Following is a translation of the campaign against Arpad and its aftermath (sections 2-4).

Translation

7b-10) In the days of Ušpilulume,[68] king of the city Kummuh, they caused Adad-nērārī (III) king of the land Assyria, (and) Sammuramat (Semiramis), the palace woman, to cross the river Euphrates.[69]

11-15a) Ataršumki, heir of Abirāmu, of the city of Arpad, together with eight kings who were with him at the city of Paqi(/a)rahubunu. Their lines with them, I have beaten. Their military camp, I took away. To save their lives they went away.

15b-18) In this year[70] this boundary (stone), between Ušpilulume, king of the city Kummuh, and (between) Qalparunda, heir of Palalam, king of the city Gurgum, they installed.[71]

---

65 Both inscriptions were attributed to the respective kings, but the real author was most probably Šamšī-ilu, an Assyrian *turtānu*. For this person, see 5.2.9.

66 For Semiramis and her role and importance in Adad-nērārī III's reign, see Timm 1993: 62-63, n. 18 with earlier literature.

67 Publication: Donbaz 1990: 5-24; Timm 1993: 55-84; Zaccagnini 1993: 53-72; Weippert 1992: 58, n. 97 (lines 4-11); *RIMA* 3, A.0.104.3; Hasegawa 2010b: 2-3; Siddall 2011: 23-27.

68 Following Timm (1993: 64), *ina ūmē Ušpilulume* is taken as a construct state. Generally, *ina ūmēšu(-ma)* is used for the meaning "at that time" in the Neo-Assyrian royal inscriptions. Donbaz (1990) and Weippert (1992: 55-56, n. 82) translated: "when Ušpilulume ..."

69 For the translation of this sentence, see the notes on this stela below.

70 For this chronological interpretation, see Timm 1993: 66-67. He interpreted this expression as chronological as well as causal.

71 The form of the verb *ušēlūni* can be interpreted either as third person plural of *elû* (Š-stem) plus ventive *-nim* or as first or third person singular of the same verb plus subjunctive marker *-ūni* (See *GAG* §83b; Hämeen-Anttila 2000: 92-93). Donbaz (1990: 9) translated: "In this (same) year this boundary stone was *set up* between Ušpilulume, king of the people of Kummuh, and Qalparuda, son of Palalam, king of the people of Gurgum." Timm (1993: 58) interpreted as did the former and translated this sentence: "In jenem Jahr stellte man diese Grenzstele zwischen Ušpilulume,

Parts of this text are syntactically problematic, rendering the historical evaluation of this stela disputable. This is exemplified by lines 7-10. Weippert (1992: 56, n. 82) suggested that it was Ušpilulume who was forced to cross the Euphrates. This interpretation, however, raises another question: was Ušpilulume deported to the eastern side of the Euphrates by Ataršumki and his allies, or was he forced to cross the Euphrates in order to join the allies in the struggle with Assyria? The first possibility is unlikely since in the Neo-Assyrian royal inscriptions (and possibly also in the Aramaic inscription of Hazael), the "crossing of the Euphrates" is commonly associated with successful or heroic military action. The second possibility is also unlikely: Ušpilulume was not punished by the Assyrians after the battle, although he had taken part in the coalition against Assyria (albeit by compulsion). Moreover, it is clear from the curses in Obv. lines 19-22 and from the geographical location of Pazarcık, that this border treaty is in favour of Kummuh.[72] Thus, Weippert's interpretation is historically improbable. Donbaz (1990: 9) and Yamada (2000a: 93) suggested that Ušpilulume was the subject of *ušēbirūni* and thus translated: "when Ušpilulume ... caused Adad-nērārī ... to cross the Euphrates".[73] This interpretation fits best the context of the inscription, which mainly concerns Ušpilulume. Ušpilulume, as a loyal vassal of Assyria, possibly requested Adad-nērārī to rescue him from the attack of the "eight kings" (Na'aman 1991: 84-85).

The aforementioned interpretation of the Obv. lines 7-10 supports the restoration of lines 14-15 of the Saba'a Stela. According to the restoration, the enemy "organised their [army]" already in Adad-nērārī III's father's reign. Adad-nērārī regarded this action as offensive and considered it a *casus belli*. This military campaign against Paqarhubuna probably took place in 805–804 BCE, when the Assyrian western frontier was endangered.[74]

In line 18, the setting of the boundary is reported. When the verb *ušēlūni* is interpreted as the third person plural form of Š-stem of *elû* plus ventive, the subject of the sentence, who set the boundary, should not be a single person.[75] According to the context in Obv. line 10, where a similar use of an Š-stem verb in the plural plus ventive is employed, the subject of the verb is to be sought after the sentence. Likewise, the subject in line 18 can be found outside the sentence,

---

dem König der Stadt der Kummuhäer, (und) zwischen Qalparu(n)da, dem Sohn des Palalam, dem König der Stadt der Gurgumäer, auf."

72   See Timm 1993: 71-72. He also drew attention to the fact that the father of Ušpilulume is not mentioned, although the father of Qalparunda is.

73   They regarded *-ūni* as a subjunctive marker of the third person singular verb *ušēbir*.

74   Weippert 1992: 55-56.

75   When interpreting it as the first or third person singular plus subjunctive marker, one should interpret that the sentence begins from line 15b with *ina* MU.AN.NA and thus the translation would be: "Boundary, which I (Adad-nērārī III) set, in this year, between ..." The possibility of third person "he" will be discarded.

for it is clear that the *persona(e)* who established the border was/were Assyrian(s). Therefore, the "they" in line 18 refers to Adad-nērārī III and Semiramis, the pair whom Ataršumki and the eight kings caused to cross the Euphrates. That this "boundary stone" belongs to both Adad-nērārī and Semiramis is clearly shown in the introduction to the text.[76]

To sum up, the obverse of the Pazarcık Stela can be dated to 805-804 BCE, when Adad-nērārī III led military campaigns against Arpad and Hazazu, or soon thereafter.

4.2.3.2.7. The Antakya Stela (A.0.104.2)

This stela was found *ca.* 1968 between Antakya and Samandağ, in Turkey. Although partially damaged, the stela is in fairly good condition. Two standing royal figures are engraved face to face across a divine symbol on the stela. The royal figures might be the two kings, Zakkur of Hamath and Ataršumki of Arpad. The text describes the establishment of the border between Hamath and Arpad by Adad-nērārī III and Šamšī-ilu, his *turtānu*.

The text consists of nineteen lines which can be divided into four sections: (1) Adad-nērārī III's genealogy (lines 1-3); (2) setting up the border between Hamath and Arpad along the Orontes River (lines 4-8a); (3) authorisation of the border of Arpad by Adad-nērārī III and Šamšī-ilu (lines 8b-11a); and (4) curses (lines 11b-19).[77] In what follows, the second part of the text, which relates the establishment of the border between Hamath and Arpad, will be examined.
Translation

> 4-8a) The boundary that Adad-nērārī (III) king of the land Assyria (and) Šamšī-ilu the field marshal set between Zakkur of the land Hamath [an]d Ataršumki, heir of Abirāmu. The city Nahlasi[78] together with its fields, orchards, [and its s]ettlements, all of it belongs to Ataršumki. They [allot] the river Orontes [eq]ually between them, and share this boundary.

Ataršumki fought against the Assyrian army in 805–804 BCE and then took part in the attack against Zakkur of Hamath in 804/3 BCE.[79] However, this event should not be the result of the siege of Hadrach, because at that time Šamšī-ilu had not yet achieved great political power in the Assyrian Empire.[80] The setting

---

76 For detailed discussion, see Hasegawa 2010b.

77 Publication: Donbaz 1990: 5-24; Siddall 2011: 23-27.

78 Lipiński (2000: 285-286) identified the city Nahlasi with the modern town Al-'Arīš on the bank of the Orontes River, while Ikeda (2003: 94*) suggested Nahliye, three kilometres northwest of modern Riha, but distant from the Orontes River.

79 Na'aman 1991: 86.

80 Nergal-ēreš held power in the Empire at least until 796 BCE, when he led the campaign against Damascus. Šamšī-ilu's name was first mentioned in the Eponym Chronicles in 780 BCE.

of the boundary can be dated after 796 BCE, for the campaign in the same year was possibly led by Nergal-ēreš, who held the power in the Empire at that time. Šamšī-ilu, having gained the power after this year, played the role of mediator between Hamath and Arpad.

This border agreement was apparently in favour of Arpad for the following two reasons.[81] First, the Antakya Stela was discovered far west of the centre of the kingdom of Arpad. Second, lines 8b-11a state that this border was given to Ataršumki and his descendants. However, it remains unclear why Assyria favoured Ataršumki and cut short the territory of Zakkur.[82] It is possible that Assyria, by supporting Ataršumki and by reducing Zakkur's territory, conciliated Arpad and wished to maintain the power balance in the region.

This border setting poses another question: why the kingdom of Unqi, which had also joined the attack on Hamath (Zakkur Inscrption A, line 6), is not mentioned in the Antakya Stela, although Kunulua, its capital, was located about twenty-five kilometres east of its discovery place.[83] Two possible interpretations could be offered. Arpad was a major power in north Syria and south Anatolia. Just as Hazael of Damascus intruded into the territories of Israel and the Philistines,[84] it is possible that during the latter half of the ninth century BCE, Ataršumki or his predecessor had expanded his territory both northward and westward. If this assumption is correct, Arpad had probably subjugated Unqi by the time of the border setting.[85] Alternatively, Zakkur of Hamath gained great

---

81   Hawkins (1995: 96) assumed that the stela was swept downstream by the river and that the original location was in the neighbourhood of Jisr esh-Shughur, the border between the two states. Given the condition of the stela, this assumption seems unlikely; the distance between Jisr esh-Shughur and Antakya is nearly fifty kilometres as the crow flies. See Lipiński 2000: 282-283, n. 188.

82   Ikeda (1999: 282-283; 2003: 91*) suggested that the intention of Šamšī-ilu to set the border in favour of Arpad was "to drive a wedge between the enemy lines", particularly between Arpad and Aram-Damascus, and that this grievance caused Hamath to revolt in the following years (772, 765, and 755 BCE according to the Eponym Chronicles). See also Dion 1997: 129. Dating the attack on Hadrach to 796 BCE, Hawkins (1982: 403-404) explained that this favourable border was granted to Arpad in order to detach it from the alliance led by Damascus. Mazzoni (2000: 48-49) argued that the Assyrian involvement in disputes between local Syrian states promoted the Assyrian hegemony over this region. She (2001: 105) also suggested that the Syrian states must have regarded Hamath under Zakkur as a more imminent threat rather than Arpad under Ataršumki. Assuming that this event occurred immediately after the siege of Hadrach, Harrison (2001: 120) interpreted this favourable treatment as a reward to Arpad from Assyria for Arpad's retreat from the siege.

83   Kunulua is generally identified with Tell Tayinat. See Hawkins 1981: 305-306.

84   Cf. 2 Kgs 10:32, 33; 12:17-18; 13:3, 7, 22. This Aramaean expansion under Hazael is generally accepted as historical fact. See most recently, Pitard 1987: 145-160; Sader 1987: 265-268; Reinhold 1989: 173-179; Lemaire 1991a; Dion 1997: 199-204; Lipiński 2000: 385-391.

85   For example, Hazazu, formerly an important city in the kingdom of Unqi/Patina supposedly belonged to Arpad in 804 BCE. See Dion 1997: 124-125; Lipiński 2000: 199.

power in the region and subjugated Unqi after the Damascene submission to Assyria in 796 BCE.[86] Zakkur's rise to power might have been the cause of the Assyrian setting of the border in favour of Arpad.

4.2.3.2.8. The Campaigns of Adad-nērārī III to Syria (805–802 BCE)

Adad-nērārī III's military campaign against Arpad in 805 BCE had a great influence on the political situation in Syria. The successive annual campaigns to this region shifted the power balance among the small kingdoms in Syria, south Anatolia, and Palestine.

In 805 BCE, Ataršumki of Arpad and eight other kings attacked Ušpilulume of Kummuh. Adad-nērārī considered this action as a *casus belli*, crossed the Euphrates and attacked them. In the following year (804 BCE), he again led his army against Arpad. They fought at Paqarhubuna and the Assyrian army defeated the north Syrian coalition. Adad-nērārī subjugated Arpad and set a borderline between Kummuh and Gurgum in favour of the former. In the following two years (803-802 BCE), he advanced far south-westward and finally reached the Mediterranean, possibly in 803 BCE. He even sailed to Arvad and set his stela there. During these years, he received tribute from various kingdoms in Syria, yet at that time, Damascus, Israel, and other kingdoms in Palestine presumably were not yet among those tributary kingdoms.

4.3. The Zakkur Inscription

The date of the siege of Hadrach as related in the Zakkur Inscription should be considered against the background of the chronological framework established above.[87]

Several dates have been suggested for the episode. Dating it to 772 BCE can safely be dismissed because Damascus had lost its leading position in Syria-Pales-

---

86   Ikeda (2003: 93*) assumed that it was Zakkur of Hamath who expanded northward and perhaps annexed a part of Unqi, and even invaded the territory of Arpad. His assumption is based on Tiglath-pileser III's summary inscription (Tadmor 1994: 146-149), in which many cities, formerly in the territory of Hamath, are allocated to Arpad. This list includes, however, also a city located far south, such as Haurani, which is identified with Hawārīn, northeast of Damascus and far south of Hamath, and thus it possibly reflects the territorial concessions by Hamath after her battle with Assyria in 772, 765, and 755 BCE and also that of Arpad in 743–740 BCE. On the other hand, Weippert (1992: 58-59 with n. 97) suggested that at the time of the erection of the stela (796 BCE), the territory of Unqi had not yet been fixed and its territory was divided by Arpad and Hamath. Harrison (2001: 120) suggested that Unqi's territory was reduced or even annexed by Arpad.

87   For general information on the Zakkur Inscription, see 3.2.4.

tine by that time.[88] Others dated it to 796 BCE, shortly before the Assyrian campaign against Damascus.[89] According to this view, Damascus tried to re-establish its hegemony over Syria-Palestine after the Assyrian retreat from the west in 803/2 BCE. Hadrach was besieged because Zakkur, the king of Hamath, had refused to take part in the anti-Assyrian coalition. Consequently, Adad-nērārī III launched a military campaign in 796 BCE against Damascus, which formed the historical background for the "miraculous deliverance" of Zakkur and the city of Hadrach from the besieging army.

However, this view confronts major problems. Ataršumki of Arpad was subjugated by Adad-nērārī III in 804 BCE, after the battle at Paqarhubuna. Arpad's re-participation in the anti-Assyrian coalition in 796 BCE is thus unlikely. Likewise, the participation of the Anatolian kingdoms, such as Que and 'Umq, in the alliance is inconceivable. In addition, Adad-nērārī III's inscriptions, describing the subjugation of Damascus in 796 BCE, does not mention any alliances; on the other hand, the Zakkur Inscription describes a large Syro-Anatolian alliance that besieged Zakkur. In light of these inconsistencies, other scholars dated the siege of Hadrach to 805 BCE, on the eve of Adad-nērārī III's campaign against Arpad.[90] However, this solution faces another problem. The Assyrian campaigns in 805/4 BCE were launched at the instigation of Ušpilulume, the king of Kummuh, and were directed against the Syro-Anatolian coalition headed by Arpad (Pazarcık Stela). The battlefield was Paqarhubuna, which lies near the northern border of Kummuh. Therefore, the "miraculous salvation" of Zakkur can hardly be consistent with the Assyrian campaign in north Syria in 805 BCE.

Na'aman (1991: 86) offered an alternative dating for the siege of Hadrach. He dated this event immediately after 805 BCE, the defeat of the Syro-Anatolian coalition by the Assyrian army. According to his view, Damascus made an effort to "unite an all-inclusive Syro-Hittite coalition against Assyria" because "it became clear that even a partial coalition of kingdoms was not strong enough to hold back the Assyrian war machine". Zakkur, however, refused to participate in the alliance and was attacked by Damascus and other coalition members.[91] Adad-nērārī III's 804/3 BCE campaign forced this coalition "to hurry northwards in order to defend their homeland and thus Hamath was saved". This dating seems

88   Lidzbarski 1915: 8-9; Noth 1929: 128-130. For more literature, see Na'aman 1991: 85, n. 19.
89   Jepsen 1941–44: 164-170; Lipiński 1971b: 397-399; Ikeda 1977: 208-209; Lemaire 1993: 153* ; Harrison 2001: 119-120. For further literature, see Na'aman 1991: 85, n. 20.
90   Dupont-Sommer 1949: 47; Cazelles 1969: 113; Millard and Tadmor 1973: 63-64.
91   Na'aman (1996: 177) suggested that after Hazael's conquest of Hamath, the capital was transferred to Hadrach.

the most probable because it produces no conflicts with the descriptions in the Assyrian inscriptions.[92]

Provided that the siege of Hadrach took place in 804/3 BCE, the absence of Joahaz from among the besieging troops in the Zakkur Inscription may indicate that the Kingdom of Israel did not take part in the siege. It might show that Joahaz had already attempted to throw off the Damascene yoke, by refusing to participate in the anti-Assyrian coalition.

4.4. The Mesha Inscription[93]

The Mesha Inscription, although not directly concerned with the relation between Israel and Aram-Damascus, demonstrates the extent of the territorial loss suffered by Israel during the reigns of Joram and Jehu. This territorial loss would certainly reflect the decline of Israel at that time. The inscription commemorates Mesha's conquest of the Israelite cities and his building activities and provides vital information on the Moabite's new territory. The main part of the text (lines 7-33) is divided into two parts: (1) Mesha's wars against Israel (lines 7-21, 31-32); (2) Mesha's building activities in Moab.

Mesha conquered the land of Medeba (lines 7-8), Ataroth (lines 10-11), Nebo (14-18), Jahaz (18-20), and Horonaim (lines 31-32). Medeba is located thirty kilometres south of Amman and twenty kilometres north of Dibon.[94] Ataroth is generally identified with Khirbet ʿAtārūz, some fifteen kilometres northwest of Dibon.[95] Nebo has generally been identified with Khribet al-Mukkhayat, due primarily to its location and the Iron Age findings from excavations at the site.[96] Jahaz, mentioned also in the Hebrew Bible,[97] should be located in the vicinity of Dibon according to lines 20-21 of the Mesha Inscription. Although Jahaz's exact location is in dispute, all the candidate sites are on the Transjordanian plateau.[98]

---

92   It should be noted that Zakkur does not mention who released Hadrach from the besieging army. 2 Kgs 13:5 likewise does not specify the "saviour" of Israel, but this verse is a later insertion (4.1.5.).

93   For the general introduction of the Mesha Inscription, see 2.4.

94   For Medeba, see Dearman 1989: 174-175; Piccirillo 1992a.

95   Dearman 1989: 177-178; Franklyn 1992.

96   For the earlier literature, see Dearman 1989: 180-181; Ferch 1992a; Piccirillo 1992b.

97   Num 21:23; Deut 2:32; Jos 13:18; 21:36; Jgs 11:20; Isa 15:4; Jer 48:21, 34.

98   Dearman (1984; 1989: 181-84; 1992a) identified it with Khirbet el-Medeiniyeh (Khirbet al-Mudayna). For the results of recent excavations of the site, see Daviau 1997; Daviau and Steiner 2000; Dion and Daviau 2000. Smelik (1992: 74-79) suggested Khribet Libb. Others suggested Jalul, ar-Remeil, Khribet ʿAleiyan and Khirbet Iskander. For the literature, see Smelik, *op. cit.*, 76, nn. 44-45; 78, n. 55; Dearman 1992a.

The conquest of Horonaim seemingly occurred later, and its location is apparently south of the Arnon.[99]

Mesha conducted construction activities at Baal-Meon,[100] Kiriathaim,[101] Qeriho, Aroer,[102] Beth-Bamoth,[103] Bezer,[104] Beth-Diblathaim,[105] and Kerioth.[106] These places are also on the Transjordanian plateau. In sum, the Mesha Inscription mentions toponyms located within the Transjordanian plateau, in the area called "Mishor" in the Bible.

However, the Moabite expansion probably continued after the composition of the Mesha Inscription. Lemaire (1987: 210-214; 1991b: 146-150) dated the composition of the Inscription to *ca.* 810 BCE, that is, during Joahaz's reign. On the other hand, Na'aman (2001b: 18-21) dated it to Jehu's reign (841–814 BCE) because the text does not seem to reflect the largest extent of the territory which the Moabites achieved.[107] Further Moabite expansion is reflected in the prophecies concerning Moab in Isa 15-16, Jer 48, Ezek 25:8-11, and Am 2:1-3.[108] In these prophecies, some of the Moabite cities (e.g., Heshbon, Elealeh, Sibma, Jazer, and Mephaath) are located beyond the region conquered by Mesha. Regardless of the details, these prophecies demonstrate well that these cities were regarded as Moabite at the time of their composition. A few cities mentioned in these prophecies are even situated on the eastern side of the Jordan Valley: Nimrim (Isa 15:12; Jer 48:34),[109] Beth-Jeshimoth (Ezek 25:9).[110] Likewise, the toponym "the plain of Moab" (ערבות מואב) – for the north-eastern plain of the Dead Sea[111] – conceivably indicates that Moab conquered that area after the composition of the Mesha Inscription.[112] In addition to this, the episode of the Moabite invasion into

---

99   For the location of Horonaim, see Dearman 1989: 188-189; 1992b; Na'aman 1994; 2001b: 11, n. 7 with earlier literature.

100   For the identification with Khirbet Ma'in, nine kilometres south of Medeba, see Dearman 1989: 175-176; Piccirillo 1992c.

101   For the proposed identifications, see Dearman 1989: 176-177; Mattingly 1992a.

102   For the identification, see above 3.1.2.; Dearman 1989: 185.

103   For the identification, see Dearman 1989: 185-186.

104   For the identification, see Dearman 1989: 186; Mattingly 1992b.

105   For the identification, see Dearman 1989: 187; Mattingly 1992c.

106   For the proposed identifications, see Dearman 1989: 178-179; Mattingly 1992d.

107   For the other dating, see Lemaire 1991b: 146-147, nn. 16-18.

108   Lemaire 1991b: 165-166; Na'aman 2001b: 18-21.

109   There is no consensus among scholars regarding the location of Nimrim. It might be either northeast or southeast of the Dead Sea. For the former view, see Glueck 1943: 11, and for the latter, see Schottroff 1966: 200-202; Ferch 1992b with earlier literature.

110   It is identified either with Khirbet es-Suweimeh or Tell 'Azeimeh, both are located in the north-eastern plain of the Dead Sea. See Glueck 1943: 23-26; Romero 1992.

111   Num 22:1; 26:3, 63; 31:12; 33:48-50; 35:1; 36:13; Deut 34:1, 8; Jos 13:32. The description of the plain is found in Glueck 1943: 10-11.

112   Weippert 1998: 548.

the western side of the Jordan in 2 Kgs 13:20-21 may support this view (see below, 5.1.3.). Yet, it is not clear that this additional conquest was achieved either by
Mesha or by his successor(s). The composition of the Mesha Inscription cannot
be dated exactly. Tentatively, I would date Mesha's death between 820 and 810
BCE, for the large extent of the Moabite expansion is best understood in the
context of the Aramaean expansion in Transjordan during the reigns of Hazael of
Damascus (see above 4.1.2).[113] It is likely that Mesha and his successor(s) took
advantage of Israel's decline during the reigns of Jehu and Joahaz and conquered
the northern Mishor after the composition of the Mesha Inscription. Consequently, by the beginning of Joash's enthronement, Moab already dominated the
entire area of the Mishor.

4.5. Synthesis

Available sources for Jehu and Joahaz's reigns reflect the decline of the Kingdom
of Israel in the late ninth century BCE. Due to the Assyrian absence from the
region, Assyrian inscriptions provide limited information on the Kingdom of
Israel. The Eponym Chronicles and Adad-nērārī III's summary inscriptions indicate his campaigns to Syria from 805 BCE on. The biblical source also delineates
the lowest ebb of the Kingdom of Israel during this period. 2 Kgs 10:32-33 and
13:3-7, 22 contribute to clarifying the status of Israel as a vassal of Aram-Damascus. The absence of Joahaz from the Zakkur Inscription indicates that he did not
participate in the siege of Hadrach (804/3 BCE). The Mesha Inscription helps to
demarcate the Moabite expansion in the latter half of the ninth century BCE and
the loss of vast Israelite territories in south Transjordan.

Jehu ascended the throne in 841 BCE and possibly paid tribute to Shalmaneser III at Ba'li-ra'si in the same year. After the Assyrian retreat from Syria, especially after 829 BCE, Hazael started invading Israel. As a result, the Israelite territory east of the Jordan was conquered by Aram-Damascus, Moab, and possibly
also Ammon.[114] The situation of Israel had not changed when Jehu was succeeded by Joahaz in 814 BCE. During Joahaz's reign, Hazael and his son Ben-
Hadad continued oppressing Israel. The shift in power balance in the Syro-
Palestinian arena took place in the year 805 BCE, when Adad-nērārī III resumed
military campaigns to the west of the Euphrates. The consecutive Assyrian four-
year-campaigns into Syria had a great influence on the kingdoms in Syria and
southern Anatolia, and possibly also in Palestine. These campaigns finally brought
a radical change in the power balance. The attempt to subjugate Arpad in 805
BCE by Adad-nērārī brought about the secession of Hamath under Zakkur (and

---

113   See also Na'aman 2001b: 37.

114   A possible mention of the Ammonite invasion of Gilead is in Am 1:13.

possibly also of Israel under Joahaz) from the anti-Assyrian coalition led by Damascus and Arpad. Consequently, Hadrach was besieged by its former allies. In the following year, Adad-nērārī III subjected Arpad, which was the second strongest power in the anti-Assyrian Syro-Anatolian alliance. As a result, the anti-Assyrian coalition headed by Damascus and Arpad broke up. Damascus was detached from its former allies and had to face the Assyrian attack alone in 796 BCE.

5. The Reign of Joash (799/798–784 BCE)

After the discussion of the lowest ebb of the Kingdom of Israel in the late ninth century BCE, this chapter will deal with the early eighth century BCE, namely the reign of Joash, son of Joahaz. Two source types are available for the historical reconstruction of Joash's reign: (1) biblical texts; (2) Assyrian texts.

5.1. The Biblical Source

The biblical texts available for the discussion are classified into two distinct types: (a) short texts which are included in the Dtr framework of Joash's reign (2 Kgs 13:10-13; 13:14-19; 13:20-21; 13:25; 14:8-14; 14:15-16; 14:17); (b) prophetic stories (1 Kgs 20; 2 Kgs 6:24-7:20; 6:8-23).

5.1.1. Synchronism between Joash and Jehoash (2 Kgs 13:10-13)

According to the synchronism (v. 10), Joash, son of Joahaz, ascended the throne of Samaria in the thirty-seventh year of Jehoash of Judah. However, Joash's enthronement falls in the thirty-ninth year of Jehoash according to the calculation of regnal data in v. 1 and 2 Kgs 14:1.[1] Some Greek manuscripts[2] and modern commentators[3] offered various solutions to this discrepancy but no consensus on Joash's dates has been achieved.

Vv. 12-13 is the reiteration of 14:15-16 and is probably a secondary attempt to conclude Joash's reign.[4] The opening formulae in 2 Kgs 13:10-11 provides

---

1   Burney 1903: 316.

2   Cf. Stade and Schwally (1904: 243).

3   For example, Gray (1977: 597) suggested Joash's co-regency with Joahaz for two years, and Kittel (1900: 258) assumed a scribal error here.

4   Montgomery 1951: 434; Gray 1977: 593; Würthwein 1984: 363; Cogan and Tadmor 1988: 145. There are only minor differences between these verses and 2 Kgs 14:15-16. The secondary origin of the 2 Kgs 13:12-13 is reflected in the unusual phrase employed for the depiction of Jeroboam's accession "וירבעם ישב על־כסאו" (v. 13).

information on the names of Joash's predecessor (Joahaz), his seat (Samaria), and the length of his reign.[5]

5.1.2. Elisha's Prophecy of Joash's Victory over Aram (2 Kgs 13:14-19)

This prophetic story of Elisha on his death bed can be divided into two redactional parts (see 3.4.5.): an original anecdote (vv. 14-17) and an interpolation (vv. 18-19). The story mentions Joash's victories over the Aramaeans. It indicates that Israel was still under the Damascene hegemony in Joash's early reign.

5.1.3. The Moabite Invasion of Cisjordan (2 Kgs 13:20-21)

The story is one of Elisha's wonder stories, in which a dead man was resurrected when his body touched that of Elisha. This story, together with vv. 14-19, seems to have been integrated into the Book of Kings by the Dtr. Our main concern here is v. 20b, which states that "Moabite bands used to invade the land at the start of the year".[6] The location of Elisha's tomb is not mentioned; however, Gilgal, the place near Jericho and the Moabite border, seems to be the best candidate.[7] This story attests to the Moabite invasion of the Israelite Cisjordanian territory in the late ninth and the beginning of the eighth centuries BCE.[8]

5.1.4. Joash's Recapture of the Israelite Cities (2 Kgs 13:25)

The verse recounts Joash's recapture of the Israelite cities from the Aramaeans. This verse is probably derived from a source which the Dtr used for the composi-

---

5   V. 11 is a schematic Dtr judgement on the religious activity of the kings of Israel.

6   Montgomery (1951: 435) and Würthwein (1984: 364) construed the phrase "בא שנה" as annual invasion. Gray (1977: 600) followed the Lucianic recension, in which the phrases are modified into "כבוא השנה"; he translated "Moabites used to come into the land at the end of the year". Following LXX and Targum renditions, Cogan and Tadmor (1988: 148) read: "בבוא השנה".

7   Gray (1977: 592-593, 600) suggested that Elisha's tomb could be located in Gilgal near Jericho (Jos 4:19), whereas Montgomery (1951: 435) located it in Abel-Meholah, Elisha's hometown (1 Kgs 19:16) situated on the west side of the Jordan. Abel Meholah was identified by Edelman (1992a:11) with Tell Abu Sus. There is another Gilgal located in the southern hills of Samaria and close to Bethel (2 Kgs 2:1, 2), but this Gilgal is too distant for the Moabite bands to raid. Cf. Kotter 1992: 1023.

8   It is probable, as Gray (1977: 600) suggested, that Hazael (and possibly Bar-Hadad as well) and Mesha attacked Israel together in Transjordan during the reigns of Jehu and Joahaz. The story of Ehud in Jgs 3:12-30, which depicts the conquest of Jericho by Moab, Ammon, and Amalek, should probably be set in the same chronological frame.

tion of vv. 22, 24-25 (see 3.4.5.). Joash's victory over Aram-Damascus would have resulted in the capture of the former Israelite cities which had been conquered by Hazael and Bar-Hadad.

5.1.5. Joash's Battle against Amaziah of Judah (2 Kgs 14:8-14)

Joash's victory over Amaziah in the battle of Beth-Shemesh is related in 2 Kgs 14:8-14.[9] The explicit attribution of Beth-Shemesh to Judah (v. 11) and the apparent sympathy with Joash show that the story originated in the Northern Kingdom. The historicity of this battle is supported by the results of the Tel Beth-Shemesh excavations. Traces of destruction were uncovered in the fortifications of Beth-Shemesh (Bunimovitz and Lederman 2001: 144; 2006: 420). The excavators dated this destruction layer (Level 3) to the first half of the eighth century BCE on the basis of the pottery assemblage and attributed it to the conflicts between Judah and Israel in the time of Amaziah (Bunimovitz and Lederman 2009: 136; 2011: 44-45). If this is indeed the case, Joash, following his victory in battle, must have attacked Beth-Shemesh and destroyed it. Joash possibly ruined other Judahite settlements on his way to Jerusalem.

Historical information from the story is summarised as follows: (1) Joash defeated Judah at Beth-Shemesh and captured Amaziah; (2) Joash attacked Jerusalem and breached part of the city wall; and (3) Joash took booty and hostages from Jerusalem and brought them to Samaria.

This battle relates the political-territorial struggle between Israel and Judah after the end of the Damascene hegemony over this region.[10] Judah's victory over Edom (vv. 7, 10) raised its status in the region.[11] Amaziah thus tried to negotiate

---

9   Würthwein (1984: 372) regarded the mention of Joash's plunder in v. 14 as schematic and attributed it to a redactional addition. However, it is natural that Joash the victor received the subjugation tax from Amaziah. The description of the plunder is not schematic either, when compared with those in the other passages (cf. 1 Kgs 14:25-26; 2 Kgs 12:19). For the historical background of the battle between Amaziah and Joash, see Na'aman 1987. Interpreting the "king" in 2 Kgs 14:22 as Joash, Na'aman (1993: 229) suggested that Israelite hegemony over Judah continued until the death of Joash.

10 The historical background for this battle suggested by scholars, such as a marriage proposal (Šanda 1912: 165) and a boundary dispute (Šanda, *op. cit.*, 166; Gray 1977: 608; Cogan and Tadmor 1988: 158), are mere speculations based either on the fable in v. 9, or on the location of the battlefield (Beth-Shemesh).

11 Amaziah's battle against Edom is related in detail in 2 Chr 25. In this episode, Amaziah hired the Israelite soldiers (vv. 6-10). Na'aman (1987: 213-214) suggested that the nucleus of the event and the results are based on an authentic source because there is no such story in the Book of Kings in which a Judahite king hires Israelite soldiers. In addition, the end of this episode contradicts the moral of the Chroniclers: that although Amaziah avoided hiring Israelite soldiers (positive action), he gained not only the reward (victory over Edom) but also the punishment (the Israelite soldiers plundered cities in Judah; v. 13).

with Joash about the political position of Judah, hoping to obtain a status of political equality. However, Joash, who had already defeated Aram-Damascus and regarded himself as the successor of the political-territorial hegemony of Damascus, dismissed the proposal for negotiation "face to face" (לכה נתראה פנים, v. 8). Instead, they "faced" at Beth-Shemesh (ויתראו פנים, v. 11) for battle (Na'aman 1987: 213).[12]

Joash's route to Beth-Shemesh was probably intentionally chosen in order to establish the Israelite hegemony in the northern Shephelah after the region was liberated from the Aramaean yoke.[13] Beth-Shemesh's proximity to Philistia and the Darb el-Ghaza route is another possible reason for Joash's attack. Amaziah's victory over Edom and his capture of Sela (2 Kgs 14:7) enabled Judah to control the commercial route to the Gulf of Aqaba. Later it facilitated the construction of Elat by Azariah (v. 22). It seems that just as Jehoshaphat, his great-great-grandfather, declined the suggested Israelite cooperation (1 Kgs 22:49-50), so Amaziah too did not allow Israel to participate in commercial enterprise through the Way of Arabah. Judah's control over this route hindered Israel from accessing the Gulf of Aqaba. Israel consequently had to seek an alternative route, possibly through Philistia (Na'aman 1987: 213). To consolidate the route to Philistia, Joash attacked Beth-Shemesh, Judah's stronghold in the northern Shephelah, located twelve kilometres southeast of the Philistine Ekron. The establishment of Kuntillet 'Ajrud, close to Darb el-Ghaza that leads from the Philistine coast to the southern Sinai, may be understood against this background.[14]

Israel's predominance is emphasised by the story.[15] Joash could regain his power only after Adad-nērārī III's conquest of Damascus in 796 BCE,[16] which was also the year of Amaziah's enthronement (v. 1). His campaign into Judah can thus be dated between 796 BCE and 783 BCE, the end of Joash's reign.

5.1.6. Dtr's Concluding Statement of Joash's Reign (2 Kgs 14:15-16)

The original concluding verses regarding Joash (vv. 15-16) are mentioned secondarily in 2 Kgs 13:12-13.[17] The Dtr mentions the peaceful death of the king, his

---

12   These two expressions form an ironical pun.

13   Hazael's invasion reached Philistine Gath (2 Kgs 12:18, see 3.3.2.10; 3.4.3.). Cf. Gray 1977: 608.

14   Since the Way of Arabah was blocked by Judah, Jeroboam II probably established and used the site as a commercial station (6.3.). For the view that the function of Kuntillet 'Ajrud as a caravanserai was secondary, see Na'aman and Lissovsky 2008.

15   This is also reflected in the mocking fable in v. 10, although the power balance of the metaphors cannot be taken at face value because the story is of Northern origin.

16   See 5.2.1.

17   See 5.1.1.

might, which is exemplified by the successful battle he waged against Amaziah, and his burial place.

5.1.7. Dtr's Calculation of Amaziah's Reign (2 Kgs 14:17)

The verse relates that Amaziah lived fifteen years after Joash's death. The calculation is based on the data in 2 Kgs 13:20 and 2 Kgs 14:1, 2: Joash reigned for sixteen years; Amaziah ascended the throne in the second year of Joash and reigned for twenty-nine years. This statement is a pure redactional note by the Dtr and can hardly be ascribed to an archival source (Begrich 1929: 149-151).[18] The verse functions as a reminder that the real subject here is Amaziah of Judah and not Joash of Israel, the actual protagonist in the preceding story (Gray 1977: 612). Hence, Lewy's suggestion (1927: 11-14) that this verse attests to Azariah's early enthronement soon after Amaziah's defeat cannot be accepted,[19] although Azariah certainly ascended the throne a long time before Amaziah's death (Chapter 1). Whether Joash dethroned Amaziah and enthroned Azariah after Amaziah's defeat cannot be verified.

5.1.8. Contribution of Prophetic Stories to the History of Joash's Reign

Three prophetic stories in the Book of Kings have often been related to the time of Joash. The literary structure and historical authenticity of these stories as well as their contribution to history will be discussed in the following three sections.

5.1.8.1. Two Battles between Israel and Aram (1 Kgs 20)

The story contains two scenes of war between Israel and Aram-Damascus (vv. 1-21 and vv. 26-34). The first scene (vv. 1-21) relates the siege of Samaria by the massive Aramaean army led by Ben-Hadad. The story culminates in the flight of the Aramaean troops as they are defeated by the Israelite forces small in number (vv. 20-21).[20] The second scene in 1 Kgs 20 relates the battle between Israel and

---

18   Würthwein 1984: 372-373.

19   Cf. Cogan and Tadmor 1988: 154. For criticism, see Begrich 1929: 150-151; Würthwein 1984: 373, n. 14.

20   The story commences with the description of the Aramaean siege of Samaria and Ben-Hadad's severe demand on the King of Israel (vv. 1-3). The Israelite king, judging from the expression in his statement (v. 4), was apparently a vassal of Ben-Hadad at that time. At the second request (vv. 5-6), he summoned the elders of the city and decided to refuse the demand (vv. 7-9). Enraged by this answer, Ben-Hadad commanded his soldiers to prepare themselves for an attack on Samaria

Aram-Damascus at Aphek, the victory of Israel, and the subsequent treaty concluded between the two kingdoms.[21] Scholars, especially those in the German
school, hypothesised that the two accounts were originally independent and that
they were later combined through vv. 22-25 (Schmitt 1972: 46-51; Würthwein
1984: 237; Stipp 1987: 230-267; Otto 2001: 212-213).[22]

However, Sroka (2006: 5-18) demonstrated that 1 Kgs 20 is a sophisticated
literary unity. He pointed out fifteen *Leitwörter* and word roots that are reiterated
in the story. These words highlight the coherent theme of the entire story and
appear also in the last part (vv. 35-43), which has been frequently regarded as a
later addition. Thematic, stylistic, and grammatical phenomena are also common
throughout chapter 20. For example, the story begins in Samaria and ends in
Samaria. In conclusion, the entire story of 1 Kgs 20 can safely be ascribed to a
single author.

Anachronistic features of the story have been widely recognised since Jepsen's article (1941–44).[23] Some scholars regarded the reference to "Ahab" in vv. 2,
13, and 14 as secondary.[24] These scholars suggested assigning the story to the
Jehuite Dynasty and identified the protagonist as either Joahaz or Joash.[25]

These identifications rest on the premise that the war narratives in 1 Kgs 20
are basically authentic. However, Sroka's close diachronic-linguistic analysis of the
text and his examination of the norms embedded in the text attest to fictional

---

(vv. 10-12). Then, a prophet came to the king of Israel and announced that God would give to
the king of Israel a victory over the massive Aramaean army (vv. 13-14). The king of Israel acted
in accordance with this oracle (vv. 15-19). The small Israelite troop defeated the vast Aramaean
army; Ben-Hadad himself had to flee (vv. 20-21).

21   For the fictional feature of the story in 1 Kgs 20, see Hasegawa *forthcoming*.

22   Some scholars counted v. 28 to a later addition. For example, see Würthwein 1984: 237. It must
be emphasised, however, that the two episodes form a literary set in the present version. The reverse of the position between the two kings and the correspondent verbs and actions are seen in
two episodes. Cf. Long 1984: 209-211; Revell 1993: 104.

23   The king of Israel depicted in this narrative presents himself as a vassal of the king of Damascus
(v. 4), which hardly reflects the power balance between the two kingdoms at Ahab's time (Cf.
Whitley 1952: 144-146). The possibility that certain anecdotes from the Elisha stories can be interpreted in the historical context of the Jehuite Dynasty was already suggested as early as the
nineteenth century (Kuenen 1890: 83, n. 13).

24   The name of the king of Israel appears only three times in the account (vv. 2, 13, and 14). In
other cases, he is merely referred to as "the king of Israel"; on the other hand, the king of Aram
is almost always mentioned with his name Ben-Hadad (thirteen times, vv. 1, 3, 5, 9, 10, 16, 17, 20,
26, 30, 32, 33 [twice]). According to Würthwein (1984: 236), vv. 13 and 14 are secondary. For
various views supporting the originality of Ahab in the story, see Gray 1977: 415, 417-418.

25   The prevailing view in research is that the vassalage situation of Israel fits the early days of the
Jehuite Dynasty when Israel was in the shadow of Aramaean hegemony (cf. Chapters 3 and 4);
hence, the anonymous king of Israel in this narrative can be one of the early Jehuite kings. Cogan
(2001: 472-474) and Sweeney (2007: 240) regarded the basic plot of the story in 1 Kgs 20 as historically authentic.

features and a late date for 1 Kgs 20 (Sroka 2006: 19-35). He found in the story seven words and expressions that are otherwise used only in secure late sources.[26] Comparison of words and expressions that appear in the story with those in the classical and Late Hebrew sources dates the story most probably to the Persian Period. In addition to the linguistic evidence, Sroka pointed out three late norms in the story (*op. cit.*, 36-37), which are likely to date it to the Persian Period. (1) The king consults with all the elders of the land and the people (vv. 7-8). (2) Anonymity of the prophets (vv. 13, 22, 28, 35, 38, and 41). (3) A prophet who appears before war without the king's summons. These features are extraordinary in the Book of Kings but are common in the Book of Chronicles.

It seems therefore that the author composed 1 Kgs 20 to convey his theological and educational messages to his contemporary readers. He composed some parts of the story by employing themes and stylistic features, including words and expressions borrowed from various passages in the Bible.[27] The source for the introduction of 1 Kgs 20 can be identified easily at 2 Kgs 6:24-7:20. The similarity between the historical circumstances of the mid-Jehuite Dynasty and those related in 1 Kgs 20 is the result of literary borrowing. The anachronisms in the story are not a result of later additions, but indicate the late date of composition. In short, it is doubtful that 1 Kgs 20 contains any historical information which could serve as a source for reconstructing the history of Israel in the time of the Jehuite Dynasty.

5.1.8.2. The Siege of Samaria (2 Kgs 6:24-7:20)

The legend describes the siege of Samaria by the Aramaean army, the famine in the city during the siege, and the surprising Aramaean withdrawal, by which the inhabitants of Samaria were released from the siege. Originally an independent story, it was later integrated into the Book of Kings by the Dtr.[28] The story probably rests on a historical event.[29] The hunger and the unanticipated relief

---

26   These words and expressions are as follows: נערי שרי (v. 10), שעלים (v. 10), אם־ישפק עפר שומרון (v. 10), הסר המלכים (vv. 23 and 25), במישור (v. 14), מי־יאסר המלחמה (vv. 14, 15, 17, and 19), המדינות (v. 24), ויחלטו הממנו (v. 33), איש ממקמו (v. 24).

27   Sroka (2006: 38-46) enumerated the possible sources for the composition of 1 Kgs 20: 2 Sam 10:1-11:1; 2 Kgs 6:24-7:20; 2 Kgs 9:1-10:28; 2 Kgs 5:7; 1 Sam 15; Gen 31; Jos 6; 1 Kgs 16:9; 1 Kgs 21:1. 1 Kgs 13 might have served as its source, although this chapter, too, shows features of a late composition.

28   Würthwein 1984: 309-310.

29   Würthwein (1984: 314-316) suggested that the involvement of Elisha in the story (6:31-7:2, 6-7, 16b-20) is fictional and may not have been in the original story. It is pointed out, already by Jepsen (1941–44: 154-155) that this account describes the same siege of Samaria described in 1 Kgs 20:1-21, and the same event was orally transferred in two different stories, described from two

from the siege must have left a strong impression on the memory of the Samarians and developed into a folkloristic legend. The author of the Book of Kings included the story within the legends attributed to the time of Joram, who can hardly be the king depicted in the story.[30] The weak status of Israel in the story reflects the time of the Jehuite Dynasty.[31] The unexpected withdrawal of the Aramaean army from besieged Samaria can best be explained by the imminent Assyrian offensive against Damascus in 796 BCE (Na'aman 1991: 86-89).[32]

Within the plot, the Aramaeans fled in panic, fearing that the kings of the Hittites and of Egypt were hired by the king of Israel (7:6-7). Cogan and Tadmor (1988: 84-85) suggested that the army was actually the Assyrians who came to relieve Israel. However, it is unlikely that this legendary story memorialises the Assyrian intervention in the siege of Samaria; rather, the mention of the kings of the Hittites and of Egypt is imaginary, invented by the story's author.[33]

5.1.8.3. The Defeat of the Aramaean Troops (2 Kgs 6:8-23)

This prophetic story is set in the period of hostility between Aram and Israel. The story begins with the description of Elisha delivering Israel from the Aramaean attacks (vv. 8-10).[34] Israel's weakness is reflected in the description of the Aramaean troops moving freely in the Israelite territory and penetrating as deep as Dothan in the northern Samarian hills.[35] The Aramaic superiority is the only chronological anchor for dating the story. Šanda (1912: 49-51) dated it, along with the event described in 2 Kgs 6:24-7:20, soon after 797 BCE.[36] Following Šanda, I

---

different viewpoints. However, literary analysis elucidates that 1 Kgs 20 borrows themes and expressions from 2 Kgs 6:24-7:20 (Sroka 2006: 38-46). Cf. 5.1.8.1.

30   Kuenen 1887: 396, n. 2.

31   Šanda (1912: 49-51) attempted to establish a more precise date of the event (shortly after 797 BCE). Cf. Gray 1977: 518. Cogan and Tadmor (1988: 84-85) dated this event to the reign of Joahaz.

32   This Assyrian campaign might have been a response to Joash's plea for help, as Na'aman suggested. The tribute of Joash is recorded in the Tell al-Rimah Inscription from the time of Adad-nērārī III (5.2.3.).

33   Würthwein 1984: 315-316.

34   The Aramaean attacks on the cities in Israel were prevented by Elisha (vv. 8-10), which infuriated the king of Aram; he sent his troops to catch Elisha (vv. 11-14). Elisha, however, with an unnatural power brought from YHWH, temporarily blinded the soldiers and led them to Samaria (vv. 15-19). The king of Israel asked Elisha's permission to kill the Aramaean soldiers, but Elisha refused it. Instead, the king of Israel served a feast for them, and sent them back to their master (vv. 20-23).

35   It is generally identified with Tel Dothan, ten kilometres south of Jenin.

36   Other scholars suggested that the legendary elements in the story, for example the lack of kings' names (both of Israel and of Aram-Damascus), hinder the precise dating of the event (Gray 1977: 512-514; Cogan and Tadmor 1988: 75). Gray (*loc. cit.*), associating the weak Israel in the

suppose that the story reflects the weak position of Israel in the time of the Jehuite Dynasty. Israel in this story is no longer a vassal of Aram-Damascus since
both kingdoms are obviously in enmity. Hence, this picture would fit the time
after the siege of Samaria (796 BCE),[37] when Joash threw off the yoke of Aram-
Damascus, although the historicity of the details of the story cannot be verified.

5.2. The Assyrian Sources

In Chapter 4, the inscriptions of Adad-nērārī III and the chronology of his military campaigns to Syria-Palestine during 805–802 BCE were discussed.[38] In this
section, his campaign to Damascus in 796 BCE will be reviewed: first, the entry
of the Eponym Chronicles in 796 BCE; then, the texts that relate the Damascene
submission to Assyria and Joash's tribute.

5.2.1. The Eponym Chronicles and the Campaign of Adad-nērārī III against Damascus

The subjugation of Damascus by Adad-nērārī III has been variously dated.[39]
Unger (1916: 16-18), on the basis of the chronological reference to Adad-nērārī's
"fifth year" in the Saba'a Stela, dated the conquest of north Syria and the subjugation of Damascus to 806 BCE. Poebel (1943: 82-84), accepting this date, explained the absence of Damascus in the Eponym Chronicles by assuming that
Adad-nērārī conducted two campaigns in a single year and only one of them, "to
Mannea", was registered in the entry.[40] Lipiński (1979: 81-93) dated the subjugation of Damascus to 803 BCE, when the Assyrian army reached "Ba'li", located
on the Mediterranean coast, and hypothesized that this is the place where Joash
paid tribute to Adad-nērārī.[41] Donner (1970: 55-57), based on the biblical chronology of Joash's reign, dated it to 802 BCE. Lemaire (1993: 149*) also dated it to
802 BCE, when other Phoenico-Palestinian kingdoms paid tribute to Adad-
nērārī.[42] However, none of these dates are decisive.

---

story with Jehu's reign, dated its *terminus post quem* to 839 BCE, when the Assyrian power withdrew from the region.

37   For the incident, see 5.1.8.2, and for the date, see 5.2.1.

38   See 4.2.3.

39   A brief history of the studies regarding the date of the Damascus campaign is also found in
Kuan 1995: 93-97.

40   Cf. Shea 1978: 101-113; Oded 1972: 28-29.

41   Also Kuan 1995: 99-106.

42   I date Joash's tribute to Adad-nērārī to 796 BCE. See 5.2.6.

Three of Adad-nērārī III's inscriptions describe the campaign against Mariʾ of Damascus and his tribute.[43] They indicate that the subjugation of Damascus was considered as one of the greatest achievements of Adad-nērārī III. The Tell Sheikh Hammad Stela mentions erecting the king's royal image in Arvad but it does not refer to the subjugation of Damascus (Siddall 2011: 27-32). It may suggest that the Sheikh Hammad Stela was erected between the two events. Provided this assumption is correct, the subjugation of Damascus must be dated after Adad-nērārī III's campaign to the Syro-Phoenician coast (803–802 BCE).[44]

Damascus is not mentioned in Adad-nērārī's entries of the Eponym Chronicles. Scholars explained the absence of Damascus by hypothesising the principle according to which the entries in the Eponym Chronicles were selected (Millard and Tadmor 1973: 62; Kuan 1995: 7-18).[45] However, very little is known about the system of selecting entries and it is impossible to clarify the principles of selection. Therefore, it is reasonable to date the campaign against Damascus according to the toponym mentioned in the Eponym Chronicles, which is geographically closer to Damascus.

The Eponym Chronicle (B1 22') refers to *a-na* KUR *man-ṣu-a-te* in the entry for 796 BCE. Two possible locations for this place have been suggested.[46] Honigmann (1924: 46) suggested the valley of Massyas/Marsyas in the southern Beqaʿ Valley, which is mentioned in the classical sources.[47] Lipiński (1971b: 393-397), based on a linguistic comparison between the two place names, identified Manṣuate with Maṣyāf, situated some forty kilometres west-south-west of Hama. This identification may be corroborated by one of Amenophis II's inscriptions and a letter from Nimrud (ND 2680; NL 22)[48] that perhaps mentions problems from the settlements of Assyrian rebels in the city of Manṣuate (Naʾaman 1999: 427-428).[49] In light of this evidence, Manṣuate may be located in the territory of Hamath.

Since Manṣuate is the closest place to Damascus in the Eponym Chronicles during Adad-nērārī III's reign after 802 BCE, I suggest dating the Assyrian campaign against Damascus in 796 BCE and use this date in the present study. Admittedly, this date is not conclusive and remains open for further discussion.

---

43   Sabaʾa Stela, lines 18-20; Tell al-Rimah Stela, lines 6-7; Nimrud Slab, lines 15-21.

44   See 4.2.3.1.

45   Cf. also Cody 1970: 328, n. 11; Oded 1972: 26.

46   For the earlier literature on the identification of Manṣuate, see Lipiński 1971b: 394-395; 2000: 304-310; Millard and Tadmor 1973: 63, n. 21.

47   Strabo, *Geography*, XVI: 2.18; Polybius, *History*, V: 45-46, 61. See Hölscher 1930: col. 1986. Weippert (1992: 50-53) and Sader (1987: 266-267) accepted this view.

48   Saggs 1955: 141, XXII 8.

49   Naʾaman assumed that these rebels may be connected to the Assyrians that Sargon II settled in Hamath.

5.2.2. The Saba'a Stela (A.0.104.6)

The inscription relates the tribute from Mari' king of Damascus as follows:[50]

"I verily commanded [to march to the land of Damascus]. [I verily confined] Mari' in the city Damascus, [... he brought to me] 100 talents of gold, 1,000 talents of silver. [I received it and took it to Assyria]" (lines 18b-20).

5.2.3. The Tell al-Rimah Stela (A.0.104.7)

The stela describes the submission of Mari' and his tribute as follows:[51]

"I verily mustered my chariots (and) camps. I verily commanded the march to the land Hatti. In one year I verily submitted the land Amurru (and) the land Hatti at my feet. I verily imposed upon them tribute of obligation for the future. He[sic] received 2,000 talents of silver, 1,000 talents of copper, 2,000 talents of iron, 3,000 multicoloured clothing and linen — the tribute of Mari' of the land Damascus. He[sic] received the tribute of Joash of the land Samaria, of the land Tyre, of the land Sidon" (lines 4-8).

5.2.4. The Nimrud Slab (A.0.104.8)

The slab relates the conquest of Damascus and tribute from Mari' as follows:[52]

"To the land Damascus, I verily marched. I verily confined Mari', the king of the land Damascus, in the city of Damascus. The fear of radiance that Aššur his[sic] lord overwhelmed him and he seized my feet, he became my vassal. 2,300 talents of silver, twenty talents of gold, 3,000 talents of bronze, 5,000 talents of iron, linen garments of multicoloured cloth, bed of ivory, couch with inlaid ivory; I received his possessions, his property without number in the city of Damascus, his royal city, inside his palace" (lines 15-21).

This is the most detailed description of the submission of Damascus. Adad-nērārī III states that he received the tribute from Mari' in his palace (line 21). This is the first time that Damascus was subjugated by the Assyrians. Adad-nērārī's predecessors did not achieve it, not even Shalmaneser III, who boasted of confining Hazael in Damascus and cutting down his orchards.[53] It was therefore a good reason for Adad-nērārī to describe this event in his inscription. The reason for the absence of this deed in the Eponym Chronicles remains unknown.

---

50   See 4.2.3.2.1.

51   See 4.2.3.2.2.

52   See 4.2.3.2.3.

53   *RIMA* 3, A.0.102.8, lines 1''''-27''''; A.0.102.10, Col iii, line 45b – Col. iv, line 15a; A.0.102.12, lines 21-30a; A.0.102.16, lines 122'b-137'a.

5.2.5. Nergal-ēreš[54]

Two out of three inscriptions describing the campaign against Damascus during Adad-nērārī III's reign (the Saba'a and Tell al-Rimah Stelae) mention the name of Nergal-ēreš.[55] He is mentioned in other various inscriptions as well as twice in the Eponym Lists,[56] and was one of the four outstanding Assyrian officials during the tumultuous period in the Assyrian Empire from 830 to 745 BCE (Grayson 1993: 26-29).[57] These officials are prominent in that "they are named in royal inscriptions or have their own private inscriptions, or both" (Grayson, *op. cit.*, 26).[58] Whether or not Nergal-ēreš engaged in the campaign against Damascus in 796 BCE is not clear. Some scholars suggested that the Saba'a and Tell al-Rimah Inscriptions indicate his intention to commemorate the military expedition in which he rendered distinguished service or which he himself led.[59] The alternation between the first and third person forms in the Tell al-Rimah Stela has been explained by such (Tadmor 1973: 142; Ruby 2001: 172).[60] If this hypothesis is correct, Mari' of Damascus paid tribute to Nergal-ēreš as representative of Adad-nērārī III.[61]

---

54   For this court official and his activities, see Fuchs 2008: 75-78.

55   The Tell Sheikh-Hammad Stela was attributed also to Nergal-ēreš by Millard (1973: 162), which turned out to be wrong by the discovery of his own inscription on the stela (Siddall 2011: 70-75).

56   Nergal-ēreš appears in the Eponym Chronicles as governor of Raṣappa (803 and 775 BCE). The list of the sources that mention his name is found in Åkerman and Baker 2002: 981-982. His name is also read as "Pālil-ēreš"; however, this reading is uncertain (Kühne and Radner 2008: 31-32). Therefore, I read "Nergal-ēreš" for practical reasons, although this reading is equally uncertain. See Åkerman and Baker, *op. cit.*, 981; Postgate 1970: 33; Tadmor 1973: 147, n. 32; Timm 1993: 65, n. 29 with earlier literature. Cf. Krebernik 2003-2005.

57   Grayson enumerated the four officials: Dayyan-Ashur (*ca.* 853–826), Šamšī-ilu (*ca.* 800–752), Nergal-ēreš, and Bel-Harran-beli-uṣur (*ca.* 782–727). He (*op. cit.*, 19; 1982: 273-279; *RIMA* 3: 200-201) pointed out that the time from Shalmaneser III's late years to the appearance of Tiglath-pileser III (830–745 BCE) was a period in which "a select few officials gained exceptional power in the state and threatened the very foundation of the Assyrian monarchy."

58   For the Assyrian magnates in this period, see the extensive studies of Blocher (2001) and Fuchs (2008).

59   See Page 1968: 153; Cody 1970: 331-332; Schramm 1973: 113. Cazelles (1969: 108) suggested that Nergal-ēreš led the campaign to Ba'li in 803 BCE (he thought it was 804 BCE), that is, the Eponym year of Nergal-ēreš himself.

60   I would like to discuss this grammatical feature elsewhere.

61   The end of Nergal-ēreš's service can be dated between 775 BCE, the last mention of him in the Eponym Lists, and 747 BCE, when Sîn-šallimanni appears as the governor of Raṣappa in the Eponym Lists. The deliberate erasure of text concerning him from the Tell al-Rimah Stela (see above) suggests that he might have fallen from power in disgrace. Cf. Grayson *RIMA* 3: 210; Page 1968: 152-153.

5.2.6. Joash's Tribute to Adad-nērārī III

The next issue is dating the two following events: (1) the receipt of the tribute from the kingdoms of Israel, Tyre, and Sidon, which is related in the Tell al-Rimah Stela (lines 8-9a); (2) the march to the Mediterranean Sea and Mt Lebanon, as related on the same stela (lines 9b-12a). Both events could be ascribed to two different (the 802 and 796 BCE) campaigns, or to one of them. Assuming that the identification of *ana tâmtim* in the Eponym Chronicles for 802 BCE with the Mediterranean is correct,[62] Adad-nērārī's march to the Mediterranean and Mt Lebanon may be dated to that year. Joash's accession to the throne was dated in this study to 798 BCE,[63] and the tribute of Israel and the Phoenician kingdoms must accordingly be dated to 796 BCE. Joash's tribute to Assyria is explained by the ancient Near Eastern custom that a new king brings tribute to his sovereign and his lord then affirms his status and authority.

5.2.7. Identification of Mari' King of Damascus

Adad-nērārī III's inscriptions call the king of Damascus by the name Mari'. The name does not appear in the Aramaic inscriptions or in the Bible. Mari''s identification can therefore be determined only upon chronological consideration. Hazael's death and Ben-Hadad's enthronement must have preceded 804/3 BCE, the date of the Zakkur Stela where Ben-Hadad is mentioned.[64] Hence, Hazael cannot be a candidate for Mari''s identification.[65] The old suggestion of identifying Mari' with the successor of Ben-Hadad cannot be excluded,[66] but more plausible is to regard Mari' as a hypocoristicon of the king's real name, and Ben-Hadad as a throne name. Mārī', meaning "my Lord" in West Semitic, probably formed a part of the real name of Ben-Hadad, son of Hazael.[67]

---

62   See 4.2.3.1.

63   See Chapter 1.

64   See 4.3. Hazael was still upon the throne until sometime after Joahaz's accession (814 BCE, cf. 2 Kgs 13:3).

65   *Contra* Unger 1957: 83, 164, n. 2; de Vaux 1934: 516-518; Lipiński 1969: 168, n. 40.

66   Pitard 1987: 165. Sader (1987: 260) regarded Mari' as another son of Hazael, who succeeded the Damascene throne after Hazael, and was excluded later by Ben-Hadad after he (Mari') paid tribute to Assyria. See Pitard, *op. cit.*, 165, n. 42, for earlier literature. Lipiński (2000: 390-393), dating the campaign against Damascus in 803 BCE, suggested that the royal title Mari' is used in Assyrian inscriptions, because Hazael died in the same year. However, this view does not explain the use of the royal title in the Assyrian inscriptions.

67   Mari'-Hadad is suggested. See Albright 1942: 28, n. 16; Page 1968: 149-150; Millard and Tadmor 1973: 63, n. 22; Millard 1987–90: 418. Cf. Hafthorsson 2006: 69-70 with n. 312.

5.2.8. The Tribute from Mari'

All three inscriptions record the inventory of the tribute of Mari' (Table 4).[68]

	Saba'a Stela	Tell al-Rimah Stela	Nimrud Slab
gold (KÙ.GI)	100?	-	20
bronze (ZABAR)	-	-	3,000
silver (KÙ.BABBAR)	1,000	2,000	2,300
copper (URUDU)	-	1,000	-
iron (AN.BAR)	-	2,000	5,000
garments (*lubulti birme*)	-	3,000	No quantity specified
bed of ivory (GIŠ.NÁ ZÚ)	-	-	No quantity specified
couch with ivory (GIŠ *nēmatti* ZÚ *ihzi tamlê*)	-	-	No quantity specified

Table 4. Tribute from Mari' king of Damascus (measures given in talents = *biltu*)[69]

The variation in the inventories and their quantities shows that these lists were probably copied from different tribute inventories.[70] During the subsequent process of recording those numbers on the stelae, the scribe(s) may have intentionally exaggerated the quantities of those items so as to enhance the achievements of the king (De Odorico 1995: 51).[71] It is thus difficult to use the numbers included in these inscriptions for the historical reconstruction.

It is noteworthy that none of Adad-nērārī III's inscriptions mention booty (*šalālu*). In his analysis of the tributes mentioned in Shalmaneser III's historical inscriptions, Yamada (2000a: 225-272) distinguished between booty and tribute (*madattu*). He suggested that the tribute can be divided into two types (*op. cit.*, 237): (1) "spot tribute" which is "received by the king (or his representative) at a particular place or spot in the course of a campaign"; (2) "annual tribute" which is "imposed on local rulers, to be delivered annually to the Assyrian capital". Adopting this categorisation, all the tributes mentioned in Adad-nērārī III's inscriptions

---

68 Saba'a Stela lines 18b-20; Tell al-Rimah Stela, lines 11-12; Nimrud Slab, lines 18-21. See also Page 1968: 144; Elat 1977: 23-24; De Odorico 1995: 51. However, the tables there must be corrected according to the new editions of the texts. For example, in the list of the Saba'a Stela, they counted sixty or one hundred talents of iron, but iron (AN.BAR) is actually not mentioned in that stela.

69 One talent is generally equivalent to about thirty kilograms. A heavy standard, equivalent to about sixty kilograms, is also attested. Cf. Powell 1987–90: 510.

70 De Odorico (1995: 51) noticed the increased quantities reported in the Nimrud Slab and suggested that these are "totals" of tribute that Adad-nērārī III received from Mari'.

71 See also Galil 2001b: 44-45 with n. 10. Examples of such manipulation are found in De Odorico 1995.

are of the "spot tribute" type, formulated as "I received X (as) the tribute of PN/GN" (*madattu ša* PN/GN ... *amhur*). Yamada further observed two different circumstances for the reception of "spot tribute": one is "tribute of surrender" or "subjugation gifts"; and the other involves "audience gifts", offered under the threat of potential Assyrian aggression.[72] The tribute from Mari' should be classified as "tribute of surrender" because the siege of Damascus and its surrender are described before the receipt of tribute (Nimrud Slab, lines 15-17). By contrast, the tribute from Joash, the Phoenician kings, Edom, and Philistia are of the "audience gifts" type, since no Assyrian assaults on these parties are mentioned.[73]

5.2.9. The Late Years of Joash and the Rise of Šamšī-ilu in Assyria

According to the Eponym Chronicles, the Assyrian army did not return to Syria until 775 BCE.[74] Adad-nērārī III was preoccupied with the east and his heirs suffered from revolts. It was against this background that Šamšī-ilu, the Assyrian *turtānu*, gained power in the West.[75]

Šamšī-ilu, the author of the Pazarcık and the Antakya Stelae, was a powerful Assyrian official from the late ninth to the mid-eighth centuries BCE.[76] His seat as Assyrian *turtānu* (field marshal) was in Til-Barsip (Tell Ahmar) and from there he exerted his power over south Anatolia and Syria-Palestine. The beginning of his office as *turtānu* can be approximately dated between 796 and 780 BCE. Considering his role as an arbitrator of the border dispute between Hamath and Arpad after 796 BCE (Antakya Stela),[77] he was nominated around that date. His name appears in the Eponym Chronicles as *turtānu* in 752 BCE but not in 742 BCE. His disappearance may be connected with Tiglath-pileser III's accession (745 BCE), who probably terminated the office of Šamšī-ilu (Hawkins 1982: 404; Lipiński 1991: 173-174).[78]

Šamšī-ilu probably led the campaign against Damascus in 773 BCE and received the tribute of Hadiānu, king of Damascus at the latter's palace (Pazarcık Stela; *RIMA* 3, A.0.105.1, Rev. lines 4-10). Further, he probably led the military campaigns against Hatarikka in 772, 765, and 755 BCE (Lipiński 1991: 174-175). Nergal-ēreš, who exerted a strong influence in the Assyrian Empire, probably fell

---

72 For the terminology, see Yamada 2000a: 236-238. Yamada's "spot tribute" is equivalent to Elat's "tribute of surrender", see Yamada, *op. cit.*, 236-237, n. 21; Elat 1982: 244-245, 249, n. 9.

73 The Scheil Fragment lines 10-11 seem to mention the "subjugation gifts" from Ataršumki.

74 The Eponym Chronicle records "to the cedar mountain" for 775 BCE; see 6.2.1.

75 For detailed analysis of his activities, see Dalley 2000; Fuchs 2008.

76 Šamšī-ilu is the one who set the borders between Arpad and Hamath (the Antakya Stela), Kummuh and Gurgum (the Pazarcık Stela, Obv.), and for Kummuh (the Pazarcık Stela, Rev.).

77 See 4.2.3.2.7.

78 Cf. Fuchs 2008: 96.

from power after 775 BCE, when his name was last mentioned in the Eponym Chronicles (see 5.2.5.). Thus, Šamši-ilu's leading role in international relations in south Anatolia and Syria-Palestine was outstanding. At a certain phase, he even made his own inscription (*RIMA* 3, A.0.104.2010) and described his successful campaign against Urartu, without mentioning the king. He undoubtedly represented the Assyrian power in the west from the early to the mid-eighth centuries BCE.[79] In short, Assyria, through Šamši-ilu, maintained its influence upon the kingdoms in Syria, especially in the north, for some twenty years after the campaign against Damascus in 796 BCE.

5.3. Synthesis

Adad-nērārī III's campaigns against Arpad in 805–804 BCE had a critical influence on all the Syro-Palestinian kingdoms. They shook the Damascene hegemony over those kingdoms, including the kingdoms of Hamath and Israel. When Joash ascended the throne in 798 BCE, he probably refused to take part in the anti-Assyrian coalition led by Ben-Hadad of Damascus. As a result, Samaria was besieged by the Aramaean army in 796 BCE. The city was relieved by the approaching Assyrian army led by Nergal-ēreš, which forced the Aramaean army to withdraw from the city.

The struggle between Damascus and Israel continued after 796 BCE. Joash defeated the Aramaean army and regained the conquered territories and established the independence of the Kingdom of Israel. Having gained a dominant power in southern Levant, Joash took over the Damascene hegemony in the region. He fought against Amaziah of Judah, who tried to obtain a political equality with Israel, and defeated him at Beth-Shemesh. As a result, Judah became, at least temporarily, a vassal kingdom of Israel (2 Kgs 14:14).[80]

---

79 Some scholars identified Bar-Ga'ya mentioned in the Sefire Inscriptions with Šamši-ilu, due to the former's significant role in northern Syria around 754 BCE (Lemaire and Durand 1984: 37-58; Ikeda 1994).

80 Vogelstein (1945: 7-20) suggested that Judah was subjugated by Israel during the reigns of Amaziah and Azariah.

6. The Reign of Jeroboam II (784–748 BCE)

Primary sources for Jeroboam II's reign are limited. The only sources that explicitly refer to him are the Book of Kings and a seal discovered at Tel Megiddo. The Book of Amos brings to light the extent of the territory and the material prosperity of Israel at that time. Assyrian inscriptions shed light on the international relations in the Syro-Palestinian region. Aramaic and Hebrew inscriptions provide information on the territorial extent of Israel during Jeroboam II's reign. The results of the archaeological excavations contribute to the understanding of the economic status and material culture of Israel at that time.

6.1. The Biblical Source

6.1.1. Biblical Description of Jeroboam's Reign (2 Kgs 14:23-29)

The passage tersely relates Jeroboam II's deeds and the Dtr's theological interpretation of them. It consists of three parts: (1) vv. 23-24; (2) vv. 25-27; and (3) vv. 28-29.

6.1.1.1. Opening and Concluding Formulae (2 Kgs 14:23-24, 29)

Vv. 23-24 form a stereotypical opening formula for an Israelite king. V. 23 presents the king's name, the name of his father, his seat, and the synchronism with the king of Judah. V. 24 is a formulaic negative judgement of Jeroboam, and v. 29 is the concluding formula for the peaceful death of the king.

6.1.1.2. Restoration of the Border (2 Kgs 14:25)

V. 25 consists of two parts. V. 25a reads: "It was he (Jeroboam II) who restored the boundaries of Israel from Lebo-Hamath to the Sea of the Arabah". V. 25b explains that Jeroboam's achievements fulfil the prophecy of YHWH's prophet, Jonah ben Amittai.

Lebo-Hamath is identified with modern Labweh in the northern Beqaʿ Valley, which is mentioned as Labʾu in the ancient sources.[1] "The Sea of the Arabah" is glossed in other biblical sources (Deut 3:17; Jos 3:16, 12:3) as "the Salt Sea", which is equivalent to the Dead Sea. This description reflects the ideal extent of the Israelite boundary and appears in the description of the prosperity in Solomon's age (1 Kgs 5:1; 8:65). The verbal form "restored" (השיב) also associates this territorial extent with Solomon's dominion.[2] In this light, scholars suggested that the territorial extent under Jeroboam II was retrospectively projected onto the ideal territorial extent in the time of Solomon.

Some scholars postulated that v. 25a was derived from an archival source and that it was later adopted by the Dtr.[3] Montgomery (1934), for example, ascribed the verse to a hypothetical lapidary source together with 2 Kgs 14:7, 22; 15:35; and 18:4, 8 because of the common formulaic terminology in those verses.[4] However, all the other texts that he cited refer to the kings of Judah.[5] The literary similarity among these texts does not necessarily indicate that this piece of information is based on an archival source. It only indicates that those texts were composed by the same author. Information on the boundaries in 2 Kgs 14:25 and its possible source must therefore be evaluated in the light of Am 6:14, which refers to a similar extent of the Israelite territory.

6.1.1.3. Theological Explanation for Jeroboam's Deeds (2 Kgs 14:26-27)

These two verses attribute Jeroboam's exploits to YHWH's mercy on Israel. According to this explanation, it is not because of Jeroboam's personal competence, but by the grace of YHWH, that Israel prospers. This explanation has nothing to do with the historical reality.[6] It only indicates that the large territory

---

1   For those classical sources, see Aḥituv 1984: 131. Cf. Donner 1977: 414; Aharoni 1979: 72; Hobbs 1985: 183; Ahlström 1993a: 617; Thomas 2003: 146-147.

2   Cogan and Tadmor 1988: 162.

3   Benzinger 1899: 165; Kittel 1900: 263; Hölscher 1923: 197; Jepsen 1934: 94; 1941–44: 153-172, esp. 154-156; Montgomery 1951: 443; Noth 1967: 75; Crüsemann 1971: 59; Gray 1977: 615; Cogan and Tadmor 1988: 163. Würthwein (1984: 374) ascribed the whole verse to the DtrP. Cf. Haran (1967: 266). Tadmor (1962: 114-122, esp. 119) regarded this report as historical. Cohen (1965: 154) interpreted it as royal boast.

4   The formulaic terminology, according to Montgomery, is הוא + suffix conjugation verb + object.

5   2 Kgs 14:7, 22 (Amaziah); 15:35 (Jotham); 18:4, 8 (Hezekiah). I follow Halpern and Vanderhooft (1992), who identified "he" in 2 Kgs 14:22 as Amaziah. Naʾaman (1993: 228-229), on the other hand, identified "he" as Azariah. Following Montgomery, Halpern (2001: 186-187, 194) categorised 2 Kgs 14:25 as "narrative statement", whose parallels can be found in other parts of the Books of Kings and regarded it as historically reliable. Halpern (op. cit., 193) suggested that 2 Kgs 14:25 relies on a source describing Jeroboam II's reign, and categorised 14:28 as "source notice".

6   Crüsemann (1971: 59) construed vv. 26-27 as a redactional comment by the Dtr. See also, Gray

conquered during Jeroboam's reign was known to the author of vv. 26-27 and that he found it necessary to explain this "bad" king's success by divine mercy.

6.1.1.4. The Restoration of Damascus and Hamath (2 Kgs 14:28)

Another description of territorial expansion during Jeroboam II's reign is found in v. 28, which forms a part of the Dtr concluding formula. According to the description, Jeroboam "fought and 'restored' Damascus and Hamath for Judah in Israel (ליהודה בישראל)". The enigmatic text has drawn scholarly attention.[7] Na'aman (1993: 231-234) tentatively restored the original text "and the war(s) of Judah against Israel" (ומלחמת יהודה בישראל). The restoration may fit the historical context, but it is impossible to verify it without further evidence. Cogan and Tadmor (1988: 162) regarded "for Judah" as "a gloss from the hand of a Judahite scribe for whom the claim to these territories in the far north rested on the achievements of David and Solomon, who were primarily kings of Judah".[8] Yet, it is possible that the territorial achievement of David and Solomon was described on the basis of Jeroboam II's conquests. In conclusion, the word "restored" was probably derived from the source that the Dtr used (v. 25) and may reflect Jeroboam's claim to "the border of Israel" (גבול ישראל).[9] Jeroboam's territorial achievement and that of David and Solomon were associated through the insertion of the phrase "for Judah" by a later editor who was inspired by the word "restored". This solution, too, is highly speculative, and I suggest it with due reservation.

Some scholars assumed that the information on the restoration of Hamath and Damascus in v. 28 was derived from an authentic source.[10] Jeroboam could

---

1977: 616. Montgomery (1951: 443) regarded vv. 25b-27 as one unit. Würthwein (1984: 375-376) ascribed vv. 26-27 to the DtrN. Gosse (1994: 169-72) suggested that v. 27 is designated not to the time of Jeroboam II, but to the posterior time, after the fulfilment of the words of Amos through the falls of Samaria and Jerusalem.

7   Burney (1903: 320) suggested reading "how he fought with Damascus and how he turned away the wrath of YHWH from Israel" (ואשר נלחם את־דמשק ואשר השיב את־חמת יהוה מישראל). Cf. Šanda 1912: 173. Vogelstein (1945: 10) suggested that this verse indicates that Judah was a province or vassalage of Israel under Jeroboam. Eissfeldt's (1968: 99-130) reading "in Ya'udi for Israel" was dismissed by Tadmor (1961: 232-271). Cf. Gordon and Rendsburg 1997: 241, n. 6.

8   Similar views were suggested by Kittel 1900: 263; Montgomery 1951: 161; Thomas 2003: 141, n. 7; 157.

9   Cf. 2 Kgs 14:25; 16:6.

10 Tadmor 1961: 238-240; 1962: 119; Haran 1967: 278-284; Soggin 1971: 434; Würthwein 1984: 375; Hentschel 1985: 66; Pitard 1987: 176-177, 179, 189; Cogan and Tadmor 1988: 163-164; Fritz 1998: 80; Halpern 2001: 191.

have conquered at least part of Damascus immediately after the Assyrian campaign by Šamšī-ilu (5.2.9.).[11] Yet, there is no source to verify these conquests.[12]

6.1.2. The Israelite Territory under Jeroboam as Reflected in the Description of Pekah's Reign (2 Kgs 15:29)

V. 29 appears in the chronological framework of the reign of Pekah, king of Israel
(737-731/730 BCE). The verse might contain information regarding the Israelite
territory at the time of Tiglath-pileser III's campaigns, about two decades after
the death of Jeroboam II. The text reads as follows:

> In the days of Pekah king of Israel came Tiglath-pileser king of Assyria, and took Ijon,
> Abel-beth-maachah, Janoah, Kedesh, Hazor, Gilead, and Galilee, all the land of
> Naphtali, and carried them captive to Assyria.

This event can be dated to 733–732 BCE, when Tiglath-pileser III led military
campaigns against Philistia and Damascus.[13] The cities mentioned in 2 Kgs 15:29
are located mostly in the Upper Galilee region.[14] Assuming that this piece of
information is historically authentic, it confirms that the Upper Galilee was within
the territorial extent of Israel in the last days of Jeroboam II.

6.1.3. Israelite Rule in Gilead under Jeroboam II (2 Kgs 15:10, 13-14, 17, 25, and 29)

Some references in the Book of Kings might allude to Israelite rule in Gilead in
the eighth century BCE (2 Kgs 15:10, 13-14, 17, 25, and 29). They have been
interpreted by some scholars as implying Israelite dominion over Gilead immediately after Jeroboam II's reign.

According to 2 Kgs 15:10, Shallum murdered Zechariah, son of Jeroboam II,
and usurped the throne. Since Jabesh, Shallum's father's name, is also the name of
a city in the northern Gilead (vv. 10, 13), some scholars identified it as a patro-
nymic/clan's name in Transjordan.[15] Shallum was murdered by Menahem whose

---

11 It is attested in v. 25 and in the Book of Amos (6.1.4.2.).

12 Halpern (2001: 199) suggested the possibility that the conquests of Hamath and Damascus were
    recorded in the "chronicles", on which 2 Kgs 14:28 relies.

13 Eponym Chronicles record the entry "to Philistia" in 734 BCE, "to Damascus" in 733 and 732
    BCE. Pekah was killed and replaced by Hoshea. This event possibly occurred during the cam-
    paign of Tiglath-pileser III in 733 BCE.

14 A concise list of the identifications of these cities is available in Younger 1998: 209, Tab. 1. Cf.
    also Becking 1992: 17-19.

15 Jgs 21:8-14; 1 Sam 11:1-10; 31:11-13; 2 Sam 2:4-5. See Šanda 1912: 181; Noth 1928: 244; Mont-
    gomery 1951: 455; Thiele 1983: 125; Würthwein 1984: 378. For the identification of Jabesh-

father's name was Gadi (vv. 14, 17). According to the same line of thought, the name Gadi may also be related to the Transjordanian tribe, Gad.[16] Pekahiah, son of Menahem, was murdered by Pekah who was aided by fifty Gileadites (v. 25). On the basis of the assumed origin of Shallum and Menahem from Transjordan, some scholars inferred that after Jeroboam II's death, the Northern Kingdom was split, so that one ruler sat in Samaria and another in Transjordan.[17]

However, there is no unequivocal evidence in the Book of Kings for regarding the name of the king's father as a patronymic/clan's name. First, none of the names of the Israelite kings' fathers can be associated with toponyms. Baasha's son (1 Kgs 16:6-13) and Hoshea's father (2 Kgs 15:30; 17:1; 18:1, 9) had a common name Elah that is identical with the name of a valley in Shephelah (1 Sam 17:12, 19; 21:10). Yet, it is unreasonable to associate them with the name of the valley that was outside of the North Israelite territory. Hence, it is unnecessary to associate Jabesh with a toponym in Transjordan. Second, none of the names of the Israelite kings' fathers or of the kings themselves in the Book of Kings designates tribe or clan names.[18] The ending "-î" in personal names must have been popular in the time of the monarchies as attested in numerous stamp seals from the period.[19] Accordingly, Gadi must have been one such name with an "-î" ending, which might have been a hypocoristicon of a name such as Gadiyahu[20] or Gadi'el.[21] Finally, there is no unequivocal explanation for the employment of patronymic/clan's names as the fathers' names of these kings.[22]

The hypothesis of an independent kingdom in Transjordan after Jeroboam II's death must be rejected. The mention of Gileadites "בני גלעדים" in v. 25 might indicate that the population in Gilead was incited by Rezin of Damascus, who had conquered Gilead and become an ally of Pekah (2 Kgs 15:37; 16:5; Isa 7:4-9).[23] The mention of "Gilead" in v. 29 as a region conquered by Tiglath-pileser III

Gilead, see Edelman 1992b: 594-595. Cf. Mittmann 1970: 214-215.
16 Cf. 1 Chr 5:18. Würthwein 1984: 378; Cogan and Tadmor 1988: 171.
17 Vogelstein 1945: 5-7, 13, 20; Cogan and Tadmor 1988: 178.
18 "Shimei the son of Gera the Benjamite" in 1 Kgs 2:8 clearly designates the name of the tribe Benjamin, but Shimei is not a king.
19 Avigad and Sass 1997. Nimshi, father or grandfather of Jehu, must be construed as such (2.1.2.2.2.).
20 Cf. Avigad and Sass 1997: 54, no. 12; 87, nos. 117, 118; 191, no. 467; 430, no. 1134.
21 Num 13:10.
22 The filiations of the kings are not always mentioned in the Book of Kings. Fathers of Zimri (1 Kgs 16:9) and Omri (1 Kgs 16:16) are not mentioned. Hence, it is not necessary to postulate that these names were invented, even if the names of the kings were unknown.
23 By that time, the inhabitants seem to have already been a mixture of the former Israelite population and the new Aramaean settlers. This hypothesis explains the existence of Aramaic inscriptions at Tell Deir 'Alla in the eighth century BCE; see 3.2.5.

must be a secondary interpolation.[24] To sum up, the references in the Book of Kings do not indicate Jeroboam's domination over Gilead.

6.1.4. Contribution of the Book of Amos to the History of Jeroboam's Reign

Am 1:1 dates the activity of the prophet to Jeroboam II's reign.[25] The prophet's message is mainly directed to the upper class in the society of the Northern Kingdom, announcing the "days of YHWH", that is, divine punishment for the social injustice that prevailed in Israel at the time. The book mentions the prosperity of the Northern Kingdom during Jeroboam II's reign. The gradual growth of the Book of Amos has repeatedly been discussed since the 1960s.[26] According to this line of research, the Book of Amos was redacted several times. Other scholars have dated large portions of the book to the late eighth century and have suggested that it originated from Amos himself.[27] The formation of the Book of Amos is thus in dispute.

Two short passages from the Book of Amos will be evaluated in the present study. (1) Am 6:13-14, which possibly alludes to the Israelite conquests in Transjordan during Jeroboam II's reign; (2) Am 1:3-5, which mentions the "transgressions" of the kingdom of Aram-Damascus. These two passages are generally ascribed to the late eighth century, if not to Amos himself.[28]

6.1.4.1. The Capture of Lo-dabar and Karnaim (Am 6:13)

V. 13 reads:

> You who rejoice of Lo-dabar, who say, "Have we not taken to us Karnaim by our own strength?"

Amos criticised the Israelites who boasted of their military achievements by mentioning the cities they captured. The two toponyms Lo-dabar and Karnaim may

---

24   Most commentators ascribed "Gilead" and "Galilee" in 2 Kgs 15:29 to the secondary interpolation for the following two reasons (Stade 1886: 160-161; Kittel 1900: 267; Šanda 1912: 188; Würthwein 1984: 383, n. 17; Cogan and Tadmor 1988: 174; Irvine 1994: 25-26; Naʾaman 1995b: 109; Younger 1998: 207). First, Gilead is mentioned in the middle of the cities lying on the west side of the Jordan River, which seems out of place in the geographical context here (Irvine, *op. cit.*, 25). Second, the extent of Galilee overlaps with that of the "land of Naphtali" which follows it. The orthography of Galilee (הגלילה) is also a late form (Cogan and Tadmor 1988: 174).

25   For the editorial history of the introductory title in Am 1:1, see Schmidt 1965: 169-173; Wolff 1969: 146-151; Paul 1991: 33-36; Willoughby 1990: 210.

26   Schmidt 1965; Wolff 1969; Coote 1981; Lust 1981.

27   Hammershaimb 1970; Gordis 1971; Limburg 1987; Paul 1991: 6; Thomas 2003: 6-8.

28   For the date of Am 6:14, see 6.1.4.2.

be a pun: "nothing" (לא-דבר) and "horns" (קרנים), a symbol of strength.[29] Most scholars construed Lo-dabar and Karnaim as two toponyms conquered by Jeroboam II in Transjordan.[30] Karnaim is identified with Sheikh es-Saʿad on a northern tributary of the middle Yarmuk River, some four kilometres north of Tell ʿAstarah, biblical Ashtaroth.[31] Lo-dabar is mentioned in various forms in the Hebrew Bible,[32] and can probably be located in the highlands area south of the Yarmuk River.[33]

Karnaim and Lo-dabar were possibly the places of concrete battles, even if those toponyms were chosen for the pun. The two cities were captured after fierce battles and were well-remembered in the Northern Kingdom. It is evident that Jeroboam II conquered Transjordan as far as the north of the Yarmuk River, including part of the district of Bashan.[34]

6.1.4.2. The Israelite Border as Reflected in the Book of Amos (Am 6:14)

The verse reads:

> Behold, I will raise up against you a nation, O house of Israel, says YHWH the God of hosts; and they shall afflict you from Lebo-Hamath unto the brook of Arabah.

This reference has generally been accepted as evidence of the territorial expansion of the Northern Kingdom during Jeroboam II's reign.[35] The two toponyms demarcate the northern and southern borders of Jeroboam's conquests. The designation "brook of the Arabah" appears only here.[36] Assuming that this expression is a variation of "the sea of the Arabah" (2 Kgs 14:25), it should be sought in the north of the Dead Sea.[37]

---

29   Cohen 1965: 156; Wolff 1969: 334-335; Paul 1991: 219; Halpern 2001: 186, n. 1; Thomas 2003: 154; Hasegawa 2007: 96-97. Cf. Zech 2:4.

30   Wolff 1969: 332, 334-335; Cogan and Tadmor 1988: 161; Paul 1991: 219.

31   Kellermann 1981.

32   Jos 13:24-28; 2 Sam 9:4-5; 17:27.

33   For the identifications of Lo-dabar by scholars, see Kallai 1962: 409-410; Edelman 1992c: 346. Edelman (1992b: 346) identified it with Tel Dover (Khribet ed-Duweir), located below the southwestern-most tip of the Golan Heights and on the west bank of the Yarmuk River. However, this identification cannot be substantiated; the recent excavation at Tel Dover uncovered remains dated to the Iron Age I but little Iron Age II material (Wolff 1998: 775; Rapuano 2001).

34   Andersen and Freedman (1989: 595-596) suggested that the conquest of Hamath and Damascus occurred after Amos's words were spoken/written. For the territory of Bashan, see Slayton 1992.

35   Montgomery 1951: 443; Wolff 1969: 334; Cogan and Tadmor 1988: 161; Paul 1991: 220.

36   Cf. Isa 15:7 "to the brook of the willows" (על נחל הערבים). Halpern (2001: 187) interpreted that the expression in Isaiah is probably "adduced in the translation of Amos as a learned explication of the *unicum*."

37   Halpern (2001: 187) interpreted as either the Arnon or the Jordan.

Due to the similarity between Am 6:14 and 2 Kgs 14:25, Gosse (1988: 30, n. 12, 38) suggested that the prophecy in the former served as a source for the latter.[38] Contrarily, Crüsemann (1971) assumed that the Dtr knew Amos's oracles predicting the doom of Israel (8:2; 9:8) and responded to them in a negative way in 2 Kgs 14:27.[39] However, since Lebo-Hamath is mentioned as an Israelite border only in the Exilic or post-Exilic texts[40] and the toponym Lebo-Hamath could appear only after the inclusion of the city Lab'u in Hamath in 720 BCE (Na'aman 1999: 417-429), its mention here as well as in 2 Kgs 14:25 can be ascribed to later editing(s) (Dietrich 1972: 110-111).[41]

Be that as it may, the descriptions in 2 Kgs 14:25, 28, and Am 6:14 were clearly written by at least two different writers holding two different points of view.[42] The Dtr emphasised the extent of the conquered territory whereas Amos avoided emphasising Jeroboam's accomplishments.

6.1.4.3. The Oracle against Damascus (Am 1:3-5)

In this passage, which is a part of the so-called "oracles against the nations" (Am 1:3-2:16), Amos pronounces punishment against Aram-Damascus.[43] The ground for the punishment is explained in v. 3, and the punishment itself is announced in vv. 4-5. The punishment in vv. 4-5 evidently refers to Tiglath-pileser III's conquest of Damascus, its annexation by Assyria, and the deportation of its population in 732 BCE.[44]

The historical background of the Aramaean "transgression" mentioned in v. 3 must be evaluated. V. 3b reads: "because they threshed Gilead with threshing iron sledges". This is a description of cruel violence in warfare likened to agricultural practice.[45] The question is, then, to which historical event this war refers.

Some scholars construeded the verse as mentioning the renewed Aramaean

---

38   Na'aman (2002a: 98-99) pointed out difficulties in the asumption of the Dtr's adoption of the prophecies of Amos and suggested the possiblity that Amos and the Dtr cited the same famous prophecy attributed to Jonah son of Amittai.

39   Also Andersen and Freedman 1989: 588. For another view, see Halpern 2001: 188-190.

40   Jos 13:5; Jgs 3:3; Ezek 47:20; 48:1; 1 Chr 13:5; 2 Chr 7:8.

41   It is not clear whether the two verses were inserted by the same editor. Dietrich ascribed it to the DtrP. See also Würthwein 1984: 375.

42   See Hasegawa 2007.

43   Geyer (2009: 80) suggested calling the prophecy "oracles about nations". All the passage is clearly targeted at Aram-Damascus. Comparing it with the Assyrian inscriptions, Höffken (1982) demonstrated that "the house of Hazael" בית חזאל represents here the territory of Hazael, namely, the kingdom of Damascus.

44   Cf. 2 Kgs 16:9.

45   See Barton (1980: 19) for earlier literature. He (op. cit., 26-31) summarised the various dates given to Amos's reference to the "threshing of Gilead" by the Aramaeans.

attack after the re-conquest of Transjordan by Jeroboam II,[46] and other scholars dated the event to the beginning of Jeroboam II's reign.[47] However, there is no evidence of an Aramaean onslaught on Gilead in Jeroboam's time.[48] It seems that the description refers to Hazael's conquest of Gilead during the latter half of the ninth century BCE (see Chapter 4).[49] The mention of Hazael's house and of Ben-Hadad's palaces in v. 4 corroborates this view.

The toponyms in vv. 4-5, on the other hand, would reflect the territorial extent of Aram-Damascus in the late eighth century BCE.[50] The Valley of Aven (בקעת און) is generally identified with the Beqaʿ Valley,[51] and Beth-Eden most probably represents the region of Baalbek in the northern Beqaʿ.[52] It seems that the Beqaʿ Valley was re-conquered and re-occupied by the Aramaeans after Jeroboam's conquest of the region. At any rate, Am 1:3-5 cannot be used as a historical source for the assumed Aramaean attack on Gilead in the last years of Jeroboam II's reign.

6.1.5. Contribution of the Book of Hosea to the History of Jeroboam's Reign

The discussion will focus on toponyms mentioned in the Book of Hosea and located in Transjordan.[53] Since the book often refers to the Israelite history beyond the scope of Jeroboam II's reign, the historical background of each passage where the toponyms appear will be analysed in detail.

---

46   Cohen 1965: 155; Wolff 1969: 182-184; Rudolf 1971: 130-131.

47   Haran 1967: 276-277; 1968: 206-207; Soggin 1971: 440-441.

48   V. 4 mentions the names of the sovereigns (Hazael and Ben-Hadad) at the apogee of Aram-Damascus.

49   Schoville 1974: 61-62 ; Galil 2000: 36. It is also possible that Ammon took part in this attack to expand its own territory, as Am 1:13 implies (Cohen 1965: 155).

50   The "oracles against the nations" seem to reflect, at least partially, the territorial reality of the Syro-Palestinian kingdoms in the eighth century BCE, since Gath is not mentioned among other Philistine cities. See 3.3.2.10., 3.4.3.

51   Wolff (1969: 190), Millard (1993: 176*), and Bordreuil (1998: 57-58) suggested Baalbek for the exact location of the Valley of Aven.

52   Bordreuil 1998: 58-59. Malamat (1953) identified Beth-Eden (בית עדן) in Am 1:5 with Bit-Adini, which is the kingdom of Aramaeans mentioned in the Assyrian inscriptions. He also related the person who held the sceptre in the same verse with Šamšī-ilu. Also, Galil 2001b: 37. Millard (1993: 176*), rejecting these identifications, suggested that Beth-Eden should be sought within the territory of Aram-Damascus at the time of Amos. Cf. Haran 1967: 276-277, n. 3; Lipiński 1991: 173, n. 12.

53   For the date of the composition of the Book of Hosea, see 2.1.3.

6.1.5.1. The Crimes in Mizpah, Tabor, and Šiṭṭim (Hos 5:1-2)

The passage tells of a divine judgment on Israel, whose crimes/sins are likened to hunters' traps. It refers to three toponyms, Mizpah,[54] Tabor,[55] and Šiṭṭim,[56] the first and the last of which are located in Transjordan. Alt (1953: 186, n. 1) suggested that these places were Israelite political centres in Gilead, Galilee, and southern Transjordan in Hosea's time and were subsequently conquered by Tiglath-pileser III in 733 BCE.[57] This suggestion has been accepted widely. Yet, it is impossible to relate these toponyms to any concrete historical events, since the accused sins at those places are metaphors.[58] At any event, it is reasonable to assume that Hosea refers to the places under the Israelite rule at his time. Hence, the mention of Mizpah and Šiṭṭim indicates Jeroboam II's (and his successors') rule over Transjordan.

6.1.5.2. The Crimes in Adam, Gilead, and Shechem (Hos 6:7-8)

In this passage, Hosea reproaches Israel with their impenitence and connects each crime to a specific toponym, namely, Adam (v. 7),[59] Gilead (v. 8), and Shechem (v. 9), the first two being located in Transjordan. Alt (1953:186, n. 1) suggested that the passage reflects the itinerary of revolutionary attacks led by Shallum (2 Kgs 15:10) and Menahem (2 Kgs 15:14).[60] Fohrer (1957: 16), while accepting Alt's theory, identified the alluded incident as Pekah's coup d'état (2 Kgs 15:25), and

---

54   Alt (1953: 187, n. 1) and Donner (1964: 44-45) identified this Mizpah as the one in Gilead. Cf. Gen 31:49; Jos 13:26; Jgs 10:17; 11:11, 29, 34.

55   Jgs 4:6, 12, 14.

56   MT reads שִׁטִּים, but the toponym שִׁטִּים fits better in the parallelism with the preceding two toponyms in v. 1. See Wellhausen 1898: 113; Elliger 1957; Wolff 1974: 94; Andersen and Freedman 1980: 387; Jeremias 1983: 73; Pentiuc 2002: 152; Rudnig-Zelt 2006: 119; Vielhauer 2007: 75-76. For more literature, see Rudnig-Zelt, *op. cit.*, 119, n. 94. *Contra* Macintosh 1997: 179. Rudnig-Zelt (*op. cit.*, 108-119) ascribed these toponyms in the passage to a redactional layer. Likewise, Vielhauer (*op. cit.*, 78) named vv. 1-2 "Überschrift" and ascribed it to a later stratum.

57   Donner (1964: 45) interpreted that the passage reflects the territorial situation of Israel after Tiglath-pileser's annexation of Gilead and Galilee; the two toponyms are represented by Mizpah and Tabor. Other scholars suggested that the three places were cult centres in Hosea's time. For literature, see Vielhauer 2007: 77, n. 67.

58   Num 25:1 relates Israel's apostasy in Šiṭṭim. Cf. Mic 6:5; Hos 9:10. Tabor might have been a cult place. Cf. Deut 33:18-19. Mizpah, if it is identified as Mizpah in Gilead, might refer to the sin mentioned in Hos 6:8 and 12:12.

59   This Adam has been widely construed as a toponym since Wellhausen's suggestion "בְּאָדָם" instead of "כְּאָדָם" (1898: 116-117). It is a city located in Transjordan (Jos 3:16). For another view, see Pentiuc 2002: 188-190. For the identification of Adam with Tell ed-Damiyeh, see Fretz 1992: 64.

60   It is unclear why Alt noted both rebels together. Cf. Day 1986: 5.

most scholars accepted this view.[61] The assumption that Hosea accused Israel by referring to contemporary incidents seems reasonable.[62]

6.1.5.3. The Battle at Beth-Arbel (Hos 10:14)

Here, the impending attack against Israel is compared to the "day of the battle" when "Shalman spoiled Beth-Arbel". Neither Shalman nor Beth-Arbel can be identified securely.[63] Shalman has been interpreted as a hypocoristic form of Shalmaneser, the name of Assyrian kings, and this Shalman could be identified either as Shalmaneser III[64] or as Shalmaneser V. Salamanu, a Moabite king, who appears as one of the tributaries in Tiglath-pileser III's inscription, is another candidate.[65] Beth-Arbel is widely identified with modern Irbid in northern Transjordan.[66] Hearers of the prophecy in the Northern Kingdom certainly knew the event, but it does not mean that the battle took place in Israelite territory, nor in the time of Jeroboam II.

6.1.5.4. Gilead as the Place of Iniquity (Hos 12:12)

Hos 12:10-12 reminds Israel of the divine fidelity.[67] V. 12 mentions Gilead as the place of iniquity (אִם־גִּלְעָד אָוֶן אַךְ־שָׁוְא הָיוּ), which might refer to the same wickedness mentioned in 6:8.[68] The mention of Gilead with Gilgal, which is evidently in Israelite territory, suggests that the former was also under Israelite rule.

6.1.5.5. Israelite Rule over Transjordan in the Light of the Book of Hosea

References to Transjordanian toponyms in the Book of Hosea indicate that part of Transjordan was ruled by Israel in the time of Hosea. It was recovered from

---

61   Jeremias 1983: 92-94; Day 1986: 5-6; Macintosh 1997: 236-237. For earlier Literature, see Vielhauer 2007: 84, n. 85.

62   Wolff (1974: 121) suggested that the lack of details about the events might show that they were contemporary ones which the hearers can perceive without details.

63   Irvine (1990: 116-117, n.12) suggested that Shalmaneser V might have attacked Israelite territory as a punishment for Hoshea's involvement in anti-Assyrian activity in the last years of Tiglath-pileser III.

64   Astour 1971.

65   Tadmor 1994: Summ. 7: r. 10´. Wolff 1974: 188.

66   For literature, see Wolff 1974: 188, n. 74.

67   Sweeney 2000: 117-130.

68   Wolff 1974: 215; Macintosh 1997: 504.

Aram-Damascus, possibly by Joash or Jeroboam II in the first half of the eighth century BCE and remained Israelite until its annexation by Rezin in the latter half of the same century. However, it is difficult to connect those toponyms to any concrete historical events in the late years of Israel.[69] They are related to sins and hence are the targets of accusation. Mention of Gilead as a region seems to indicate that Israel ruled over the entire Gilead region, or most of it. Šiṭṭim and Adam are located on the eastern side of the Jordan Valley. The location of Mizpah of Gilead cannot be determined with certainty, but one may search for it not far from Mahanaim (Tell edh-Dhahab), on the northern side of the Jabbok River (Na'aman 1995b: 105-106, 110-113).[70] Hence, Israelite rule in Gilead encompassed the area between Mizpah of Gilead in the north to Šiṭṭim in the south.

6.1.6. The Extent of Jeroboam II's Dominion according to the Bible

Lack of sources will not allow us to delineate the Israelite territorial extent during Jeroboam II's reign. Available sources explicitly indicate the Israelite expansion eastward, namely, into northern Transjordan. Jeroboam also expanded northward and might have occupied part of the territories of Damascus for a short period of time. The eastern territory most probably encompasses the entire Gilead region, or most of it, down to the Moabite border in the south. It seems, however, that the inhabitants of Transjordan wrote Aramaic even under the Israelite rule. The Deir 'Alla Inscription and another unearthed Aramaic inscription attest to the Aramaean influence in Transjordan at that time (3.2.5.). Until now, no Hebrew inscriptions dating to the eighth century BCE have been found in the region. There is no evidence that attests to Jeroboam's conquest of Ammonite or Moabite territories.[71] Jeroboam's relations with Phoenicia, Philistia, and Judah are not mentioned in the Bible and any theory on this issue must remain conjectural.

6.2. The Assyrian Sources

Assyrian inscriptions refer neither to Jeroboam II nor to Israel under his rule. Only the Eponym Chronicles, the Pazarcık Stela, and the Nimrud Wine Lists

---

69 The attempts to set each passage in a certain historical setting is seen most prominently in Alt (1953: 163-187), Wolff (1974: 110-112, 172-173), and Donner (1964: 42-59). Good (1966: 275-278) suggested that the passage in Hos 5:8-6:6 can alternatively be interpreted apart from the historical point of view.

70 Among the candidates are Tell Maṣfah, El-Mishrifeh, Khirbet Jel'ad, and Er-Reshuni, see Na'aman 1995b: 106, n. 5; MacDonald 2000: 199-200, with earlier literature.

71 *Contra* Cohen (1965: 154), who suggested that Israel recovered all the territories lost in the time of Jeroboam's ancestors, including the border between Moab and Israel. Cf. Hübner 1992: 186.

bring some light to the political situation and international relations during his reign.

6.2.1. The Eponym Chronicles

The Eponym Chronicles in the corresponding years of the reign of Jeroboam II (*ca.* 784–748 BCE) run as follows (Table 5):

Name of King	Year	Event Entry
Adad-nērārī III	784	to Hubuškia
	783	to Itu'a
Shalmaneser IV	782	to Itu'a
	781	to Urartu
	780	to Urartu
	779	to Urartu
	778	to Urartu
	777	to Itu'a
	776	to Urartu
	775	to the cedar mountain
	774	to Namri
	773	to Damascus
Ashur-dān III	772	to Hatarikka
	771	to Gananati
	770	to Marad
	769	to Itu'a
	768	in the land
	767	to Gananati
	766	to Media
	765	to Hatarikka; plague
	764	in the land
	763	revolt in the citadel; in Siwan the sun had an eclipse
	762	revolt in the citadel
	761	revolt in Arrapha
	760	revolt in Arrapha
	759	revolt in Guzana; plague
	758	to Guzana; peace in the land
	757	in the land
	756	in the land
	755	to Hatarikka
Ashur-nērārī V	754	to Arpad; return from Ashur
	753	in the land
	752	in the land
	751	in the land
	750	in the land
	749	to Namri
	748	to Namri

Table 5. The Eponym Chronicles between 784-748 BCE

As seen from the list, Assyria was less involved in Syria-Palestine than in the previous period. It also suffered from revolts in the years 763–759 BCE.[72] Hence, there is little evidence for an Assyrian presence in the west during these years. Under Shalmaneser IV, Assyria conducted campaigns to the west in the years 775, 773–772 BCE. Ashur-dān III led two campaigns against Hatarikka: in the years 765 and 755 BCE, and one campaign against Arpad in 754 BCE.

Scholars have explained the territorial expansion of Israel under Jeroboam II by citing the influence of Assyria in the West in his time. Haran (1967: 279-280) dated the Israelite expansion under Jeroboam to 754–748 BCE, when Assyrian influence on the Syro-Palestinian region was reduced.[73] In his view, the Israelite expansion was independent of the Assyrian influence on the region. Lipiński (1991: 175) and Halpern (2001: 192) suggested that Jeroboam II could recover the Transjordanian territory because Assyria defeated its major rival kingdoms in the region (Arpad, Hamath, and Damascus). According to Halpern, the Beqaʿ was given to Israel by Assyria as a reward for loyalty, which can be dated as early as the time of Adad-nērārī III (810–783 BCE), or as late as that of Ashur-dān III (773–755 BCE).[74] Lipiński and Halpern thus assumed an Israeli-Assyrian alliance behind the Israelite expansion under Jeroboam.

In reviewing these reconstructions, we must emphasise that it is hard to assume a vacuum of Assyrian power in the Syro-Palestinian region. Strong Assyrian influence in the region is indicated by the Assyrian campaign against Damascus related in the Pazarcık Stela (6.2.2.). Jeroboam's territorial expansion is therefore best explained by collaboration between Israel and Assyria (Šamšī-ilu).

6.2.2. The Pazarcık Stela (Reverse A.0.105.1)[75]

The text on the reverse of the stela has twenty lines, which can be divided into the following four sections: (1) Shalmaneser IV's genealogy and mention of Šamšī-ilu as field marshal (lines 1-4a); (2) campaign against Damascus and the

---

72 The Eponym Chronicles refer to "in the land" nine times during the reigns of Ashur-dān III and Ashur-nērārī V (768, 764, 757, 756, 753–750, and 747 BCE).

73 Also Hallo 1960: 44-46. Cogan and Tadmor (1988: 164), assuming the large Israelite expansion during the reign of Jeroboam II even "beyond Damascus" (Am 5:27), set it in the early and middle days of his reign. Similarly, Vogelstein (1945: 17-20) dated it between 773–765 BCE.

74 This dating is based on the active role of Adad-nērārī III and his son in establishing borders in the West, as reflected in the Pazarcık and Antakya Stelae. However, it was actually done by Šamšī-ilu. Lipiński (1991: 174-175) suggested that it was probably Šamšī-ilu who actually led the military campaigns against Hatarikka in 772, 765, and 755 BCE. Halpern connected the cession of Beqaʿ to Ashur-dān III's campaign in 772 BCE against Hatarikka. Hadrach is also mentioned in Zech 9:1. Halpern (*op. cit.*, 193) suggested that the Transjordanian territory was conquered by Jeroboam as reflected in the Book of Amos.

75 For basic information of the Pazarcık stela, see 4.2.3.2.6.

tribute paid by Hadiānu of Damascus (lines 4b-10); (3) the granting of this boundary stone to Ušpilulume of Kummuh (lines 11-13a); and (4) curses (lines 13b-21). The following translation is that of section 2.

Translation:[76]

> 4b-10) When they (= Shalmaneser IV and Šamšī-ilu) went to Damascus, the tribute of Hadiānu of the land Damascus, silver, gold, copper, his royal bed, his royal couch, his daughter with her abundant dowry, the property of his palace without number, I received from him.

> 11-13a) On my return, this boundary (stone) to Ušpilulume, king of the city Kummuh, I gave.

The side of the stela composed on the occasion of the successful campaign against Damascus, was given to Ušpilulume of Kummuh as a boundary stone (lines 11-13a). Although the inscription was engraved soon after the campaign (773 BCE), the reference to the subjugation of the Damascene king is brief (lines 4b-10) and refers only to his tribute.[77]

In light of this inscription, it seems that the Israelite expansion northward under Jeroboam is best understood against the background of the Assyrian 773 BCE campaign.

6.2.3. The Nimrud Wine Lists

About sixty tablets bearing wine rations to approximately 6,000 people belonging to the Assyrian king's household were discovered in the 1950s–1960s excavations at Fort Shalmaneser in Nimrud. The tablets were published by Kinnier Wilson (1972) and later revised by Dalley and Postgate (1984). These tablets, designated as the "Nimrud Wine Lists", were dated to the eighth century BCE.[78] Kinnier Wilson (*op. cit.*, 92-94) suggested that the foreign gentility mentioned in the lists were captives from military campaigns. The Samarians (*Samerināya*) are mentioned three times in lists dating to the early eighth century BCE (ND 6229, Col. iv, 4; ND 6212, Rev. 15; ND 10032, Obv. 7).[79] Their professions are not specified, but they apparently fulfilled official functions in the Assyrian king's household.[80] The stay of the Samarians in the Assyrian capital may show that Joash and/or Jero-

---

76 Publication: Hasegawa 2010b: 5-6.

77 The quantities of tribute are not given either, except for "without number" in line 10.

78 Kinnier Wilson (1972: 2-3) dated the tablets to the last years of Adad-nērārī III and the early years of Shalmaneser IV (791–779 BCE) but it later became clear that the tablets covered a longer period than Kinnier Wilson had suggested (Dalley and Postgate 1984: 22-24).

79 ND 10047, Rev. 15, referring to Samarians, was originated in NE 48III, which can be dated to the late eighth century BCE (Dalley and Postgate 1984: 23).

80 The foreign gentility mentioned in the lists includes foreign leaders and ambassadors (Tadmor 1975: 42; Dalley and Postgate 1984: 24).

boam II sent them to Assyria either to bring the tax or to carry out a diplomatic mission.

6.3. The Kuntillet ʿAjrud Inscriptions

Kuntillet ʿAjrud is located in southern Sinai, about fifty kilometres south of Kadesh-barnea. It was excavated by Meshel in 1975–76 and results were published in preliminary reports (Meshel 1992). The site was used only for a short period of time and then deserted.[81] It was dated on the basis of three criteria: (1) On the basis of the pottery analysis it was dated to the end of the ninth or the beginning of the eighth century BCE.[82] (2) On the basis of radiocarbon dating it was dated between *ca.* 820 to later than 745 BCE.[83] (3) On the basis of palaeographical analysis it was dated to the first three quarters of the eighth century BCE.[84]

The influence of the Northern Kingdom is reflected especially in the inscriptions discovered at the site. Most remarkable is the mention of "YHWH of Samaria" in the Phoenician script.[85] In addition, the theophoric names with *-yaw* (יו-) ending suggest that their dedicators came from the Northern Kingdom.[86] Although most of the pottery originated in Judah (Singer-Avitz 2006: 198-207), petrographic analyses indicate that part of the pottery, especially small vessels, originated in northern Israel (Gunneweg, Perlman, and Meshel 1985; Goren 1995). Due to these facts, some scholars regarded the findings at Kuntillet ʿAjrud as evidence for Israelite expansion and prosperity during the time of Jeroboam II.[87]

The excavator suggested a religious function of the site.[88] However, most scholars have interpreted the site as being a fortified caravanserai for travellers to

---

81   On the date of the abandonment of the site, see Freud 2008.

82   Ayalon 1995. Singer-Avitz (2006) dated the pottery assemblage of Kuntillet ʿAjrud to the end of eighth to beginning of the seventh centuries BCE. She (*op. cit.*, 212-213) related the site to Assyrian activity in the Empire's peripheral regions. For the criticism of Singer-Avitz's dating, see Freud 2008.

83   Finkelstein and Piasetzky 2008. Some scholars dated the site on the basis of radiocarbon dating. Segal (1995) dated it to first half of the eighth century BCE. Meshel, Carmi, and Segal (1995) dated it to around 800 BCE. Later, they (Carmi and Segal 1996) dated more narrowly to 801–770 BCE.

84   Lemaire 1984: 134-136. Renz (1995: 51, 60, n. 7) dated it to *ca.* 800 BCE. However, such a narrow dating based solely on palaeography is hardly possible.

85   For the script and language of the inscriptions, see Mastin 2009.

86   The theophoric name endings are written as *-yahu* (יהו) in the Judahite tradition.

87   The excavator considered that the site was built by the Northern Kingdom under Joash (Meshel 1992: 109). Hadley (1987: 207-208; 1993) suggested that the site is a caravanserai. Cf. Beck (1982: 61); Naʾaman (1993: 232).

88   Meshel 1992: 108-109; Weinfeld 1984: 127.

Elat on the way called Darb el-Ghaza.[89] Lemaire (1984: 136-139) suggested a commercial joint enterprise between Phoenicians and Israelites and dated the inscriptions to the time of Jeroboam II, more precisely between 776 and 750 BCE. Na'aman (1993: 232-234) first suggested that Amaziah blocked the Way of Arabah after Joash's death and did not allow Jeroboam II to use it. Jeroboam was forced to use the western route via Darb el-Ghaza to reach Elat and thus built Kuntillet 'Ajrud near the road.[90] Later, Na'aman and Lissovsky (2008) associated the various artefacts from Kuntillet 'Ajrud with the cult of sacred trees in Levant, and emphasised the religious function of the site. They pointed out that the site's function as a caravanserai was only secondary. Its distant location from Darb el-Ghaza (about twelve kilometres), the relatively small number of cooking-pots unearthed there, and an abundance of unique material discovered at the site may support this view. At any event, the view does not contradict the dating of the site and its construction by the Northern Kingdom. I follow the view of Lemaire and Na'aman and date the site to the time of Jeroboam II.

The divergent origin of the findings in this remote site can be explained by the multi-cultural background of the travellers who visited it. Inscriptions in Phoenician script may indicate the Phoenicians' visit to the site. The origin of most of the pottery in Judah shows that Judaeans visited the place or provided travellers on their way to Kuntillet 'Ajrud with food and drink.[91] If the site was used also by Phoenicians and Judaeans, it might reflect a peaceful relationship between Israel and these two neighbours during Jeroboam II's reign. The use of Darb el-Ghaza further indicates peaceful relations between the travellers and the Philistines who lived on the outskirts of the route.

6.4. The Samaria Ostraca

Sixty-six ostraca with Hebrew inscriptions were uncovered during the excavation of Samaria in 1910. These ostraca provide information on the delivery of wine and oil to Samaria during the ninth, tenth, and fifteenth years of a king, who is usually identified with Jeroboam II. They no doubt served as an administrative record, although their exact function is in dispute.[92] The contents of the ostraca contribute little to our understanding of the political history of Israel during the time of Jeroboam II. The distribution of the toponyms in the ostraca encom-

---

89   Zwickel 2000: 139; Finkelstein and Piasetzky 2008. A list of the literature for the view is found in Na'aman and Lissovsky 2008: 187.
90   This view is followed by Zwickel (2000: 140-141). Cf. Weinfeld (1984: 127). He related the inscriptions to the expeditions towards Elat (2 Kgs 8:20-22; 14:7, 22).
91   Goren 1995.
92   See Kaufman 1992: 923-925.

passes only part of the territory of western Manasseh, which certainly does not reflect the extent of the Israelite kingdom at the time.

6.5. The Seal of Shemaʿ

Schumacher's excavations at Tel Megiddo unearthed a seal with a roaring lion at its centre and the inscription "belonging to Shemaʿ, servant of Jeroboam" (לשמע עבד ירבעם).[93] The majority of scholars believe this "Jeroboam" to be Jeroboam II.[94] This seal cannot be ascribed to Jeroboam I, as no seals with personal names dating before the mid-eighth century BCE have been found so far.[95] This is the earliest known seal from the Kingdom of Israel bearing the name of an Israelite king.

6.6. Archaeological Evidence

Construction of strongly fortified cities and large public and private buildings, or the discovery of many prestige artefacts of local and foreign origin, indicates a period of ascent and prosperity in the land. To examine the prosperity under Jeroboam II, archaeological evidence from the early eighth century BCE will be reviewed below. Only the Cisjordanian sites will be analysed, for archaeological information of the Iron Age sites in northern Transjordan is limited (Hindawi 2007). It should be noted that the Low Chronology system usually does not affect the date of the eighth century strata.

6.6.1. Tel Dan

Tel Dan (Tell el-Qadi) is located at the foot of Mt Hermon, close to one of the sources of the Jordan River. An important road connecting the Mediterranean

---

93   Schumacher and Steuernagel 1908: 99-100, Fig. 47. The present whereabouts of the seal are unknown.

94   See Ussishkin (1994: 420) for earlier literature.

95   Yeivin (1960) and Ahlström (1993b), examining the seal from the palaeographical, iconographical, and stratigraphical point of view, concluded that the seal cannot be dated later than the ninth century BCE. Renz and Röllig (2003: 398) dated it to the mid-eighth century BCE, based on its iconography (cf. Lemaire 1990; Avigad 1992). Ussishkin (1994) re-examined the stratigraphy of the discovery place of the seal and ascribed the seal to Jeroboam I. Different opinions on the stratigraphical status of the seal merely show that the early excavations at Megiddo were methodologically problematic, and did not provide any decisive date regarding the seal of Shemaʿ (Finkelstein, Ussishkin, and Halpern 2006b: 854).

with Damascus passes near the site. Excavations at the site began in 1966 and continued until 1999 under the direction of Biran (Biran, Ilan, and Greenberg 1996; Biran and Ben-Dov 2002). According to the excavator (Biran 2002: 4), Stratum II dates to the second and third quarters of the eighth century BCE, which roughly overlaps the reign of Jeroboam II.[96] Arie (2008) re-examined the pottery of the Iron Age strata and dated Stratum IVA to the time of Hazael and his son Bar-Hadad. If his stratigraphy is adopted, two strata (III and II) should be assigned to the period between the destruction of Hazael's city (Stratum IVA) and Tiglath-pileser III's destruction of 732 BCE.[97] I tentatively relate Stratum III to the time of Joash, who conquered the Aramaean city (Stratum IVA), smashed the Tel Dan Stela, and rebuilt the city (Stratum III). The renovation of the city can be attributed to the time of Jeroboam II (Stratum II).[98] The stratigraphical affiliation of monumental buildings, such as the city gate complex, fortification system and piazza, is not clear in the publication (Biran 2002: 4). Part of these buildings may have been built during the reign of Jeroboam II (Stratum II).

6.6.2. Tel Hazor

Tel Hazor is the largest tell in Palestine, located in the Upper Galilee, north of the Sea of Galilee. Excavation at Hazor was first launched by Yadin (1955–1958, 1968) and by Ben-Tor (from 1991 to the present) (Yadin *et al.* 1958, 1960, 1961, Ben-Tor 1989, 1996; Ben-Tor and Ben-Ami 1998; Ben-Tor and Bonfil 1997).

According to the Low Chronology, Strata VIII-VII were built by the Aramaeans. Finkelstein and Piasetzky (2007: 271-272) ascribed the destruction of Stratum VII to either Joash or Jeroboam II. Yadin (1972b: 179) observed that the city of Stratum VI was rebuilt in an entirely different layout than its predecessor and suggested that it was built by Jeroboam II and destroyed by an earthquake *ca.* 760 BCE.[99]

The buildings in Stratum VI are the best constructed among the Iron Age buildings at Hazor (Yadin 1972b: 179, 182, and 185). Luxury objects, including

---

96 In the chronicle of the excavations (Biran 2002), however, the excavator did not assign each building to a certain stratum, but only dated each building. This makes it difficult to connect those buildings to Biran's stratigraphy.

97 Mazar (2005: 24) dated Stratum IV to Iron IIA (1000/980–840/830 BCE) and Stratum III as only before the Assyrian attack in 732 BCE. This dating – Stratum II as after 732 BCE – is not convincing because the loci, where the Tel Dan Inscription fragments were uncovered, apparently belong to Stratum II, most possibly destroyed in 732 BCE.

98 Arie (2008: 37-38) dated Stratum III to the time of Joash and Stratum II to Jeroboam II. However, there is no sufficient data to separate the two strata, as he himself stated (*op. cit.*, 33).

99 Yadin *et al.* 1960: 24, 26; Yadin 1975: 157.

ivory vessels, were discovered in this stratum and attest to the prosperity of the city at this time.[100]

6.6.3. Tel Kinrot[101]

Stratum II at Tel Kinrot covers the period from the end of the ninth century BCE to 732 BCE. During this period, only the upper mound was inhabited. Two pillared buildings, a city-gate, and a solid wall were discovered (Fritz 1990; Münger, Zangenberg, and Pakkala 2011: 70, 73). The destruction of Stratum II was assigned to Tiglath-pileser III's campaign. Hebrew inscriptions unearthed in this stratum may suggest that the site was inhabited by the Israelites (Fritz, *op. cit.,* 209-211).[102] Assuming that the city of Stratum II was Israelite, the upper mound served as a fortress under Jeroboam II.

6.6.4. Tel Bethsaida[103]

Stratum V at Tel Bethsaida encompasses the eighth century BCE. The site seems to have been occupied by Aramaeans (3.3.2.3.) until its destruction by Tiglath-pileser III in 732 BCE.[104]

6.6.5. Tel ʿEn Gev

The destruction of the lower city of ʿEn Gev (Stratum III by Mazar) may be the result of the campaign of Adad-nērārī III in 796 BCE, or that of Joash of Israel in the early eighth century BCE (3.3.2.4.). It seems that the Aramaeans rebuilt the city soon thereafter (Stratum IV on the acropolis and Stratum II in the lower city).

---

100 The dating of the Late Iron Age strata at Hazor was recently challenged by James (2008: 153-154), who dated Stratum VIII to Jeroboam II's time. If so, the large-scaled water system (Ben-Tor and Bonfil 1997: 239-246) was hewn in the time of Jeroboam.

101 For general information on the site, see 3.3.2.2.

102 It is worth noting that Hebrew inscriptions were also found in the equivalent stratum at Hazor. See 6.6.2. However, despite its geographical proximity to Hazor, no destruction layer was exposed at Tel Kinrot equivalent to the one between Strata VI and V at Hazor. This fact makes it difficult to explain the destruction of Hazor by an earthquake.

103 For general information on Bethsaida, see 3.3.2.3.

104 The jar handle impression of *zkryw* found at the site does not necessarily indicate that Bethsaida was incorporated into the Israelite kingdom in the eighth century BCE (*contra* Brandl 2009). The population of this region was mixed, as the other seals indicate (Knauf 2006: 315, n. 130).

There is no archaeological evidence to indicate Israelite occupation of the site during the eighth century BCE.

6.6.6. Tel Beth-Shean[105]

Mazar (2005: 24) dated Strata Upper V-IV and Strata P-8-7 at Tel Beth-Shean to *ca.* 830 to 732 BCE.[106] The violent destruction of stratum P-8 may reflect Joash's/Jeroboam's military campaign to regain Israelite domination in the Beth-Shean Valley. The large dwelling exposed in Stratum P-7 (Mazar 2006: 33) is "one of the largest and most impressive Iron Age dwelling structures excavated in Israel", and may represent more of the prosperity of Jeroboam's reign.

6.6.7. Tel Rehov[107]

Stratum III at Tel Rehov is contemporaneous with the other strata dated to *ca.* 830–732 BCE in this region. This Stratum, which was found only at the upper mound, is characterised by the construction of new buildings including a massive mud brick fortification wall (Mazar 1999: 36; 2003b: 157-158). The destruction of the city is associated with Tiglath-pileser III's campaign in 732 BCE. In light of the stratigraphic sequence of the nearby site of Beth-Shean, it seems that Tel Rehov was rebuilt during the time of Jeroboam II.[108] If this is indeed the case, there is a settlement gap at Tel Rehov for about half a century from Hazael's conquest (Stratum IV) until Jeroboam's rebuilding of the city (Stratum III).[109]

6.6.8. Tel Megiddo

Tel Megiddo (Tell el-Mutesellim) is located in the west Jezreel Valley. It was excavated in 1903–1905 by Schumacher (Schumacher and Steuernagel 1908), in the 1920s–1930s by the Chicago Oriental Institute (Fischer 1929; Guy 1931; Lamon and Shipton 1939; Loud 1948), and between 1960 and 1972 by Yadin (1960; 1970; 1972b). The renewed excavations by the Tel Aviv University began in 1992

---

105 For general information on the site, see 3.3.2.6.

106 Strata Upper V-IV were named by the excavation by the University of Pennsylvania and Strata P-8-7 were named by the Hebrew University excavation.

107 For general information on the site, see 3.3.2.7.

108 The massive mud brick wall may be an offset-inset wall (Mazar 1999: 36), which is also found in Megiddo IVA.

109 An occupation gap between Strata IV and III is not observed by the excavator.

and is ongoing (Finkelstein, Ussishkin, and Halpern 2000; 2006a). The Chicago Oriental Institute established a pottery chronology of the strata. The new excavators carefully co-related their strata with those of the old excavations. According to their observation, Stratum IVA by the Chicago stratigraphy corresponds to H-3 and H-4, and a stratum in Area L by the renewed excavation. These strata, more particularly H-3, represent the time of Jeroboam II.

Monumental stables were uncovered in Area L and they were well furnished for breeding and handling horses. Cantrell and Finkelstein (2006) hypothesised that the horses were bred by the Northern Kingdom for export in the eighth century BCE. If so, the stables at Megiddo suggest that under the reign of Jeroboam II, the Northern Kingdom had commercial relations with the neighbouring political powers – especially Egypt and Assyria. This view accords well with the assumed good relations between Jeroboam II and Šamšī-ilu of Assyria. Other buildings from Stratum IVA, such as inset-offset city walls, the gate complex, and a massive water system, show that the city was well-planned and prosperous.[110]

6.6.9. Tel Yoqneʿam

Tel Yoqneʿam, identified with biblical Jokneam, is a large mound, located at a point along the abutment of Mt Carmel and the Jezreel Valley. The site was excavated from 1977 to 1988 by Ben-Tor (Ben-Tor and Rosenthal 1978; 1979; 1983; Ben-Tor, Zarzecki-Peleg, and Cohen-Anidjar 2005).

Stratum XII at Tel Yoqneʿam corresponds to the time of Jeroboam II. The city was well planned, with a "gallery wall", towers, piazza, and perimeter-street. The excavator dated the beginning of Stratum XII to the latter half of the ninth century BCE, under the reigns of Jeroboam's predecessors. However, the similarity in pottery assemblage between Strata XV-XIV and Rehov Strata V-IV (Zarzecki-Peleg 1997; Mazar *et al.* 2005:243) suggests that Stratum XIII, which shows the IAIIA-IIB transitional features (Zarzecki-Peleg 2005b), can be dated, in conformity with the recent modified chronology, to the time of Jeroboam II's predecessors.[111] If so, it is peferable to date the buildings of Stratum XII to Jeroboam II's reign.

---

110 Ussishkin (Finkelstein, Ussishkin, and Halpern 2006b: 856) suggested that Megiddo was an Israelite garrison city in the eighth century BCE.

111 The excavator described Stratum XIII as ephemeral, which seems to agree with the period of Jeroboam's predecessors (*ca.* 840–780 BCE).

6.6.10. Tel Ta'anach

Tel Ta'anach (Tell Ta'annek) is biblical Ta'anach, located in the southern Jerzreel Valley, about eight kilometres southeast of Tel Megiddo. The site was excavated in 1902-1904 by Sellin (1904; 1905) and in 1963–1968 by Lapp (1964; 1967; 1969). Finkelstein (1998) ascribed the destruction of the flourishing city of stratum IIB[112] to Hazael's military campaign.[113] The following strata (III and IV) are quite poor. Several loci from stratum IV show signs of destruction, which can be connected to the Assyrian campaign in 732 BCE (Rast 1978: 45). It indicates that Tel Ta'anach became an insignificant site during stratum IV, which corresponds to the time of Jeroboam II.

6.6.11. Samaria

The most important site for examining the material culture of the time of Jeroboam II is Samaria, the capital of the Northern Kingdom. The site of Samaria was first excavated in 1908 by Schumacher, from 1909 to 1910 by Reisner and Fisher (Reisner, Fisher, and Lyon 1924), and from 1932 to 1935 by Crowfoot, Sukenik, and Kenyon (Crowfoot and Crowfoot 1938; Crowfoot, Kenyon, and Sukenik 1942; Crowfoot, Crowfoot, and Kenyon 1957). Minor archaeological campaigns were also conducted in 1965–67 and in 1968 (Zayadine 1967–68; Hennessy 1970). Kenyon established a stratigraphy of nine building phases and pottery periods at Samaria, which for a time became the "standard" stratigraphy of Samaria (Table 8).[114]

Pottery Period	I	II	III	IV	V	VI	VII
Kenyon	Omri	Ahab	Jehu, Joahaz, Joash	Jeroboam II and his successors	Assyrian hegemony	Assyrian hegemony	Assyrian administration
Tappy	11th century to *ca.* 875		*ca.* 875 to 800	*ca.* 800-722			722-

Table 8. Schematic Table of the Suggested Stratigraphy by Kenyon and Tappy

One of the problems of Kenyon's stratigraphy is her excessive tendency to relate the strata to certain Israelite rulers. Tappy (1992; 2001), using unpublished field

---

112 The strata are pottery strata.

113 The pottery assemblage of Periods IIa-IIb appears to correspond to Rehov Strata VI-IV, which confirms to date the end of IIb to *ca.* 840/830 (Mazar *et al.* 2005: 243).

114 Wright (1959) dated the construction activities differently, and proposed a different view concerning the relations between the construction phases and the pottery periods.

notes of the British expedition, considerably changed Kenyon's stratigraphy of the Iron Age Samaria. Yet, his new stratigraphy has little effect on the strata attributed to the time of Jeroboam II. Both Kenyon and Tappy dated Stratum IV[115] to the time of Jeroboam II and his successors.

Almost all the main buildings, fortification walls and city gates of Stratum IV had been constructed during the previous periods and only repaired and renovated during the eighth century BCE. But some buildings were newly constructed. Stratum IV does not reflect well the prosperity under Jeroboam II, despite Samaria's status as the capital of the Northern Kingdom. This may be explained by the fact that the later buildings used the earlier remains as building material. The conquering Assyrians took most of the prestigious objects from Samaria as booty. For these reasons, luxurious artefacts were rarely found at the site.

6.6.12. Tell el-Far'ah (North)

The site of Tell el-Far'ah (North), which lies eleven kilometres northeast of Nablus, is generally identified with biblical Tirzah.[116] The site is located at the source of Wadi Far'ah, flowing into the Jordan River; the Samarian mountains rise just west of the site. A good view toward the east suggests its strategic control over the route from/to the Jordan Valley in the east.

De Vaux conducted nine seasons of excavation at Tell el-Far'ah from 1946 to 1960 (de Vaux 1951; 1952; 1955; 1956; 1957; 1961; 1962; de Vaux and Steve 1947; 1948; 1949). Chambon (1984) subsequently published the final report of the Tell el-Far'ah excavations concerning the Iron Age strata.[117] Stratum VII corresponds to the Iron Age I-II and is divided into five sub-strata (VIIa-e).[118] Stratum VIId, dated to the eighth century BCE, indicates the flourishing period of the site. The houses were better constructed and also larger than those of the preceding stratum. This stratum ended perhaps with the Assyrian conquest in the late eighth century BCE.

---

115   The strata are pottery strata.
116   For the identification of Tirzah, see Manor 1992: 573-574.
117   See also McClellan 1987.
118   Stratum VIIb corresponds to Rehov Strata VI-IV (Mazar *et al.* 2005: 243).

6.6.13. Tel Gezer[119]

The Iron Age II Strata VII-VI at Tel Gezer show the heyday of the site. A newly built outer wall strengthened the city fortification,[120] and the city was enlarged to about eight hectares. Finkelstein (2002: 285-286) dated Strata VII-VI to the eighth century BCE.[121] The prosperity of these strata at Gezer is also reflected in the increased number of rural sites in the vicinity (Shavit 2000: 217-229).[122]

6.6.14. Conclusion

The strata at various sites in the territory of the Northern Kingdom, dating to the time of Jeroboam II, show a large-scale, extensive building activity.[123] Cities were well planned, new buildings constructed, and fortifications strengthened. Prolific building activity can be achieved only in time of economic growth, social stability, and sufficient manpower. This may suggest that Jeroboam II, in addition to military success, had established close amicable relations – both commercially and politically – with Assyria.[124]

6.7. Synthesis

After ascending the throne in 784 BCE, Jeroboam II established amicable relations with the Assyrian Empire. He co-operated with the Assyrian *turtānu* Šamšī-ilu, who had a great influence on the Syro-Palestinian kingdoms at that time. The Assyrian military campaigns against Arpad, Hamath, and Damascus in the years 775–754 BCE opened the way for Jeroboam. Following the conquests of Joash, his father, Jeroboam was able to expand the Israelite territory in Gilead further and possibly also in the Bashan. Jeroboam's territorial expansions brought great prosperity to the Kingdom of Israel, and this is reflected in the building activities at various sites throughout his kingdom.

---

119   For general information of Tel Gezer, see 3.3.2.9.

120   Finkelstein 1994.

121   For criticism, see Dever 2003: 267-270.

122   Shavit (*op. cit.*, tab. 4) observed that the numbers of settlements both in the Ayalon Valley and the Lower Galilee increased more in the eighth century BCE than in the ninth (cf. Gal 1992: 94-109).

123   Finkelstein and Singer-Avitz (2009) re-examined the pottery assemblage from Bethel and concluded that the site was prosperous in the eighth century BCE.

124   Israel probably had commercial relations also with Egypt, as implied in Hos 12:2.

7. The End of the Jehuite Dynasty (747 BCE)

The Jehuite Dynasty came to an end with Zechariah's murder. The Book of Kings is the single source that refers to his name and this event.

7.1. The Biblical Source

2 Kgs 15:8-12 describes the reign of Zechariah (748–747 BCE), the successor of Jeroboam II, and the last king of the Jehuite Dynasty. V. 10 is a short report on the conspiracy.

7.1.1. The Murder of Zechariah (2 Kgs 15:10)

The verse originally derives from an archival source of the Northern Kingdom, which related a series of conspiracies (vv. 14, 25). It mentions Ibleam as the place of Zechariah's murder. This was the place where Jehu killed Ahaziah, king of Judah (2 Kgs 9:27).[1] Based on the Lucianic recension, modern commentators support the reading of "Ibleam" (יבלעם), instead of "before people" (קבל־עם) in the Masoretic text.[2]

7.1.2. The End of the Jehuite Dynasty as Fulfilment of YHWH's Words (2 Kgs 15:12)

With Zechariah's murder, the Jehuite Dynasty came to an end. 2 Kgs 15:12 mentions the fulfilment of YHWH's words, as announced to Jehu (2 Kgs 10:30). Hence, the two verses form the "prophecy and fulfilment" pattern. These two verses are obviously *post factum* statements, added by the Dtr. The Dtr's authorship of 2 Kgs 10:30 is indicated in the way that the words of YHWH were directly conveyed to the king, and not through a prophet.

---

1   Cogan and Tadmor 1988: 171; Hasegawa 2006.
2   Montgomery 1951: 453-454; Gray 1977: 620; Würthwein 1984: 377-378; Cogan and Tadmor 1988: 169-170. There are two reasons that make it difficult to accept קבל־עם here: קבל is a late Aramaic word; עם needs the definite article ה before it.

7.2. Synthesis

The lack of sources does not allow a detailed sketch of the end of the Jehuite Dynasty. The political instability in the Northern Kingdom after the end of the Jehuite Dynasty is reflected in repeated coups d'état (2 Kgs 15:14, 25, 30). According to the Book of Kings, Zechariah was the first king who was murdered in a conspiracy after Joram's murder of 841 BCE – almost a century before. The reason for the murder is unknown. The rise of Urartu under Sarduri II (764–734 BCE) brought about the decline of the Assyrian Empire in the last years of Jeroboam II, which reduced Assyria's political influence in the Syro-Palestinian arena. It opened the way for the rise of Rezin who ascended the Damascene throne in the mid-eighth century BCE. Damascus under Rezin exerted considerable influence on the political situation in the kingdoms of Israel and Judah. We may thus suggest that Rezin's political intervention in the Northern Kingdom formed the background for Zechariah's murder. Shallum, who might have been an ally of Rezin, set an ambush for Zechariah at Ibleam and killed him, thereby bringing the Dynasty of Jehu to an end.

Conclusion

Critical reading and analysis of the Book of Kings enable to some extent a sifting of texts and isolation of historically credible material. 2 Kgs 9-15 provides the basic information about the kings of the Jehuite Dynasty: affiliations, lengths of reigns, and deeds of the kings. The prophetic stories in the Book of Kings and the prophecies in the books of Hosea and Amos present the relations between Aram-Damascus and Israel from different perspectives.

Aramaic, Moabite, and Assyrian texts elucidate the chain of political events in Syria-Palestine and the international affairs of the region during the Jehuite Dynasty.

Archaeology casts light on two political historical aspects: Hazael's military conquests of the Israelite territory and the prosperity during the reign of Jeroboam II. The former is reflected in the destruction layers, dated to the same period at various sites. The large scale building activity, dating to the eighth century BCE at key sites in northern Israel corroborates the political stability and material prosperity under Joash and Jeroboam II.

Only through a combination of these three types of sources can the political-historical relationship and the shifts in the power-balance between Assyria, Aram-Damascus, and Israel during the Jehuite Dynasty be reconstructed. The following description is a concise political history of Aram-Damascus and Israel in chronological order.

Shortly before Jehu's coup d'état, Israel fought against Hazael, the new king of Aram, in Transjordan. After Jehu took the throne, Hazael invaded the Israelite territory. Then, either in the late years of Jehu or during the reign of Joahaz, Israel became a vassal kingdom of Aram-Damascus. After Hazael's death, Bar-Hadad succeeded to the Damascene throne and later besieged Joash in Samaria. The latter, however, survived the siege and succeeded in defeating the Aramaean army. It was during his reign that Israel threw off the Aramaean yoke, recovered its independence and even re-conquered parts of its former territory. Jeroboam II also fought against Aram-Damascus and conquered the former Israelite territory in Transjordan and possibly in the southern Bashan. The date of the loss of the conquered territories, either in the late years of Jeroboam or in the time of his successors, remains unknown. The Jehuite Dynasty came to an end with Zechariah's murder by Shallum, who possibly cooperated with Rezin, the king of Aram-Damascus.

As demonstrated in every chapter, Assyria played a major role in the international affairs of Syria-Palestine during the Jehuite Dynasty. In 841 BCE, Jehu paid tribute to Shalmaneser III when the latter reached the border of his kingdom, whereas Hazael did not pay the tribute and remained as an opponent of Assyria. After 838–837 BCE, Assyria withdrew from Syria-Palestine. Hazael took advantage of the political situation and became the dominant power in the region between southern Palestine and the Euphrates. Since 805 BCE, Adad-nērārī III resumed the Assyrian military campaigns to Syria. In 796 BCE, he subjugated Bar-Hadad and, for the first time, the king of Damascus paid tribute to Assyria, side by side with Joash and the Phoenician kingdoms. Šamši-ilu exerted the Assyrian power over Syria-Palestine during the first half of the eighth century BCE. He led campaigns to Damascus, Hamath, and Arpad. Jeroboam II possibly established amicable relations with Šamši-ilu, and took advantage of the political situation to expand the Israelite territory northward. It might have been the instability in Assyria in the mid-eighth century BCE that enabled Rezin, the new king in Damascus, to rise to power, possibly in the late years of Jeroboam.

This study has sought to show the value of meticulous and cautious analysis of all the available sources – biblical, extra-biblical, and archaeological – before suggesting a reconstruction of the history of Israel. Shortened means will not do justice to the complexity of the sources. Only comprehensive and systematic work can bring results that might stand the test of time and illuminate this significant period in the history of ancient Israel.

Bibliography

Abel, F.M. 1938. *Geographie de la Palestine, Tome II*. Paris.

Abu Taleb, M. 1973. *Investigations in the History of North Syria 1115–717 B.C.* Unpublished Ph.D. Thesis. University of Pennsylvania.

Aharoni, Y. 1965a. The Carmel as the Israel-Tyre Border. In: *Western Galilee and the Coast of Galilee: The Nineteenth Archaeological Convention, October 1963.* Jerusalem: 56-62 (Hebrew).

—— 1965b. Hermon. *Encyclopaedia Biblica* 3: 294-297 (Hebrew).

—— 1970. Mount Carmel as Border. In: Kuschke, A. and Kutsch, E. Eds. *Archäologie und Altes Testament. Festschrift für Kurt Galling zum 8. Januar 1970.* Tübingen: 1-7.

—— 1979. *The Land of the Bible: A Historical Geography.* Revised and Enlarged Ed. Philadelphia.

Aḥituv, S. 1984. *Canaanite Toponyms in Ancient Egyptian Documents.* Leiden.

Ahlström, G.W. 1993a. *The History of Ancient Palestine from the Palaeolithic Period to Alexander's Conquest.* (JSOTS 146). Sheffield.

—— 1993b. The Seal of Shemaʿ. *SJOT* 7: 208-215.

Åkerman, K. and Baker, H.D. 2002. Pālil-ēreš. In: Baker, H.D. Ed. *The Prosopography of the Neo-Assyrian Empire.* Volume 3/I P-Ṣ. Helsinki: 981-982.

Albright, W.F. 1942. A Votive Stele Erected by Ben-Hadad I of Damascus to the God Melcarth. *BASOR* 87: 23-29.

Alt, A. 1953. Hosea 5,8-6,6: Ein Krieg und seine Folgen in prophetischer Beleuchtung. *KLG II*: 163-187.

Amadasi-Guzzo, M.G. 1996. In: Bacchielli, L. and Bonanno Aravantions, M. Eds. *Studi di antichità in memoria di Sandro Stucchi* I. Studi Miscellanei 29. Rome: 329-338.

Andersen, F.I. and Freedman, D.N. 1980. *Hosea.* New York.

—— 1989. *Amos.* New York.

Arav, R. 1995. Bethsaida Excavations: Preliminary Report, 1987-1993. In: Arav, R. and Freund, R.A. Eds. *Bethsaida. A City by the North Shore of the Sea of Galilee.* Vol. 1. Kirksville: 3-63.

—— 1999. Bethsaida Excavations: Preliminary Report, 1994-1996. In: Arav, R. and Freund, R.A. Eds. *Bethsaida. A City by the North Shore of the Sea of Galilee.* Vol. 2. Kirksville: 3-113.

—— 2004. Toward a Comprehensive History of Geshur. In: Arav, R. and Freund, R.A. Eds. *Bethsaida. A City by the North Shore of the Sea of Galilee.* Vol. 3. Kirksville: 1-48.

—— 2009. Final Report on Area A, Stratum V: The City Gate. In: Arav, R. and Freund, R.A. Eds. *Bethsaida. A City by the North Shore of the Sea of Galilee.* Vol. 4. Kirksville: 1-122.

Arav, R. and Bernett, M. 1997. An Egyptian Figurine of Pataikos at Bethsaida. *IEJ* 47: 198-213.

—— 2000. The *bīt hilāni* at Bethsaida: Its Place in Aramaean/Neo-Hittite and Israelite Palacea Architecture in the Iron Age II. *IEJ* 50: 47-81.

Arie, E. 2008. Reconsidering the Iron Age II Strata at Tel Dan: Archaeological and Historical Implications. *TA* 35: 6-64.

Astour, M. 1971. 841 B.C.: The First Assyrian Invasion in Israel. *JAOS* 91: 383-389.

Athas, G. 2003. *The Tel Dan Inscription – A Reappraisal and a New Interpretation.* (JSOTS 360. Copenhagen International Seminar 12). Sheffield.

Aufrecht, W.E. 1986. A Bibliography of the Deir 'Alla Plaster Texts. *News Letter for Targumic and Cognate Studies,* 1986 September. Lethbridge.

Avigad, N. 1992. A New Seal Depicting a Lion. *Michmanim* 6: 33*-36*.

Avigad, N. and Sass, B. 1997. *Corpus of West Semitic Stamp Seals.* Jerusalem.

Ayalon, E. 1995. The Iron Age II Pottery Assemblage from Horvat Teiman (Kuntillet 'Ajrud) Pottery. *TA* 22: 141-205.

Baker, H.D. 2000. Hazā-il. In: Baker, H.D. Ed. *The Prosopography of the Neo-Assyrian Empire.* Volume 2/I H-K. Helsinki: 467-469.

Barré, L.M. 1988. *The Rhetoric of Political Persuasion: The Narrative Artistry and Political Intentions of 2 Kings 9-11.* (CBQMS 20). Washington D.C.

Barton, J. 1980. *Amos's Oracles against the Nations: A Study of Amos 1.3-2.5.* Cambridge.

Beck, P. 1982. The Drawings from Horvat Teiman (Kuntillet 'Ajrud). *TA* 9: 3-68.

Becking, B. 1992. *The Fall of Samaria: An Historical and Archaeological Study.* (SHANE 2). Leiden/New York/Köln.

—— 1999. Did Jehu Write the Tel Dan Inscription? *SJOT* 13: 187-201.

Begrich, J. 1929. *Die Chronologie der Könige von Israel und Juda, und die Quellen des Rahmens der Königsbücher.* (BHT 3). Tübingen.

Ben-Ami, D. 2004. The Casemate Fort at Tel Harashim in Upper Galilee. *TA* 31: 194-208.

Ben-Ruven, S. 2004. The Position of Chariot in the Story of Jehu's Revolution. *Al Haperek* 20: 51-53 (Hebrew).

Ben-Shlomo, D., Shai, I., and Maier, A. 2004. Late Philistine Decorated Ware ('Ashdod Ware'): Typology, Chronology, and Production Centers. *BASOR* 335: 1-34.

Ben-Tor, A. Ed. 1989. *Hazor III-IV (Texts): The James A. de Rothschild Expedition at Hazor: An Account of the Third and Fourth Seasons of Excavation, 1957-1958.* Jerusalem.

—— 1996. Hazor Excavations in Memory of Yigael Yadin - Aims and Preliminary Results. *EI* 25: 67-81.

—— 2000. Hazor and the Chronology of Northern Israel: A Reply to Israel Finkelstein. *BASOR* 317: 9-15.

Ben-Tor, A. and Ben-Ami, D. 1998. Hazor and the Archaeology of the Tenth Century B.C.E. *IEJ* 48: 1-37.

Ben-Tor, A. and Bonfil, R. Eds. 1997. *Hazor V: The James A. de Rothschild Expedition at Hazor: An Account of the Fifth Season of Excavation, 1968.* Jerusalem.

Ben-Tor, A. and Rosenthal R. 1978. The First Season of Excavation at Tel-Yoqneʿam, 1977. *IEJ* 28: 57-82.

—— 1979. The Second Season of Excavation at Tel-Yoqneʿam, 1978. *IEJ* 29: 65-83.

—— 1983. The Third and Fourth Seasons of Excavation at Tel-Yoqneʿam, 1979 and 1981. *IEJ* 33: 30-54.

Ben-Tor, A., Zarzecki-Peleg, A., and Cohen-Anidjar, S. 2005. *Yoqneʿam II: The Iron Age and the Persian Period. Final Report of the Archaeological Excavations (1977– 1988).* (Qedem Reports 6). Jerusalem.

Benz, F.L. 1972. *Personal Names in the Phoenician and Punic Inscriptions.* Studia Pohl 8. Rome.

Benzinger, I. 1899. *Die Bücher der Könige.* Leipzig/Tübingen.

Ben-Zvi, E. 1990. Tracing Prophetic Literature in the Book of Kings: The Case of II Kings 15,37. *ZAW* 102: 100-105.

Biran, A. 1994. *Biblical Dan.* Jerusalem.

—— 1999. Two Bronze Plaques and the *Ḥuṣṣot* of Dan. *IEJ* 49: 43-54.

—— 2002. Part I: A Chronicle of the Excavations. In: Biran, A. and Ben-Dov, R. *Dan II. A Chronicle of the Excavations and the Late Bronze Age "Mycenaean Tomb".* Jerusalem: 3-32.

Biran, A. and Ben-Dov, R. 2002. *Dan II. A Chronicle of the Excavations and the Late Bronze Age "Mycenaean Tomb".* Jerusalem.

Biran, A., Ilan, D., and Greenberg, R. 1996. *Dan I. A Chronicle of the Excavations, the Pottery Neolithic, the Early Bronze Age and the Middle Bronze Age Tombs.* Jerusalem.

Biran, A. and Naveh, J. 1993. An Aramaic Stele Fragment from Tel Dan. *IEJ* 43: 81-98.

—— 1995. The Tel Dan Inscription: A New Fragment. *IEJ* 45: 1-18.

Blocher, F. 2001. Assyrische Würdenträger und Gouverneure des 9. Und 8. Jh.: Eine Neubewertung ihrer Rolle. *AoF* 28: 298-324.

Blum, E. 1997. Der Prophet und das verderben Israels: Eine ganzheitliche, historisch-kritische Lektüre von 1 Regum XVII-XIX. *VT* 47: 277-292.

—— 2000. Die Nabothüberlieferungen und die Kompositionsgeschichte der Vorderen Propheten. In: Kratz, G.R., Krüger, T., and Schmid, K. Eds. *Schriftauslegung in der Schrift. Festschrift für Odil Hannes Steck zu seinem 65. Geburtstag.* (BZAW 300). Berlin/New York: 111-128.

Boaretto, E. 2006. Radiocarbon Investigations. In: Finkelstein, I., Ussishkin, D. and Halpern, B. Eds. *Megiddo IV: 1998-2002 Seasons.* Tel Aviv: 550-557.

Boaretto, E., Jull, A.J.T., Gilboa, A., and Sharon, I. 2005. Dating the Iron Age I/II Transition in Israel: First Intercomparison Results. *Radiocarbon* 47: 39-55.

Boas, A.J. and Maeir, A. 1998. The Renewed Excavations at Tell e-Safi/Gath. In: Ackermann, O. Ed. *The Judaean Shephelah – Man, Nature and Landscape. Proceedings of the Eighteennth Annual Conference of the Martin (Szusz) Department of Land of Israel Studies. May 19th 1998.* Ramat-Gan: 31-37 (Hebrew).

Bohlen, R. 1978. *Der Fall Nabot. Form, Hintergrund und Werdegang einer alttestamentlichen Erzählung (1 Kön 21).* (TThSt 35). Trier.

Bordreuil, P. 1998. Amos 1:5: la Beqaʿ septentrionale de l'Eden au paradis. *Syria* 75: 55-59.

Borger, R. 1956. *Die Inschriften Asarhaddons, Königs von Assyrien* (AfOB 9). Osnabrück.

—— 1967. *Handbuch der Keilschriftliteratur, I. Repertorium der sumerischen und akkadischen Texte.* Berlin.

Borger, R. and Tadmor, H. 1982. Zwei Beiträge zur alttestamentlichen Wissenschaft aufgrund der Inschriften Tiglathpilesers III. *ZAW* 94: 244-251.

Brandl, B. 2009. An Israelite Administrative Jar Handle Impression from Bethsaida (et-Tell). In: Arav, R. and Freund, R.A. Eds. *Bethsaida. A City by the North Shore of the Sea of Galilee.* Vol. 4. Kirksville: 136-146.

Briend, J. 1981. Jéroboam II, sauveur d'Israël. In: Caquot, A. and Delcor, M. Eds. *Mélanges bibliques et orientaux en l'honneur de M. Henri Cazelles.* (AOAT 212). Neukirchen-Vluyn: 41-49.

Brinkman, J.A. 1968. *A Political History of Post-Kassite Babylonia 1158-722 B.C.* (AnOr 43). Rome.

Bron, F. and Lemaire, A. 1989. Les inscriptions araméennes de Hazaël. *RA* 83: 35-44.

Bruins, J.H., van der Plicht, J. and Mazar, A. 2003. ^{14}C Dates from Tel Rehov: Iron-Age Chronology, Pharaohs, and Hebrew Kings. *Science* 300: 315-318.

Bruins, J.H., van der Plicht, J., Mazar, A., Ramsey, C.B., and Manning, S.W. 2005. The Groningen Radiocarbon Series from Tel Reḥov: OxCal Bayesian Computations for the Iron IB-IIA Boundary and Iron IIA Destruction Events. In: Levy, T.E. and Higham, T. Eds. *The Bible and Radiocarbon Dating: Archaeology, Text and Science.* London: 271-293.

Buccellati, G. 1967. *Cities and Nations of Ancient Syria.* Rome.

Bunimovitz, S. and Faust, A. 2001. Chronological Separation, Geographical Segregation, or Ethnic Demarcation? – Ethnography and the Iron Age Low Chronology. *BASOR* 322: 1-10.

Bunimovitz, S. and Lederman, Z. 2001. The Iron Age Fortifications of Tel Beth Shemesh: A 1900-2000 Perspective. *IEJ* 51: 121-147.

—— 2006. The Early Israelite Monarchy in the Sorek Valley: Tel Beth-Shemesh and Tel Batash (Timanh) in the 10th and 9th Centuries BCE. In: Maeir, A.M. and de Miroschedji, P. Eds. *"I Will Speak the Riddle of Ancient Times": Archaeological and Historical Studies in Honor of Amihai Mazar on the Occasion of His Sixtieth Birthday*, Vol. 2. Winona Lake: 407-428.

—— 2009. The Archaeology of Border Communities: Renewed Excavations at Tel Beth-Shemesh, Part 1: The Iron Age. *NEA* 72: 114-142.

—— 2011. Close Yet Apart: Diverse Cultural Dynamics at Iron Age Beth-Shemesh and Lachish. In: Finkelstein, I. and Na'aman, N. Eds. *The Fire Signals of Lachish: Studies in the Archaeology and History of Israel in the Late Bronze Age, Iron Age and Persian Period in Honor of David Ussishkin.* Winona Lake: 33-53.

Burney, C.F. 1903. *Notes on the Hebrew Text of the Book of Kings with an Introduction and Appendix*. Oxford.

Cahill, J.M. 2006. The Excavations at Tell el-Hammah: A Prelude to Amihai Mazar's Beth-Shean Valley Regional Project. In: Maeir, A.M. and de Miroschedji, P. Eds. *"I Will Speak the Riddles of Ancient Times": Archaeological and Historical Studies in Honor of Amihai Mazar*, Vol. 2. Winona Lake: 429-459.

Campbell, A.F. 1986. *Of Prophets and Kings. A Late Ninth-Century Document (1 Samuel 1-2 Kings 10)*. (CBQMS 17). Washington.

Campbell, A.F. and O'Brien, M.A. 2000. *Unfolding the Deuteronomistic History: Origins, Upgrades, Present Text*. Minneapolis.

Cantrell, D.O. and Finkelstein, I. 2006. A Kingdom for a Horse: the Megiddo Stables and Eighth Century Israel. In: Finkelstein, I., Ussishkin, D. and Halpern, B. Eds. *Megiddo IV: 1998-2002 Seasons*. Tel Aviv: 643-665.

Caquot, A. 1961. Osée et la royauté. *RHPR* 41: 123-146.

Caquot, A. and Lemaire, A. 1977. Les texts araméens de Deir 'Alla. *Syria* 54: 189-208.

Carmi, I. and Segal, D. 1996. ^{14}C Dating of an Israelite Biblical Site at Kuntillet 'Ajrud (Horvat Teiman): Correction, Extension and Improved Age Estimate. *Radiocarbon* 38: 385-386.

—— 2000. Radiocarbon Dates. In: Finkelstein, I., Ussishkin, D. and Halpern, D. Eds. *Megiddo III: The 1992-1996 Seasons*. Tel Aviv: 502-503.

Cazelles, H. 1969. Une nouvelle stèle d'Adad-nirari d'assyrie et Joas d'Israël. *CRAIBL*: 106-114.

Chambon, A. 1984. *Tell el-Far'ah I – l'âge du fer*. Éditions Recherche sur les Civilisations 31. Paris.

Charbonnet, A. 1986. Le dieu aus lions d'Erétrie. *Annali del Dipartimento di Studi del Mondo Classico e del Mediterraneo Antico, Sezione di Archeologia e Storia Antica de l'Université de Naples* 8: 117-156, Pls. 33-41.

Charlesworth, J.H. 1992. Rechabites, History of. *ABD* V: 632-633.

Cody, A. 1970. A New Inscription from Tell āl-Rimaḥ and King Jehoash of Israel. *CBQ* 32: 325-340.

Cogan, M. 1983. "Ripping Open Pregnant Women" in Light of an Assyrian Analogue. *JAOS* 103: 755-757.

—— 2001. *I Kings*. New York.

Cogan, M. and Tadmor, H. 1988. *II Kings*. New York.

Cohen, S. 1965. The Political Background of the Words of Amos. *HUCA* 36: 153-160.

Cole, S.W. 1997. The Destruction of Orchards in Assyrian Warfare. In: Parpola, S. and Whiting, R.M. Eds. *Assyria 1995: Proceedings of the 10th Anniversary Symposium of the Neo-Assyrian Text Corpus Project, Helsinki, September 7–11, 1995.* Helsinki: 29-40.

Coote, R.B. 1981. *Amos Among the Prophets: Composition and Theology.* Philadelphia.

Cross, F.M. 1973. *Canaanite Myth and Hebrew Epic. Essays in the History of the Religion of Israel.* Harvard.

Crowfoot, J.W. and Crowfoot, G.M. 1938. *Early Ivories from Samaria.* London.

Crowfoot, J.W., Crowfoot, G.M., and Kenyon, K.M. 1957. *The Objects from Samaria.* London.

Crowfoot, J.W., Kenyon, K.M., and Sukenik, E.L. 1942. *The Buildings of Samaria.* London.

Crüsemann, F. 1971. Kritik an Amos im deuteronomistischen Geschichtswerk. Erwägungen zu 2. Könige 14,27. In: Wolff, H.W. Ed. *Probleme biblischer Theologie. Gerhard von Rad zum 70. Geburtstag.* München: 57-63.

Cryer, F.H. 1994. On the Recently-Discovered "House of David" Inscription. *SJOT* 8: 3-19.

—— 1995. King Hadad. *SJOT* 9: 223-235.

—— 1996. Of Epistemology, Northwest-Semitic Epigraphy and Irony: The *'bytdwd*/House of David' Inscription Revisited. *JSOT* 69: 3-17.

Culley, R.C. 1976. *Studies in the Structure of Hebrew Narrative.* (Semeia Supplements 3). Missoula.

Dalley, S. 2000. Shamshi-ilu, Language and Power in the Western Assyrian Empire. In: Bunnens, G. Ed. *Essays on Syria in the Iron Age.* (ANESS 7). Louvain/Paris/Sterling: 79-88.

Dalley, S. and Postgate, J.N. 1984. *The Tablets from Fort Shalmaneser.* (CTN III). Oxford.

Daviau, P.M.M. 1997. Moab's Borthern Border: Khirbat al-Mudayna on the Wadi ath-Thamad. *BA* 60: 222-228.

Daviau, P.M.M. and Steiner, M. 2000. A Moabite Sanctuary at Khirbat al-Mudayna. *BASOR* 320: 1-21.

Davies, P.R. 1992. *In Search of "Ancient Israel".* (JSOTS 148). Sheffield.

Davis, J.D. 1891. The Moabite Stone and the Hebrew Records. *Hebraica* 7: 178-182.

Day, J. 1986. Pre-Deuteronomic Allusions to the Covenant in Hosea and Psalm LXXVIII. *VT* 36: 1-12.

Dearman, J.A. 1984. The Location of Jahaz. *ZDPV* 100: 122-126.

—— 1989. Historical Reconstruction and the Mesha Inscription. In: Dearman, J.A. Ed. *Studies in the Mesha Inscription and Moab*. Atlanta: 155-210.

—— 1992a. Jahaz. *ABD* III: 612.

—— 1992b. Horonaim. *ABD* III: 289.

Debus, J. 1967. *Die Sünde Jerobeams. Studien zur Darstellung Jerobeams und der Geschichte des Nordreichs in der deuteronomistischen Geschichtsschreibung*. Göttingen.

Delsman, W.C. 1985. Aramäische historische Inschriften. *TUAT I*, 6: 625-637.

Demsky, A. 1995. On Reading Ancient Inscriptions: The Monumental Aramaic Stele Fragment from Tel Dan. *JNES* 23: 29-35.

De Odorico, M. 1995. *The Use of Numbers and Quantifications in the Assyrian Royal Inscriptions*. (SAAS 3). Helsinki.

Dever, W.G. 1993. Gezer. *NEAEHL* 2: 496-506.

—— 2003. Visiting the Real Gezer: A Reply to Israel Finkelstein. *TA* 30: 259-282.

Dietrich, W. 1972. *Prophetie und Geschichte. Eine redactionsgeschichtliche Untersuchung zum deuteronomistischen Geschichtswerk*. Göttingen.

Dion, P.-E. 1995. Syro-Palestinian Resistance to Shalmaneser III in the Light of New Documents. *ZAW* 107: 482-489.

—— 1997. *Les Araméens à l'âge du fer. Histoire politique et structures sociales* (Études bibliques nouvelle série 34). Paris.

—— 1999. The Tel Dan Stele and Its Historical Significance. In: Avishur, Y. and Deutsch, R. Eds. *Michael. Historical, Epigraphical and Biblical Studies in Honor of Prof. Michael Heltzer*. Tel Aviv: 145-156.

Dion, P.E. and Daviau, P.M.M. 2000. An Inscribed Incense Altar of Iron Age II at *Hirbet el-Mudēyine* (Jordan). *ZDPV* 116: 1-13, Pls. 1-2.

Donbaz, V. 1990. Two Neo-Assyrian Stelae in the Antakya and Kahramanmaraş Museums. *ARRIM* 8: 5-24.

Donner, H. 1964. *Israel unter den Völkern: Die Stellung der klassischen Propheten des 8. Jahrhunderts v.Chr. zur Aussenpolitik der Könige von Israel und Juda*. (VTS 11). Leiden.

—— 1970. Adadnirari III. und die Vasallen des Westens. In: Kuschke, A. and Kutsch, E. Eds. *Archäologie und Altes Testament* (Festschrift für Kurt Galling zum 8. Januar 1970). Tübingen.

—— 1977. The Separate States of Israel and Judah. In: Hayes, J.H. and Miller, J.M. Eds. *Israelite and Judean History*. London: 381-434.

Drinkard, J.F. 1989. The Literary Genre of the Mesha Inscription. In: Dearman, A. Ed. *Studies in the Mesha Inscription and Moab.* Atlanta: 131-154.

Dupont-Sommer, A. 1949. *Les Araméens.* Paris.

Dussaud, R. 1922. La stele araméenne de Zakir. *Syria* 3: 175-176.

—— 1927. *Topographie historique de la Syrie antique et médiévale.* Paris.

—— 1952. Review: "Avi-Yonah, Mount Carmel and the God of Baalbek, Extr. d'Israel Exploration Journal, II, 2 (1952), pp. 118-124". *Syria* 29: 384-386.

Edelman, D.V. 1992a. Abel-Meholah. *ABD* I: 11-12.

—— 1992b. Jabesh-Gilead. *ABD* III: 594-595.

—— 1992c. Lo-debar. *ABD* IV: 345-346.

Ehrlich, C.S. 2002. Die Suche nach Gat und die neuen Ausgrabungen auf Tell eṣ-Ṣāfī. In: Hübner, U. And Knauf, E.A. Eds. *Kein Land für sich allein – Studien zum Kulturkontakt in Kanaan, Israel/Palästina und Ebirnâri für Manfred Weippert zum 65. Geburtstag.* (OBO 186). Freiburg Schweiz/Göttingen: 56-69.

Eissfeldt, O. 1965. *The Old Testament. An Introduction.* New York.

—— 1968. *Kleine Schriften zum Alten Testament,* IV. Tübingen.

Elat, M. 1975. The Campaigns of Shalmaneser III against Aram and Israel. *IEJ* 25: 25-35.

—— 1977. *Economic Relations in the Lands of the Bible, c. 1000–539 B.C.* Jerusalem. (Hebrew).

—— 1982. The Impact of Tribute and Booty on Countries and People within the Assyrian Empire. In: Hirsch, H. and Hunger, H. Eds. *Vorträge gehalten auf der 28. Rencontre Assyriologique Internationale in Wien 6.-10. Juli 1981.* (AfOB 19). Horn: 244-251.

Elayi, J. 1981. Ba'lira'si, Rêsha, Reshba'l, étude de toponymie historique. *Syria* 58: 331-341.

Elliger, K. 1957. Eine verkannte Kunstform bei Hosea (Zur Einheit von Hos 5₁f.). *ZAW* 69: 151-160.

Emmerson, G.I. 1984. *Hosea: An Israelite Prophet in Judean Perspective.* (JSOTS 28). Sheffield.

Eph'al, I. 1984. *The Ancient Arabs: Nomads on the Borders of the Fertile Crescent 9th–5th Century B.C.* Jerusalem.

—— 1991. "The Samarian(s)" in the Assyrian Sources. In: Cogan, M. and Eph'al, I. Eds. *Ah, Assyria… Studies in Assyrian History and Ancient Near Eastern Historiography Presented to Hayim Tadmor.* (ScrHier 33). Jerusalem: 36-45.

Eph'al, I. and Naveh, J. 1989. Hazael's Booty Inscriptions. *IEJ* 39: 192-200, Pls. 24-25.

—— 1993. The Jar of the Gate. *BASOR* 289: 59-65.

Eskhult, M. 1990. *Studies in Verbal Aspect and Narrative Technique in Biblical Hebrew Prose.* Uppsala.

Ferch, A.J. 1992a. Nebo. *ABD* IV: 1056.

—— 1992b. Nimrim, the Waters of. *ABD* IV: 1116.

Finkelstein, I. 1988. *The Archaeology of the Israelite Settlement.* Jerusalem.

—— 1994. Penelope's Shroud Unravelled: Iron II Date of Gezer's Outer Wall Established. *TA* 21: 276-282.

—— 1995. The Date of the Settlement of the Philistines in Canaan. *TA* 22: 213-239.

—— 1996. The Archaeology of the United Monarchy: An Alternative View. *Levant* 28: 177-187.

—— 1998. Notes on the Stratigraphy and Chronology of Iron Age Ta'anach. *TA* 25: 208-218.

—— 1999. Hazor and the North in the Iron Age: A Low Chronology Perspective. *BASOR* 314: 55-70.

—— 2000. Omride Architecture. *ZDPV* 116: 114-138.

—— 2002. Gezer Revisited and Revised. *TA* 29: 262-296.

—— 2004. Tel Rehov and Iron Age Chronology. *Levant* 36: 181-188.

—— 2005. A Low Chronology Update: Archaeology, History and Bible. In: Levy, T.E. and Higham, T. Eds. *The Bible and Radiocarbon Dating: Archaeology, Text and Science.* London: 31-42.

Finkelstein, I. and Na'aman, N. 1994. *From Nomadism to Monarchy: Archaeological and Historical Aspects of Early Israel.* Jerusalem.

—— 2005. Shechem of the Amarna Period and the Rise of the Northern Kingdom of Israel. *IEJ* 55: 172-193.

Finkelstein, I. and Piasetzky, E. 2003a. Recent Radiocarbon Results and King Solomon. *Antiquity* 77: 771-779.

—— 2003b. Comment on "14C Dates from Tel Rehov: Iron-Age Chronology, Pharaohs, and Hebrew Kings". *Science* 302: 568.

—— 2003c. Wrong and Right; High and Low 14C Dates from Tel Rehov and Iron-Age Chronology. *TA* 30: 283-295.

—— 2006a. The Iron I-IIA in the Highlands and Beyond: 14C Anchors, Pottery Phases and the Shoshenq I Campaign. *Levant* 38: 45-61.

——— 2006b. ¹⁴C and the Iron Age Chronology Debate: Rehov, Khirbet en-Nahas, Dan, and Megiddo. *Radiocarbon* 48: 373-386.

——— 2007. Radiocarbon, Iron IIa Destructions and the Israel – Aram Damascus Conflicts in the 9th Century BCE. *UF* 39: 261-276.

——— 2008. The Date of Kuntillet 'Ajrud: The ¹⁴C Perspective. *TA* 35: 175-185.

——— 2009. Radiocarbon-Dated Destruction Layers: A Skeleton for Iron Age Chronology in the Levant. *Oxford Journal of Archaeology* 28: 255-274.

——— 2010a. Radiocarbon Dating the Iron Age in the Levant: A Bayesian Model for Six Ceramic Phases and Six Transitions. *Antiquity* 84: 374-385.

——— 2010b. The Iron I/IIA Transition in the Levant: A Reply to Mazar and Ramsey and a New Perspective. *Radiocarbon* 52: 1667-1680.

——— 2011. The Iron Age Chronology Dabate: Is the Gap Narrowing? *NEA* 74: 50-54.

Finkelstein, I. and Singer-Avitz, L. 2009. Reevaluating Bethel. *ZDPV* 125: 33-48.

Finkelstein, I., Ussishkin, D., and Halpern, B. Eds. 2000. *Megiddo III: 1992–1996 Seasons.* Tel Aviv.

——— 2006a. *Megiddo IV: 1998–2002 Seasons.* Tel Aviv.

——— 2006b. Archaeological and Historical Conclusions. In: Finkelstein, I., Ussishkin, D. and Halpern, B. Eds. *Megiddo IV: 1998–2002 Seasons.* (MSIATU 24). Tel Aviv: 843-859.

Fischer, C.S. 1929. *The Excavation of Armageddon.* Chicago.

Fitzmyer, J.A. 1978. Review of Hoftijzer and van der Kooij 1976. *CBQ* 40: 93-95.

Fohrer, G. 1957. *Elia.* (ATHANT 53). Zürich.

Franklin, N. 2008. Jezreel: Before and after Jezebel. In: Grabbe, L.L. Ed. *Israel in Transition: From Late Bronze II to Iron IIa (c. 1250–850 B.C.E.). Volume 1. The Archaeology.* (LHBOTS 491). New York/London: 45-53.

Franklyn, P.N. 1992. Ataroth. *ABD* I: 510.

Fretz, M.J. 1992. Adam. *ABD* I: 64.

Freud, L. 2008. The Date of Kuntillet 'Ajrud: A Reply to Lily Singer-Avitz. *TA* 35: 169-174.

Friedrich, J. 1966. Zu der altaramäischen Stele des ZKR von Hamat. *AfO* 21: 83.

Fritz, V. 1990. *Kinneret: Ergebnisse der Ausgrabungen auf dem Tell el-'Oreme am See Gennesaret, 1982–1985.* (ADP 15). Wiesbaden.

——— 1993. Kinneret: Excavations at Tell el-'Oreimeh (Tel Kinrot) 1982–1985 Seasons. *TA* 20: 187-215.

——— 1998. *Das Zweite Buch der Könige.* Zürich.

Fritz, V. and Davies, P.R. Eds. 1996. *The Origins of the Ancient Israelite States.* (JSOTS 228). Sheffield.

Fritz, V. and Münger, S. 2002. Vorbericht über die zweite Phase der Ausgrabungen in Kinneret (Tell el-'Orēme) am See Gennesaret, 1994–1999. *ZDPV* 118: 2-32.

Fuchs, A. 1994. *Die Inschriften Sargons II. aus Khorsabad.* Göttingen.

—— 2008. Der Turtan Šamšī-ilu und die große Zeit der assyrischen Großen (830–746). *WO* 38: 61-145.

Gal, Z. 1992. *Lower Galilee during the Iron Age.* (ASOR Dissertation Series. Vol. 8). Winona Lake.

Galil, G. 1996. *The Chronology of the Kings of Israel and Judah.* (SHANE 9). Leiden/New York/Köln.

—— 2000. The Boundaries of Aram-Damascus in the 9th-8th Centuries BCE. In: Galil, G. and Weinfeld, M. Eds. *Studies in Historical Geography and Biblical Historiography Presented to Zecharia Kallai.* (VTS 81). Leiden/Boston/Köln: 35-41.

—— 2001a. *Israel and Assyria.* Haifa/Tel Aviv (Hebrew).

—— 2001b. A Re-arrangement of the Fragments of the Tel Dan Inscription and the Relations between Israel and Aram. *PEQ* 133: 16-21.

—— 2002. Shalmaneser III in the West. *RB* 109: 40-56.

—— 2007. David and Hazael: War, Peace, Stones and Memory. *PEQ* 139: 79-84.

Garelli, P. 1971. Nouveau coup d'œil sur Muṣur. In: Caquot, A. and Philonenko, M. Eds. *Hommages à A. Dupont-Sommer.* Paris: 37-48.

—— 1982. La propaganda royale assyrienne. *Akkadica* 27: 16-29.

Geyer, J.B. 2009. Another Look at the Oracles about the Nations in the Hebrew Bible. A Response to A. C. Hagedorn. *VT* 59: 80-87.

Gibson, J.C.L. 1971. *Textbook of Syrian Semitic Inscriptions. Volume I. Hebrew and Moabite Inscriptions.* Oxford.

—— 1975. *Textbook of Syrian Semitic Inscriptions. Volume II. Aramaic Inscriptions Including Inscriptions in the Dialect of Zenjirli.* Oxford.

Gilboa, A. and Sharon, I. 2001. Early Iron Age Radiometric Dates from Tel Dor: Preliminary Implications for Phoenicia and Beyond. *Radiocarbon* 43: 1343-1451.

—— 2003. An Archaeological Contribution to the Early Iron Age Chronological Debate: Alternative Chronologies for Phoenicia and Their Effects on the Levant, Cyprus, and Greece. *BASOR* 332: 7-80.

Gilboa, A., Sharon, I. and Zorn, J. 2004. Dor and Iron Age Chronology: Scarabs, Ceramic Sequence and ¹⁴C. *TA* 31: 32-59.

Glueck, N. 1943. Some Ancient Towns in the Plains of Moab. *BASOR* 91: 7-26.

Good, E.M. 1966. Hosea 5 ₈-6 ₆: An Alternative to Alt. *JBL* 85: 273-286.

Gordis, R. 1971. The Composition and Structure of Amos. In: Gordis, R. Ed. *Poets, Prophets and Sages: Essays in Biblical Interpretations.* Blooming-ton/London: 217-229.

Gordon, C.H. and Rendsburg, G. 1997. *The Bible and the Ancient Near East.* New York.

Goren, Y. 1995. Petrographic Analyses of Horvat Teiman (Kuntillet ʿAjrud) Pot-tery. *TA* 22: 206-207.

Gosse, B. 1988. Le recueil d'oracles contre les nations du livre d'Amos et l'"histoire deuteronomistique". *VT* 38: 22-40.

—— 1994. 2 Rois 14:27 et l'influence des livres prophétiques sur la rédaction du dexième livre des Rois. *OTE* 7: 167-174.

Gray, J. 1977. *I & II Kings. A Commentary.* 3rd, Fully Revised Ed. London.

Grayson, A.K. 1975. *Assyrian and Babylonian Chronicles.* Locus Valley/A.K. 1976. Glückstadt.

—— 1976. Studies in Neo-Assyrian History: The Ninth Century B.C. *BiOr* 33: 134-145.

—— 1993. Assyrian Officials and Power in the Ninth and Eighth Centuries. *SAAB* 7: 19-52.

Green, A.R. 1979. Sua and Jehu: The Boundaries of Shalmaneser's Conquest. *PEQ* 111: 35-39, Pls. IV-VI.

Greenfield, J.C. 1980. Review of Hoftijzer and van der Kooij 1976. *JSS* 25: 248-252.

Gressmann, H. 1921. *Die älteste Geschichtschreibung und Prophetie Israels.* 2nd Ed. Göttingen.

Gross, W. 1981. Syntaktische Erscheinungen am Anfang althebräischer Er-zählungen: Hintergrund und Vordergrund. In: Emerton, J.A. Ed. *Congress Volume Vieena 1980.* (VTS 32). Leiden: 131-145.

Gunkel, H. 1906. *Elia, Yahwe und Baal.* Tübingen.

—— 1913. Die Revolution des Jehu. *Deutsche Rundschau* 40: 289-308.

Gunneweg, J., Perlman, I. and Meshel, Z. 1985. The Origin of the Pottery of Kuntillet ʿAjrud. *IEJ* 35: 270-283.

Guy, P.L.O. 1931. *New Light from Armageddon.* (OIC 9). Chicago.

Hackett, J.A. 1984a. *The Balaam Text from Deir 'Alla.* (HSM 31). Chico.

——— 1984b. The Dialect of the Plaster Text from Tell Deir 'Alla. *Or* 53: 57-65.

Hadley, J.M. 1987. Some Drawings and Inscriptions on two Pithoi from Kuntillet 'Ajrud. *VT* 37: 180-213.

——— 1993. Kuntillet 'Ajrud: Religious Centre or Desert Way Station? *PEQ* 125: 115-124.

Hafthorsson, S. 2006. *A Passing Power: An Examination of the Sources for the History of Aram-Damascus in the Second Half of the Ninth Century B.C.* (CB 54). Stockholm.

Hallo, W.W. 1960. From Qarqar to Carchemish: Assyria and Israel in the Light of New Discoveries. *BA* 23: 34-61.

Halpern, B. 1987. Dialect Distribution in Canaan and the Deir Alla Inscriptions. In: Golomb, D.M. Ed. *"Working With No Data": Semitic and Egyptian Studies Presented to Thomas O. Lambdin.* Winona Lake: 119-139.

——— 1994. The Stela from Dan: Epigraphic and Historical Considerations. *BASOR* 296: 63-80.

——— 2001. The Taking of Nothing: 2 Kings 14.25, Amos 6.14 and the Geography of the Deuteronomistic History. In: Daviau, P.M.M., Wevers, J.W., and Weigl, M. Eds. *The World of the Aramaeans I: Biblical Studies in Honour of Paul-Eugène Dion.* (JSOTS 324). Sheffield: 186-204.

Halpern, B. and Vanderhooft, D.A. 1992. The Editions of Kings in the 7th–6th Centuries B.C.E. *HUCA* 62: 179-244.

Hämeen-Anttila, J. 2000. *A Sketch of Neo-Assyrian Grammar.* (SAAS 13). Helsinki.

Hammershaimb, E. 1970. *The Book of Amos.* Oxford.

Handy, L.K. Ed. 1997 *The Age of Solomon: Scholarship at the Turn of the Millennium.* (SHANE 11). Leiden/New York/Köln.

Haran, M. 1967. The Rise and Decline of the Empire of Jeroboam Ben Joash. *VT* 17: 266-297.

——— 1968. Observations on the Historical Background of Amos 1:2-2:6. *IEJ* 18: 201-212.

Harrak, A. 1992. Des noms d'année araméen? *WO* 23: 67-73.

Harrison, T.P. 2001. Tell Ta'yinat and the Kingdom of Unqi. In: Daviau, P.M.M., Wevers, J.W., and Weigl, M. Eds. *The World of the Aramaeans II: Studies in History and Archaeology in Honour of Paul-Eugène Dion.* (JSOTS 324). Sheffield: 115-132.

Hasegawa, S. 2006. Historical Reality vs. Theological Message: Deuteronomist's Insertions in 2 Kgs 9:27-28. *AJBI* 32: 5-14.

—— 2007. The Relations between Amos 6:13-14 and 2 Kgs 14:25-28. *AJBI* 33: 93-102.

—— 2008. Adad-nērārī III's Fifth Year in the Saba'a Stela: Historiographical Background. *RA* 102: 89-98.

—— 2010a. The Numbers of the Israelite Army in the Time of Joahaz: Is II Reg 13,7 Derived From an Archival Source? *Orient* 45: 35-39.

—— 2010b. Historical and Historiographical Notes on the Pazarcık Stela. *Akkadica* 131: 1-9.

—— *forthcoming*. Looking for Aphek in 1 Kgs 20. *VT*.

Hasegawa, S. and Paz, Y. 2009. Tel 'En Gev: Preliminary Report. *HA-ESI* 121.

Hawkins, J.D. 1972-75a. Hattin. *RlA* 4: 160-162.

—— 1972-75b. Hazazu. *RlA* 4: 240.

—— 1974. Assyrians and Hittites. *Iraq* 36: 67-83.

—— 1981. Kullani(a). *RlA* 6: 305-306.

—— 1982. The Neo-Hittite States in Syria and Anatolia. In: *The Cambridge Ancient History*, Vol. III, Part I. Cambridge: 372-441.

—— 1983. Kummuḫ. *RlA* 6: 338-340.

—— 1995. The Political Geography of North Syria and South-East Anatolia in the Neo-Assyrian Period. In: Liverani, M. Ed. *Neo-Assyrian Geography*. Roma: 87-101.

Hennessy, J.B. 1970. Excavations at Samaria-Sebaste, 1968. *Levant* 2: 1-21.

Hentschel, G. 1977. *Die Elijaerzählungen zum Verhältnis von historischem Geschehen und geschichtlicher Erfahrung*. Leipzig.

—— 1985. *2 Könige*. Würzburg.

Herzog, Z. and Singer-Avitz, L. 2004. Redefining the Centre: The Emergence of State in Judah. *TA* 31: 209-244.

Hindawi, A.N. 2007. The Iron Age of the Northern Jordanian Plateau. *UF* 39: 451-479.

Hobbs, T.R. 1985. *2 Kings*. (WBC 13). Waco.

Höffken, P. 1982. Eine Bemerkung zum »Haus Hasaels« in Amos 1₄. *ZAW* 94: 413-415.

Hoffmann, H.-D. 1980. *Reform und Reformen. Untersuchungen zu einem Grundthema der deuteronomistischen Geschichtsschreibung*. (ATHANT 66). Zürich.

Hoftijzer, J. and van der Kooij, G. 1976. *Aramaic Texts from Deir 'Alla*. (DMOA 19). Leiden.

Holden, C. 2003. Dates Boost Conventional Wisdom about Solomon's Splendor. *Science* 300: 229, 231.

Hölscher, G. 1923. Das Buch der Könige, seine Quellen und seine Redaktion. In: Schmidt, H. Ed. *Eucharisterion*. Fs. H. Gunkel. (FRLANT 36/1). Göttingen: 184-186.

—— 1930. *Marsyas. 5. Paulys Real-Encyclopädie der classischen Altertumswissenschaft*, XIV/2, Stuttgart: Col. 1986.

Hommel, F. 1885. *Geschichte Babyloniens und Assyriens*. Berlin.

Honigmann, E. 1924. Historische Topographie von Nordsyrien im Altertum. *ZDVP* 47: 1-64.

—— 1928. Ba'albek. *RlA* 1: 327-328.

—— 1938. Danabi. *RlA* 2: 116.

Horowitz, W. and Oshima, T. 2006. *Cuneiform in Canaan: Cuneiform Sources from the Land of Israel in Ancient Times*. Jerusalem.

Hrozný, F.(B). 1904. Keilschrifttexte aus Ta'annek; Nr. 1-4. Wien.

Hübner, U. 1992. *Die Ammoniter. Untersuchungen zur Geschichte, Kultur und Religion eines transjordanischen Volkes im 1. Jahrtausend v.Chr.* (ADP 16). Wiesbaden.

Hughes, J. 1990. *Secrets of the Times: Myth and History in Biblical Chronology*. (JSOTS 66). Sheffield.

Ibrahim, M.M. and van der Kooij, G. 1991. The Archaeology of Deir 'Alla Phase IX. In: Hoftijzer, J. and van der Kooij, G. Eds. *The Balaam Text from Deir 'Alla Re-Evaluated. Proceedings of the International Symposium Held at Leiden 21–24 August 1989*. Leiden: 16-29.

Ikeda, Y. 1977. *The Kingdom of Hamath and Its Relations with Aram and Israel*, Unpublished Ph.D. Thesis. Jerusalem (Hebrew).

—— 1978. Hermon, Sirion and Senir. *AJBI* 4: 32-44.

—— 1994. Once Again *KTK* in the Sefire Inscriptions. *EI* 24: 104*-108*.

—— 1999. Looking from Til Barsip on the Euphrates: Assyria and the West in Ninth and Eighth Centuries B.C. In: Watanabe, K. Ed. *Priests and Officials in the Ancient Near East. Papers of the Second Colloquium on the Ancient Near East – The City and its Life held at the Middle Eastern Culture Center in Japan (Mitaka, Tokyo). March 22–24, 1996*. Heidelberg: 271-302.

—— 2003. "They Divided the Orontes River between them." Arpad and its Borders with Hamath and Patin/Unqi in the Eighth Century BCE. *EI* 27: 91*-99*.

Ilan, D. 1999. *Northeastern Israel in the Iron Age I: Cultural, Socioeconomic and Political Perspectives*. Vol. I. Unpublished Ph. D. Thesis, Tel Aviv University. Tel Aviv.

Irvine, S.A. 1990. *Isaiah, Ahaz, and the Syro-Ephraimitic Crisis*. (SBLDS 123). Atlanta

——— 1994. The Southern Border of Syria Reconstructed. *CBQ* 56: 21-41.

——— 1995. The Threat of Jezreel (Hosea 1:4-5). *CBQ* 57: 494-503.

——— 2001. The Rise of the House of Jehu. In: Dearman, J.A. and Graham, M.P. Eds. *The Land that I Will Show You: Essays on the History and Archaeology of the Ancient Near East in Honour of J. Maxwell Miller.* (JSOTS 343). Sheffield: 104-118.

——— 2005. The Last Battle of Hadadezer. *JBL* 124: 341-347.

Ishida, T. 1969. The House of Ahab. *IEJ* 19: 135-137.

——— 1977. *The Royal Dynasties in Ancient Israel: A Study of the Formation and Development of Royal-Dynastic Ideology.* (BZAW 142). Berlin/New York.

James, F.W. 1966. *The Iron Age at Beth-Shan: A Study of Levels VI-IV.* Philadelphia.

James, P. 2008. The Alleged "Anchor Point" of 732 BC for the Destruction of Hazor V. *Antiguo Oriente* 6: 137-183.

Jepsen, A. 1934. *Nabi. Soziologische Studien zur alttestamentlichen Literatur und Religionsgeschichte.* München.

——— 1941-44. Israel und Damaskus. *AfO* 14: 153-172.

——— 1970. Ein neuer Fixpunkt für die Chronologie der israelitischen Könige? *VT* 20: 359-361.

Jeremias, J. 1983. *Der Prophet Hosea.* (ATD 24/1). Göttingen.

Kallai, Z. 1962. Lo-dabar. *Encyclopaedia Biblica* 4: 409-410 (Hebrew).

Katzenstein, H.J. 1997. *The History of Tyre, from the Beginning of the Second Millennium B.C.E. until the Fall of the Neo-Babylonian Empire in 538 B.C.E.* 2nd and Revised Ed. Beer Sheva.

Kaufman, I.T. 1992. Samaria (Ostraca). *ABD* V: 921-926.

Kaufman, S.A. 1980. Review Article: The Aramaic Texts from Deir ʿAllā. *BASOR* 239: 71-74.

——— 1986. The Pitfalls of Typology: On the Early History of the Alphabet. *HUCA* 57: 1-14.

Keel, O. and Uehlinger, C. 1994. Der Assyrerkönig Salmanassar III. und Jehu von Israel auf dem Schwarzen Obelisken aus Nimrud. *ZKTh* 116: 391-420.

Kellermann, D. 1981. ʿAštārōt – ʿAštərōt Qarnayim – Qarnayim. *ZDPV* 97: 45-61.

Kessler, K. 1998-2001. Namar/Namri. *RlA* 9: 91-92.

Kinnier Wilson, J.V. 1972. *The Nimrud Wine Lists: A Study of Men and Administration at the Assyrian Capital in the Eighth Century B.C.* (CTN 1). London.

Kittel, R. 1900. *Die Bücher der Könige*. Handkommentar zum Alten Testament. Göttingen.

Klengel, H. 1992. *Syria 3000 to 300 B.C.: A Handbook of Political History*. Berlin.

Knauf, E.A. 2000. Kinneret and Naftali. In: Lemaire, A. and Sæbø, M. Eds. *Congress Volume. Oslo 1998*. (VTS 80). Leiden/Boston/Köln: 219-233.

―――― 2006. Bethel: The Israelite Impact on Judean Language and Literature. In: Lipschits, O. and Oeming, M. Eds. *Judah and the Judeans in the Persian Period*. Winona Lake: 291-349.

Knauf, E.A., de Pury, A., and Römer, T. 1994. *BaytDawîd ou *BaytDaōd? Une relecture de la nouvelle inscription de Tel Dan. *BN* 72: 60-69.

Knott, III, J.B. 1971. *The Jehu Dynasty: An Assessment Based upon Ancient Near Eastern Literature and Archeology*. Unpublished Ph.D. Thesis. Emory University.

Koch, K. 1976. Die Rolle der hymnischen Abschnitte in der Komposition des Amos-Buches. *ZAW* 86: 504-537

Kochavi, M. 1989. The Land of Geshur Project: Regional Archaeology of the Southern Golan (1987-1988 Seasons). *IEJ* 39: 1-17.

―――― 1991. The Land of Geshur Project, 1989-1990. *IEJ* 41: 180-184.

―――― 1993a. ʿEn Gev: Recent Excavations. *NEAEHL* 2: 411-412.

―――― 1993b. The Land of Geshur Project, 1992. *IEJ* 43: 185-190.

―――― 1994. The Land of Geshur Project, 1993. *IEJ* 44: 136-141.

―――― 1996. The Land of Geshur: History of a Region in the Biblical Period. *EI* 25: 184-201.

Kochavi, M., Renner, T., Spar, I., and Yadin, E. 1992. Rediscovered! The Land of Geshur. *BARev* 18-4: 30-44, 84-85.

Kochavi, M. and Tsukimoto, A. 2008. ʿEn Gev. *NEAEHL* 5: 1724-1726.

Kotter, W.R. 1992. Gilgal. *ABD* I: 1022-1024.

Kottsieper, I. 1998. Die Inschrift vom Tell Dan und die politischen Beziehungen zwischen Aram-Damaskus und Israel in der 1. Hälfte des 1. Jahrtausends vor Christus. In: Dietrich, M. and Loretz, O. Eds. *"Und Mose schrieb dieses Lied auf." Studien zum Alten Testament und zum Alten Orient*. (Festschrift für Oswald Loretz). (AOAT 250). Münster: 475-500.

―――― 2007. The Tel Dan Inscription (*KAI* 310) and the Political Relations between Aram-Damaskus and Israel in the First Half of the First Millennium BCE. In: Grabbe, L.L. Ed. *Ahab Agonistes: The Rise and Fall of the Omride Dynasty* (LHBOTS 421). London: 104-134.

Kraeling, E.G.H. 1918. *Aram and Israel or the Aramaeans in Syria and Mesopotamia*. (Reprinted in 1966). New York.

Kratz, R.G. 2000. *Die Komposition der erzählenden Bücher des Alten Testaments. Grundwissen der Bibelkritik.* (UTB 2157). Göttingen.

Krebernik, M. 2003-2005. ᵈPALIL(IGI.DU). *RlA* 10:281.

Kuan, J.K. 1995. *Neo-Assyrian Historical Inscriptions and Syria-Palestine.* (Jian Dao Dissertation Series 1). Hong Kong.

Kuenen, A. 1887. *The Prophets and Prophecy in Israel.* London.

—— 1890. *Historisch-kritische Einleitung in die Bücher des Alten Testaments hinsichtlich ihrer Entstehung und Sammlung.* I, 2. Leipzig.

Kühne, H. and Radner, K. 2008. Das Siegel des Išme-ilu, Eunuch des Nergal-ēreš, aus Dūr-Katlimmu. *ZA* 98: 26-44.

Kyrieleis, H. and Röllig, W. 1988. Ein altorientalischer Pferdeschmuck aus dem Heraion von Samos. *Mitteilungen des deutschen archäologischen Instituts, athenische Abteilung* 103:37-75, Pls. 9-15.

Lamb, D.T. 2007. *Righteous Jehu and His Evil Heirs: The Deuteronomist's Negative Perspective on Dynastic Succession.* Oxford.

Lamon, R.S. and Shipton, G.M. 1939. *Megiddo I.* (OIP 42). Chicago.

Lapp, P. 1964. The 1963 Excavations at Taʿannek. *BASOR* 173: 4-44.

—— 1967. The 1966 Excavations at Taʿannek. *BASOR* 185: 2-39.

—— 1969. The 1968 Excavations at Taʿannek. *BASOR* 195: 2-49.

Lehnart, B. 2003. *Prophet & König im Nordreich Israel. Studien zur sogenannten vorklassischen Prophetie im Nordreich Israel anhand der Samuel-, Elija- & Elischa-Überlieferungen.* (VTS 96). Leiden/Boston.

Lemaire, A. 1973. À propos d'une inscription de Tel ʿAmal. *RB* 80: 559.

—— 1977. *Inscriptions hébraïques I, Les Ostraca.* (LAPO 9). Paris.

—— 1984. Date et origine des inscriptions hebraiques et pheniciennes de Kuntillet ʿAjrud. *SEL* 1: 131-143.

—— 1985a. Notes d'épigraphie nord-ouest sémitique. *Semitica* 35: 13-17.

—— 1985b. Les inscriptions de Deir ʿAlla et la literature araméenne antique. *CEAIBL:* 270-285.

—— 1985c. Fragments from the Book of Balaam Found at Deir ʿAlla. *BARev* 11/5: 27-39.

—— 1987. Notes d'épigraphie nord-ouest sémitique. *Syria* 64: 205-216.

—— 1990. Trois sceaux inscrits inédits avec lion rugissant. *Semitica* 39: 12-22.

—— 1991a. Hazaël de Damas, roi d'Aram. In: Charpin, D. et Joannès, F. Eds. *Marchands, diplomats et empereurs. Études sur la civilisation mésopotamienne offertes à Paul Garelli.* Paris: 91-108.

—— 1991b. La stèle de Mésha et l'histoire de l'ancien Israël. In: Garrone, D. and Israel, F. Eds. *Storia e tradizioni di Israele. Scritti in onore di J. Alberto Soggin.* Brescia: 143-169.

—— 1991c. Les inscriptions sur plâtre de Deir 'Alla. In: Hoftijzer, J. and van der Kooij, G. Eds. *The Balaam Text from Deir 'Alla Re-Evaluated. Proceedings of the International Symposium held at Leiden 21-24 August 1989.* Leiden: 33-57.

—— 1993. Joas de Samarie, Barhadad de Damas, Zakkur de Hamat. La Syrie-Palestine vers 800 av. J.-C. *EI* 24: 148*-157*.

—— 1994. Épigraphie palestinienne: Nouveaux documents. I. Fragment de stele araméenne de Tell Dan (IXe s. av. J.-C.). *Henoch* 16: 87-93.

—— 1998. The Tel Dan Stela as a Piece of Royal Historiography. *JSOT* 81: 3-14.

—— 1999. Nouveaux sceaux et bulles paléo-hébraïques. *EI* 26: 106*-115*.

Lemaire, A. and Durand, J.-M. 1984. *Les inscriptions araméennes de Sfiré et l'Assyrie de Shamshi-ilu.* (Hautes etudes orientales 20). Paris.

Lemche, N.P. 1995. Bemerkungen über einen Paradigmenwechsel aus Anlaß einer neuentdecken Inschrift. In: Weippert, M. and Timm, S. Eds. *Meilenstein. Festgabe für Hebert Donner zum 16. Feburar 1995.* Wiesbaden: 99-108.

—— 1998. *The Israelites in History and Tradition.* Louisville.

Lemche, N.P. and Thompson, T.L. 1994. Did Biran Kill David? The Bible in the Light of Archaeology. *JSOT* 64: 3-22.

Levine, B.A. 1981. Review Article: The Deir 'Alla Plaster Inscriptions. *JAOS* 101: 195-205.

—— 1985. The Balaam Inscription from Deir 'Alla: Historical Aspects. In: *Biblical Archaeology Today. Proceedings of the Internatinal Congress on Biblical Archaeology. Jerusalem, April 1984.* Jerusalem: 326-339.

Levy, S. and Edelstein, G. 1972. Cinq années de fouilles à Tel 'Amal (Nir David). *RB* 79: 325-367.

Levy, T.E. and Higham, T. 2005. Introduction: Radiocarbon Dating and the Iron Age of the Southern Levant: Problems and Potentials for the Oxford Conference. In: Levy, T.E. and Higham, T. Eds. *The Bible and Radiocarbon Dating: Archaeology, Text and Science.* London: 3-14.

Lewy, J. 1927. *Die Chronologie der Könige der Könige von Israel und Juda.* Gießen.

Lidzbarski, M. 1915. *Ephemeris für semitische Epigraphik*, III. Gießen.

Lieberman, S.J. 1985. Giving Directions on the Black Obelisk of Shalmaneser III. *RA* 79: 88.

Limburg, J. 1987. Sevenfold Structures in the Book of Amos. *JBL* 106: 217-222.

Lipiński, É. 1969. Le Ben-hadad II de la bible et l'histoire. *Proceedings of the Fifth World Congress of Jewish Studies. The Hebrew University, Mount Scopus—Givat Ram, Jerusalem. Jerusalem, 3–11 August 1969.* Jerusalem. 1969: 157-173.

—— 1971a. Ba'li-ra'ši et Ra'šu Qudšu. *RB* 78: 84-92.

—— 1971b. The Assyrian Campaign to Manṣuate in 796 B.C. and the Zakir Stela. *AION* 31: 393-399.

—— 1979. Aram et Israël du Xᵉ au VIIIᵉ siècle av. N.È. *Acta Antiqua* 27: 47-102.

—— 1991. Jéroboam II et la Syrie. In: Garrone, D. and Israel, F. Eds. *Storia e tradizioni di Israele. Scritti in onore di J. Alberto Soggin.* Bresica: 171-176.

—— 1994. *Studies in Aramaic Inscriptions and Onomastics* II. (OLA 57). Leuven.

—— 1999. Ba'il. In: Radner, K. Ed. *The Prosopography of the Neo-Assyrian Empire.* Volume 1, Part II. Helsinki: 242.

—— 2000. *The Aramaeans. Their Ancient History, Culture, Religion.* (OLA 100). Leuven.

—— 2004. *Itineraria Phoenicia.* (OLA 127, Studia Phoenicia 18). Leuven/Paris/Dudley.

Lissovsky, N. and Na'aman, N. 2003. A New Outlook at the Boundary System of the Twelve Tribes. *UF* 35: 291-332.

Liverani, M. 1992. *Studies on the Annals of Ashurnasirpal II, 2: Topographical Analysis.* (Quaderni di Geografica Storica 4). Roma.

Long, B.O. 1976. Recent Field Studies in Oral Literature and Their Bearing on OT Criticism. *VT* 26: 187-198.

—— 1984. *1 Kings with an Introduction to Historical Literature.* Grand Rapids.

—— 1991. *2 Kings.* Grand Rapids.

Lord, A.B. 1960. *The Singer of Tales.* Cambridge.

Loud, G. 1948. *Megiddo II.* (OIP 62). Chicago.

Lust, J. 1981. Remarks on the Redaction of Amos v 4-6, 14-15. In: Albrektson, B. et al. *Remembering All the Way: A Collection of Old Testament Studies Published on the Occasion of the Fortieth Anniversary of the Oudtestamentisch Werkgezelschap in Nederland.* (OtSt 21). Leiden: 129-154.

MacDonald, B. 2000. *"East of the Jordan": Territories and Sites of the Hebrew Scriptures.* (ASOR Books 6). Boston.

Macintosh, A.A. 1997. *A Critical and Exegetical Commentary on Hosea.* (ICC). Edinburgh.

Maeir, A.M. 2001. The Philistine Culture in Transformation: A Current Perspective Based on the Results of the First Sessions of Excavations at Tell es-

Safi/Gath. In: Maeir, A.M. and Baruch, E. Eds. *Settlement, Civilization and Culture. Proceedings of the Conference in Memory of David Alon.* Ramat-Gan: 111-129. (Hebrew).

—— 2003. Notes and News: Tell eṣ-Ṣafi/Gath, 1996-2002. *IEJ* 53: 237-246.

—— 2004. The Historical Background and Dating of Amos VI 2: An Archaeological Perspective from Tell eṣ-Ṣâfî/Gath. *VT* 54: 319-334.

Maeir, A.M., Ackermann, O., and Bruins, H.J. 2006. The Ecological Consequences of a Siege: A Marginal Note on Deuteronomy 20:19-20. In: Gitin, S., Wright, J.E., and Dessel, J.P. Eds. *Confronting the Past: Archaeological and Historical Essays on Ancient Israel in Honor of William G. Dever.* Winona Lake: 238-243.

Maeir, A.M. and Ehrlich, C.S. 2001. Excavating Philistine Gath. Have We Found Goliath's Hometown? *BARev* 27-6: 22-31.

Maeir, A.M. and Gur-Arieh, S. Comparative Aspects of the Aramean Siege System at Tell eṣ-Ṣāfi/Gath. In: Finkelstein, I. and Na'aman, N. Eds. *The Fire Signals of Lachish: Studies in the Archaeology and History of Israel in the Late Bronze Age, Iron Age and Persian Period in Honor of David Ussishkin.* Winona Lake: 227-244.

Malamat, A. 1953. Amos 1:5 in the Light of the Til-Barsip Inscriptions. *BASOR* 129: 25-26.

—— 1964. Wars of Israel and Assyria. In: Liver, J. Ed. *Military History of the Land of Israel in Biblical Times.* Tel Aviv: 241-260 (Hebrew).

—— 1965a. The Campaign of the Mesopotamian Kings to the Phoenician Coast before the Rise of the Assyrian Empire. In: *West Galilee and the Coast of Galilee. The Nineteenth Archaeological Convention. October 1963.* Jerusalem: 76-93 (Hebrew).

—— 1965b. Campaigns to the Mediterranean by Iahdunlim and Other Early Mesopotamian Rulers. In: Güterbock, H.G. and Jacobsen, T. Eds. *Studies in Honor of Benno Landsberger on His Seventy-Fifth Birthday. April 21. 1965.* (Assyriological Studies 16). Chicago: 365-373.

Mallowan, M.E.L. 1966. *Nimrud and its Remains* 2. London.

Manor, D.W. 1992. Tirzah. *ABD* VI: 573-577.

Ma'oz, Z.U. 1992. Geshur. *ABD* II: 996.

Marcus, M.I. 1987. Geography as an Organizing Principle in the Imperial Art of Shalmaneser III. *Iraq* 49: 77-90, Pls. XVI-XXII.

Margalit, B. 1994. The OAram. Stele from t. Dan. *NABU* 1994/1: 20-21.

Master, D.M. 2001. State Formation Theory and the Kingdom of Ancient Israel. *JNES* 60: 117-131.

Mastin, B.A. 2009. The Inscriptions Written on Plaster at Kuntillet ʿAjrud. *VT* 59: 99-115.

Mattila, R. and Radner, K. 1998. Abi-rāmu or A(b)-rāmu. In: Radner, K. Ed. *The Prosopography of the Neo-Assyrian Empire*. Volume 1, Part I. Helsinki: 12-14.

Mattingly, G.L. 1992a. Kiriathaim. *ABD* IV: 85.

—— 1992b. Bezer. *ABD* I: 718-719.

—— 1992c. Beth-Diblathaim. *ABD* I: 683-684.

—— 1992d. Kerioth. *ABD* IV: 24.

Mazar, A. 1993. Beth Shean in the Iron Age: Preliminary Report and Conclusions of the 1990-1991 Excavations. *IEJ* 43: 201-229.

—— 1997. Iron Age Chronology: A Reply to I. Finkelstein. *Levant* 29: 157-167.

—— 1999. The 1997-1998 Excavations at Tel Rehov: Preliminary Report. *IEJ* 49: 1-42.

—— 2003a. Three 10th–9th Century B.C.E. Inscriptions From Tel Rehov. In: den Hertog, C.G., Hübner, U., and Münger. S. Eds. *Saxa loquentur: Studien zur Archäologie Palälastinas/Israels – Festchrift für Volkmar Fritz*. (AOAT 302). Münster: 171-184.

—— 2003b. The Excavations at Tel Reḥov and Their Significance for the Study of the Iron Age in Israel. *EI* 27: 143-160 (Hebrew).

—— 2005. The Debate over the Chronology of the Iron Age in the Southern Levant: Its History, the Current Situation, and a Suggested Resolution. In: Levy, T.E. and Higham, T. Eds. *The Bible and Radiocarbon Dating: Archaeology, Text and Science*. London: 15-30.

—— 2006. *Excavations at Tel Beth-Shean 1989–1996. Volume 1. From the Late Bronze Age IIB to the Medieval Period*. Jerusalem.

—— 2007. The Spade and the Text: The Interaction between Archaeology and Israelite History Relating to the Tenth-Ninth Centuries BCE. In: Williamson, H.G.M. Ed. *Understanding of the History of Ancient Israel*. (Proceedings of the British Academy 143). Oxford/New York: 143-171.

—— 2008. From 1200 to 850 B.C.E.: Remarks on Some Selected Archaeological Issues. In: Grabbe, L.L. Ed. *Israel in Transition: From Late Bronze II to Iron IIa (c. 1250–850 B.C.E.). Volume 1. The Archaeology*. (LHBOTS 491). New York/London: 86-120.

—— 2011. The Iron Age Chronology Debate: Is the Gap Narrowing? Another Viewpoint. *NEA* 74: 105-111.

Mazar, A., Bruins, H.J., Panitz-Cohen, N., and van der Plicht, J. 2005. Ladder of Time at Tel Reḥov. In: Levy, T.E. and Higham, T. Eds. *The Bible and Radiocarbon Dating: Archaeology, Text and Science*. London: 193-255.

Mazar, A. and Carmi, I. 2001. Radiocarbon Dates from Iron Age Strata at Tel Beth Shean and Tel Rehov. *Radiocarbon* 43-3: 1333-1341.

Mazar, A. and Ramsey, C.B. 2008. ¹⁴C Dates and the Iron Age Chronology of Israel: A Response. *Radiocarbon* 50: 159-180.

—— 2010. A Response to Finkelstein and Piasetzky's Criticism and "New Perspective". *Radiocarbon* 52: 1681-1688.

Mazar, B. 1961. Geshur and Maacha. *JBL* 80: 16-28.

—— 1962. The Aramean Empire and its Relations with Israel. *BA* 25: 98-120.

Mazar, B., Biran, A., Dothan, M., and Dunayevsky, I. 1964. 'Ein Gev. Excavations in 1961. *IEJ* 14: 1-49.

Mazzoni, S. 2000. Syria and the Periodization of the Iron Age. In: Bunnens, G. Ed. *Essays on Syria in the Iron Age.* (ANESS 7). Louvain/Paris/Sterling: 31-59.

McCarter, P.K. 1974. 'Yaw, Son of Omri': A Philological Note on Israelite Chronology. *BASOR* 216: 5-7.

—— 1980. The Balaam Texts from Deir 'Alla: The First Combination. *BASOR* 239: 49-60.

—— 1991. The Dialect of the Deir 'Alla Texts. In: Hoftijzer, J. and van der Kooij, G. Eds. *The Balaam Text from Deir 'Alla Re-Evaluated. Proceedings of the International Symposium held at Leiden 21–24 August 1989.* Leiden: 87-99.

McClellan, T.L. 1987. Review Article: Tell el-Far'ah I: L'âge du fer, by Alain Chambon. (Editions Recherche sur les Civilisations, Memoire no. 31). Paris. *BASOR* 267: 84-86.

McComiskey, T.E. 1993. Prophetic Irony in Hosea 1.4: A Study of the Collocation פקד על and Its Implications for the Fall of Jehu's Dynaty. *JSOT* 58: 93-101.

McKenzie, S.L. 1991. *The Trouble with Kings. The Composition of the Book of Kings in the Deuteronomistic History.* (VTS 42). Leiden.

Meshel, Z. 1992. Kuntilet 'Ajrud. *ABD* IV: 103-109.

Meshel, Z., Carmi, I., and Segal, D. 1995. ¹⁴C Dating of an Israelite Biblical Site at Kuntillet Ajrud (Horvat Teman). *Radiocarbon* 37: 205-212.

Millard, A.R. 1970. Recension: J.A. Brinkman, A Political History of Post-Kassite Babylonia. 1158–722 B.C. (AnOr 43). Roma 1968. *Orientalia* 39: 445-450.

—— 1973. Adad-nirari III, Aram, and Arpad. *PEQ* 105: 161-164.

—— 1987-90. Mari². *RlA* 7: 418-419.

—— 1993. Eden, Bit Adini and Beth Eden. *EI* 24: 173*-177*.

—— 1994. *The Eponyms of the Assyrian Empire. 910–612 BC.* (SAAS 2). Helsinki.

Millard, A.R. and Tadmor H. 1973. Adad-nirari III in Syria. *Iraq* 35: 57-64.

Miller, J.M. 1966. The Elisha Cycle and the Accounts of the Omride Wars. *JBL* 85: 441-454.

—— 1967. The Fall of the House of Ahab. *VT* 17: 307-324.

—— 1968. The Rest of the Acts of Jehoahaz. *ZAW* 80: 337-342.

—— 1974. The Mesha Inscription as a Memorial Inscription. *PEQ* 106: 9-18.

Miller, J.M. and Hayes, J.H. 1986. *A History of Ancient Israel and Judah*. Philadelphia.

Minokami, Y. 1989. *Die Revolution des Jehu*. (GTA 38). Göttingen.

Mittmann, S. 1970. *Beiträge zur Siedlungs- und Territorialgeschichte des nördlichen Ostjordanlandes*. Wiesbaden.

Miyazaki, S. and Paz, Y. 2005. Tel 'En Gev. *HA-ESI* 117.

Montgomery, J.A. 1934. Archival Data in the Book of Kings. *JBL* 53: 46-52.

—— 1951. *A Critical and Exegetical Commentary on the Book of Kings*. (Gehman, H.S. Ed.). (ICC). Edinburgh.

Mulzer, M. 1992. *Jehu schlägt Joram. Text-, literar- und structurkritische Untersuchung zu 2 Kön 8,25-10,36*. (ATS 37). St Ottilien.

Münger, S. 2003. Egyptian Stamp-Seal Amulets and Their Implications for the Chronology of the Early Iron Age. *TA* 30: 66-82.

—— 2005. Stamp-Seal Amulets and Early Iron Age Chronology: An Update. In: Levy, T.E. and Higham, T. Eds. *The Bible and Radiocarbon Dating: Archaeology, Text and Science*. London: 381-404.

Münger, S., Zangenberg, J. and Pakkala, J. 2011. Kinneret – An Urban Center at the Crossroads: Excavations on Iron IB Tel Kinrot at the Lake of Galilee. *NEA* 74: 68-90.

Na'aman, N. 1976. Two Notes on the Monolith Inscription of Shalmaneser III from Kurkh. *TA* 3: 89-106.

—— 1986. Historical and Chronological Notes on the Kingdoms of Israel and Judah in the Eighth Century B.C. *VT* 36: 71-92.

—— 1987. The Historical Background of the Battle between Amaziah and Jehoash. *Shnaton. An Annual for Biblical and Ancient Near Eastern Studies* 9: 211-217 (Hebrew).

—— 1991. Forced Participation in Alliances in the Course of the Assyrian Campaigns to the West. In: Cogan, M. and Eph'al, I. Eds. *Ah, Assyria... Studies in Assyrian History and Ancient Near Eastern Historiography Presented to Hayim Tadmor*. (ScrHier 33). Jerusalem: 80-98.

—— 1993. Azariah of Judah and Jeroboam II of Israel. *VT* 43: 227-234.

—— 1994. The Campaign of Mesha against Horonaim. *BN* 73: 27-30.

—— 1995a. Hazael of ʿAmqi and Hadadezer of Beth-rehob. *UF* 27: 381-394.

—— 1995b. Rezin of Damascus and the Land of Gilead. *ZDPV* 111: 105-117.

—— 1995c. The Deuteronomist and Voluntary Servitude to Foreign Powers. *JSOT* 65: 37-53.

—— 1996. Sources and Composition in the History of David. In: Fritz, V. and Davies, P.R. Eds. *The Origins of the Ancient Israelite States*. (JSOTS 228). Sheffield: 170-186.

—— 1997a. Prophetic Stories as Sources for the Histories of Jehoshaphat and the Omrides. *Biblica* 78: 153-173.

—— 1997b. Historical and Literary Notes on the Excavation of Tel Jezreel. *TA* 24: 122-128.

—— 1997c. The Historical Background of the Aramaic Inscription from Tel Dan. *EI* 26: 112-118 (Hebrew).

—— 1997d. Transcribing the Theophoric Element in North Israelite Names. *NABU* 1997/1: 19-20.

—— 1998. Jehu Son of Omri: Legitimizing a Loyal Vassal by His Lord. *IEJ* 48: 236-238.

—— 1999. Lebo-Hamath, Ṣubat-Hamath, and the Northern Boundary of the Land of Canaan. *UF* 31: 417-441.

—— 2000. Three Notes on the Aramaic Inscription from Tel Dan. *IEJ* 50: 92-104.

—— 2001a. Historical Analysis of the Book of Kings in the Light of Royal Inscriptions of the Ninth Century BCE. *Cathedra* 102: 90-108 (Hebrew).

—— 2001b. Royal Inscription versus Prophetic Story: Mesha's Rebellion in Historical Writing. *Zion* 66: 5-40 (Hebrew).

—— 2002a. *The Past that Shapes the Present. The Creation of Biblical Historiography in the Late First Temple Period and after the Downfall.* Jerusalem (Hebrew).

—— 2002b. In Search of Reality behind the Account of David's Wars with Israel's Neighbours. *IEJ* 52: 200-224.

—— 2006. The Story of Jehu's Rebellion: Hazael's Inscription and the Biblical Narrative. *IEJ* 56: 160-166.

—— 2007. Sources and Composition in the Book of Kings: The Introductory and Final Verses of the Kings of Judah and Israel. In: Bar-Asher, M., Rom-Shiloni, D., Tov, E. and Wazana, N. Eds. *Shai le-Sara Japhet: Studies in the Bible, its Exegesis and its Language.* Jerusalem: 97-118 (Hebrew).

—— 2008. Naboth's Vineyard and the Foundation of Jezreel. *JSOT* 33: 197-218.

Na'aman, N. and Lissovsky, N. 2008. Kuntillet 'Ajrud, Sacred Trees and the Asherah. *TA* 35: 186-208.

Naveh, J. 1979. Review of Hoftijzer and van der Kooij 1976. *IEJ* 29: 133-136.

—— 1999. Marginalia on the Inscriptions from Dan and Ekron. *EI* 26: 119*-122*.

Nielsen, E. 1954. *Oral Tradition: A Modern Problem in Old Testament Introduction.* (Studies in Biblical Theology 11). London.

Noll, K.L. 1998. The God Who Is among the Danites. *JSOT* 80: 3-23.

Noth, M. 1928. *Die israelitischen Peronennamen im Rahmen der gemeinsemitischen Namengebung.* (*BWANT* III 10). Stuttgart.

—— 1929. La'asch und Hazrak. *ZDPV* 52: 124-141.

—— 1967. *Überlieferungsgeschichtliche Studien. Die sammelnden und bearbeitenden Geschichtswerke im Alten Testament.* 3rd Ed. Tübingen.

Oded, B. 1971. Darb el-Hawarneh – An Ancient Route. *EI* 10: 191-197 (Hebrew).

—— 1972. The Campaigns of Adad-nirari III into Syria and Palestine. *Studies in the History of the Jewish People and the Land of Israel* 2: 25-34 (Hebrew).

—— 1992. *War, Peace and Empire: Justifications for War in Assyrian Royal Inscriptions.* Wiesbaden.

Olmstead, A.T. 1904–1905. The Fall of Samaria. *AJSL* 21: 179-182.

—— 1921. Shalmaneser III and the Establishment of the Assyrian Power. *JAOS* 41: 345-382.

Olyan, S. 1984. *Hăšālôm:* Some Literary Considerations of 2 Kings 9. *CBQ* 46: 652-668.

Otto, S. 2001. *Jehu, Elia und Elisa. Die Erzählung von der Jehu-Revolution und die Komposition der Elia-Elisa-Erzählungen.* (BWANT 152). Stuttgart.

—— 2003. The Composition of the Elijah-Elisha Stories and the Deuteronomistic History. *JSOT* 27: 487-508.

Ottosson, M. 1969. *Gilead: Traditioin and History.* (CB 3). Lund.

Page, S. 1968. A Stela of Adad-nirari III and Nergal-ereš from Tell al Rimah. *Iraq* 30: 139-153, Pls. XXXVIII-XLI.

Pakkala, J., Münger, S., and Zangenberg, J. 2004. *Kinneret Regional Project: Tel Kinrot Excavations. Tel Kinrot – Tell el 'Orēme – Kinneret. Proceedings of the Finnish Institute in the Middle East.* Vantaa.

Pardee, D. 1991. The Linguistic Classification of the Deir 'Alla Text Written on Plaster. In: Hoftijzer, J. and van der Kooij, G. Eds. *The Balaam Text from*

Deir 'Alla Re-Evaluated. Proceedings of the International Symposium Held at Leiden 21–24 August 1989. Leiden: 101-105.

Parker, B. 1963. Economic Tablets from the Temple of Mamu at Balawat. *Iraq* 25: 86-103, Pls. XIX-XXVI.

Parker, S.B. 2006. Ancient Northwest Semitic Epigraphy and the "Deuteronomistic" Tradition in Kings. In: Witte, M., Schmid, K., Prechel, D. and Gertz, J.-C. Eds. *Die deuteronomistischen Geschichtswerke. Redaktions- und religionsgeschichtliche Perspektiven zur "Deuteronomismus"-Diskussion in Tora und Vorderen Propheten.* (BZAW 365). Berlin/New York: 213-227.

Parpola, S. 1970. *Neo-Assyrian Toponyms.* (AOAT 6). Neukirchen-Vluyn.

Parpola, S. And Porter, M. Eds. 2001. *The Helsinki Atlas of the Near East in the Neo-Assyrian Period.* Helsinki.

Parpola, S. and Watanabe, K. 1988. *Neo-Assyrian Treaties and Loyalty Oaths.* (SAA 2). Helsinki.

Paul, S.M. 1991. *Amos.* Minneapolis.

Pentiuc, E.J. 2002. *Long-Suffering Love: A Commentary on Hosea with Patristic Annotations.* Brookline.

Piasetzky, E. and Finkelstein, I. 2005. ¹⁴C Results from Megiddo, Tel Dor, Tel Rehov and Tel Hadar: Where Do They Lead Us? In: Levy, T.E. and Higham, T. Eds. *The Bible and Radiocarbon Dating: Archaeology, Text and Science.* London: 294-301.

Piccirillo, M. 1992a. Medeba. *ABD* IV: 656-658.

—— 1992b. Nebo, Mount. *ABD* IV: 1056-1058.

—— 1992c. Baal-Meon. *ABD* I: 552.

Pitard, W.T. 1987. *Ancient Damascus: A Historical Study of the Syrian City-State from Earliest Times until its Fall to the Assyrians in 732 B.C.E.* Winona Lake.

—— 1994. Arameans. In: Hoerth, A.J., Mattingly, G.L., and Yamauchi, E.M. Eds. *People of the Old Testament World.* Grand Rapids: 207-230.

Plein, O. 1966. Erwägungen zur Überlieferung von I Reg 11,26-14,20. *ZAW* 78: 8-24.

Poebel, A. 1943. The Assyrian King List from Khorsabad — Concluded. *JNES* 2: 56-85.

Pognon, H. 1907-08. *Inscriptions sémitiques de la Syrie, de la Mésopotamie, et de la region de Mossoul.* Paris.

Porada, E. 1983. Remarks about Some Assyrian Reliefs. *AnSt* 33: 15-18.

Postgate, J.N. 1970. A Neo-Assyrian Tablet from Tell al Rimah. *Iraq* 32: 31-35, Pl. XI.

Powell, M.A. 1987-90. Masse und Gewichte. *RIA* 7: 457-517.

Pruin, D. 2007. What Is a Text? – Searching for Jezebel. In: Grabbe, L.L. Ed. *Ahab Agonistes: The Rise and Fall of the Omride Dynasty.* (LHBOTS 421). London/New York: 208-235.

Puech, É. 1981. L'ivoire inscrit d'Arslan Tash et les rois de Damas. *RB* 88: 544-562, Pls. 12-13.

——— 1994. La stele araméenne de Dan: Bar Hadad II et la coalition des Omrides et de la maison de David. *RB* 101: 215-241.

Radner, K. 2002. *Die Neuassyrischen Texte aus Tall Šēḫ Ḥamad.* (Berichte der Ausgrabung Tell Schech Hammad / Dur Katlimmu 6). Berlin.

Rahlfs, A. 1911. *Septuaginta-Studien*, Heft 3. Lucians Rezension der Königsbücher. Göttingen.

Rainey, A.F. 1975. The Identification of Philistine Gath. *EI* 12:63-67 (Hebrew).

——— 1999. Taanach Letters. *EI* 26: 153*-162*.

Ramsey, C.B. 2005. Improving the Resolution of Radiocarbon Dating by Statistical Analysis. In: Levy, T.E. and Higham, T. Eds. *The Bible and Radiocarbon Dating: Archaeology, Text and Science.* London: 57-64.

Rapuano, Y. 2001. Tel Dover. *HA-ESI* 113: 21-23 (Hebrew).

Rast, W.E. 1978. *Taanach I. Studies in the Iron Age Pottery.* Cambridge.

Reade, J.E. 1978. Assyrian Campaigns, 840–811 B.C., and the Babylonian Frontier. *ZA* 68: 251-260.

Reinhold, G.G.G. 1989. *Die Beziehungen Altisraels zu den aramäischen Staaten in der israelitisch-judäischen Königszeit.* Frankfurt am Main/Bern/New York/Paris.

Reisner, G.A., Fisher, C.S., and Lyon, D.G. 1924. *Harvard Excavations at Samaria.* Cambridge.

Renz, J. 1995. Die althebräischen Inschriften. I. Text und Kommentar. In: Renz, J. and Röllig, W. Eds. *Handbuch der althebräischen Epigraphik.* I. Darmstadt.

Renz, J. and Röllig, W. 2003. Materialien zur althebräischen Morphologie. II: Siegel und Gewichte. In: Renz, J. and Röllig, W. *Handbuch der althebräischen Epigraphik.* II/2. Darmstadt.

Revell, E.J. 1993. Language and Interpretation in 1 Kings 20. In: Walfish, B. Ed. *The Frank Talmage Memorial Volume I.* Haifa: 103-113.

Richelle, M. 2010a. *Le testament d'Élisée. Texte massorétique et septante en 2 Rois 13.10-14.16* (Cahiers de la Revue Biblique 76). Pendé.

——— 2010b. Les conquêtes de Hazaël selon la recension lucianique en 4 Règnes 13,22. *BN* 146: 19-25.

Rofé, A. 1988. *The Prophetical Stories. The Narratives about the Prophets in the Hebrew Bible. Their Literary Types and History.* Jerusalem.

—— 2001. *Introduction to the Historical Literature of the Hebrew Bible.* Jerusalem (Hebrew).

Röllig, W. 1957-71. Gilzānu. *RlA* 3: 375.

—— 1974. Alte und neue Elfenbeinschriften. In: Degen, R., Müller, W.W. and Röllig, W. Eds. *Neue Ephemeris für semitische Epigraphik II.* Wiesbaden: 37-64.

—— 1988. Ein Altorientalischer Pferdeschmuck aus dem Heraion von Samos. *Mitteilungen des Deutschen Archäologischen Instituts, Athenische Abteilung* 103: 37-75.

Romero, C.G. 1992. Beth-Jeshimoth. *ABD* I: 689.

Ruby, J. 2001. Assyrian Provincial Governors in Syria. *BCSMS* 36: 169-174.

Rudnig-Zelt, S. 2006. *Hoseastudien: Redaktionskritische Untersuchungen zur Genese des Hoseabuches.* (FRLANT 213). Göttingen.

Rudolf, W. 1971. *Joel-Amos-Obadja-Jona.* (KAT 13/2). Gütersloh.

Sader, H. 1987. *Les étas araméens de Syrie depuis leur foundation jusqu'à leur transformation en provinces assyriennes.* Beirut.

Saggs, H.W.F. 1955. The Nimrud Letters, 1952 – Part II. *Iraq* 17: 126-154, Pls. XXX-XXXV.

Šanda, A. 1911. *Die Bücher der Könige: Das erste Buch der Könige.* Band I. Münster.

—— 1912. *Die Bücher der Könige: Das zweite Buch der Könige.* Band II. Münster.

Scheil, V. 1917. Fragment d'une inscription de Salmanasar, fils d'Aššurnaṣirpal. (Notules 35), *RA* 14: 159-160.

Schenker, A. 2004. *Älteste Textgeschichte der Königsbücher: Die hebräische Vorlage der ursprünglichen Septuaginta als älteste Textform der Königsbücher.* (OBO 199). Fribourg/Göttingen.

Schiffer, S. 1911. *Die Aramäer — Historisch-Geographische Untersuchungen.* Leipzig

Schmidt, W.H. 1965. Die deuteronomistische Redaktion des Amosbuches: Zu den theologischen Unterschieden zwischen dem Prophetenwort und seinem Sammler. *ZAW* 77: 168-193.

Schmitt, H.-C. 1972. *Elisa. Traditionsgeschichtliche Untersuchungen zur vorklassischen nordisraelitischen Prophetie.* Gütersloh.

Schneider, T.J. 1996. Rethinking Jehu. *Biblica* 77: 100-107.

Schniedewind, W.M. 1996. Tel Dan Stela: New Light on Aramaic and Jehu's Revolt. *BASOR* 302: 75-90.

—— 1998. The Geopolitical History of Philistine Gath. *BASOR* 309: 69-79.

Schniedewind, W.M. and Zuckerman, B. 2001. A Possible Reconstruction of the Name of Haza'el's Father in the Tel Dan Inscription. *IEJ* 51: 88-91.

Schottroff, W. 1966. Horonaim, Nimrim, Luhith und der Westrand des "Landes Ataroth": Ein Beitrag zur historischen Topographie des Landes Moab. *ZDPV* 82: 163-208.

Schoville, K.N. 1974. A Note on the Oracles of Amos against Gaza, Tyre, and Edom. In: *Studies on Prophecy: A Collection of Twelve Papers.* (VTS 26). Leiden: 55-63.

Schramm, W. 1973. *Einleitung in die Assyrischen Königsinschriften, zweiter Teil, 934–722 v. Chr.* (HO, Section 1 The Near and Middle East, Ergänzungsband, 5/2). Leiden/Köln.

Schumacher, G. and Steuernagel, C. 1908. *Tell el-Mutesellim I. Band, Fundbericht A. Text.* Leipzig.

Segal, D. 1995. ^{14}C Dates from Horvat Teiman (Kuntillet 'Ajrud) and Their Archaeological Correlation. *TA* 22: 208-209.

Sekine, M. 1975. Literatursoziologische Beobachtungen zu den Elisaerzählungen. *AJBI* 1: 39-62.

―――― 1977. Elias Verzweiflung. – Erwägungen zu 1.Kö XIX –. *AJBI* 3: 52-68.

Sellin, E. 1904. *Tell Ta'annek. Bericht über eine mit Unterstützung der Kaiserlichen Akademie der Wissenschaften und des K. K. Ministeriums für Kultus und Unterricht unternommene Ausgrabung in Palästina.* Wien.

―――― 1905. *Eine Nachlese auf dem Tell Ta'annek in Palästina.* 2 vols. Vienna.

Seux, M.-J. 1980-83. Königtum: B. II. und I. Jahrtausend. *RlA* 6: 140-173.

Sharon, I., Gilboa, A., and Boaretto, E. 2007. ^{14}C and Early Iron Age of Israel – Where Are We Really at? A Commentary on the Tel Rehov Radiometric Dates. In: Bietak, M. Ed. *The Synchronization of Civilizations in the Eastern Mediterranean in the Second Millennium B.C. III.* Vienna: 150-155.

Sharon, I., Gilboa, A., Jull, A.J.T., and Boaretto, E. 2007. Report on the First Stage of the Iron Age Dating Project in Israel: Supporting a Low Chronology. *Radiocarbon* 49: 1-46.

Shavit, A. 2000. Settlement Patterns in the Ayalon Valley in the Bronze and Iron Ages. *TA* 27: 189-230.

Shea, W.H. 1978. Adad-nirari III and Jehoash of Israel. *JCS* 30: 101-113.

Siddall, L.R. 2011. A Historical and Ideological Analysis of the Reign of Adad-nīrārī III, King of Assyria. Unpublished Ph.D. Thesis. The University of London.

Singer-Avitz, L. 2006. The Date of Kuntillet 'Ajrud. *TA* 33: 196-228.

Slayton, J.C. 1992. Bashan. *ABD* I: 623-624.

Smelik, K.A.D. 1992. *Converting the Past: Studies in Ancient Israelite and Moabite Historiography*. (OtSt 28). Leiden/New York/Köln.

Smith, G.A. 1894. *The Historical Geography of the Holy Land*. London.

Soggin, J.A. 1971. Amos VI:13-14 und I:3 auf dem Hintergrund der Beziehungen zwischen Israel und Damaskus im 9. und 8. Jahrhundert. In: Goedicke, H. Ed. *Near Eastern Studies in Honor of William Foxwell Albright*. Baltimore/London: 433-441.

Sroka, D. 2006. *Kings, Wars and Prophets: Historiography, Literature and Ideology in 1 Kgs 20*. Unpublished MA Thesis. Tel Aviv University. (Hebrew).

Stade, B. 1885. Anmerkungen zu 2 Kö. 10-14. *ZAW* 5: 275-297.

—— 1886. Ammerkungen zu 2 Kö. 15-21. *ZAW* 6: 156-189.

—— 1889. *Geschichte des Volkes Israel*. I. 2nd Ed. Berlin.

Stade, B. and Schwally, F. 1904. *The Books of Kings. Critical Edition of the Hebrew Text*. Leipzig.

Staszak, M. 2009. Zu einer Lesart und dem historischen Hintergrund des Fragments B der Stele von Tel Dan. *BN* 142: 67-77.

Steck, O.H. 1968. *Überlieferung und Zeitgeschichte in den Elia-Erzählungen*. Neukirchen-Vluyn.

Steuernagel, C. 1912. *Lehrbuch der Einleitung in das Alte Testament mit einem Anhang über die Apokryphen und Pseudepigraphen*. Tübingen.

Stipp, H.-J. 1987. *Elischa – Propheten – Gottesmänner. Die Kompositionsgeschichte des Elischazyklus und verwandter Texte, rekonstruiert auf der Basis von Text- und Literarkritik zu 1 Kön 20.22 und 2 Kön 2-7*. (ATS 24). St. Ottilien.

Stith, D.M. 2008. *The Coups of Hazael and Jehu: Building an Historical Narrative*. (Georgias Dissertations 37. Biblical Studies 3). Piscataway.

Sugimoto, T. 1999. Iron Age Potteries from Tel En-Gev, Israel: Seasons 1990–1992. *Orient* 34: 1-21.

—— 2010. Tel 'En Gev: Preliminary Report. *HA-ESI* 122.

Suriano, M.J. 2007. The Apology of Hazael: A Literary and Historical Analysis of the Tel Dan Inscription. *JNES* 66: 163-176.

Sweeney, M.A. 2000. *Twelve Prophets. Vol. I: Hosea, Joel, Amos, Obadiah, Jonah*. (Berit Olam: Studies in Hebrew Narrative & Poetry). Collegeville.

—— 2007. *I & II Kings*. Louisville/London.

Tadmor, H. 1958. The Campaigns of Sargon II of Assur: A Chronological-Historical Study. *JCS* 12: 22-40, 77-100.

—— 1961. Azriyau of Yaudi. (ScrHier 8). Jerusalem: 232-271.

—— 1962. The Southern Border of Aram. *IEJ* 12: 114-122.

—— 1969. A Note on the Saba'a Stele of Adad-nirari III. *IEJ* 19: 46-48.

—— 1973. The Historical Inscriptions of Adad-nirari III. *Iraq* 35: 141-150.

—— 1975. Assyria and the West: The Ninth Century and Its Aftermath. In: Goedicke, H. and Roberts, J.J.M. Eds. *Unity and Diversity: Essays in the History, Literature, and Religion of the Ancient Near East.* Baltimore/London: 36-48.

—— 1979. The Chronology of the First Temple Period. In: Malamat, A. Ed. *The Age of the Monarchies: Political History. The World History of the Jewish People* IV/I. Jerusalem: 44-60.

—— 1983. Autobiographical Apology in the Royal Assyrian Literature. In: Tadmor, H. and Weinfeld, M. Eds. 1983. *History, Historiography and Interpretation. Studies in Biblical and Archaeological Literatures.* Jerusalem: 36-57.

—— 1994. *The Inscriptions of Tiglath-pileser III King of Assyria.* Jerusalem.

—— 1997. Propaganda, Literature, Historiography: Cracking the Code of the Assyrian Royal Inscriptions. In: Parpola, S. and Whiting, R.M. Eds. *Assyria 1995.* Helsinki: 325-338.

Takata, G. 2005. Problems in the Chronology of the Iron Age IIA in Palestine and Research on *bīt-hilāni. Orient* 40: 91-104.

Tappy, R.E. 1992. *The Archaeology of Israelite Samaria, Volume I: Early Iron Age through the Ninth Century BCE.* (HSS 44). Atlanta.

—— 2001. *The Archaeology of Israelite Samaria, Volume II: The Eighth Century BCE.* (HSS 50). Winona Lake.

Thenius, O. 1873. *Die Bücher der Könige.* Leipzig.

Thiel, W. 1992. Jehu. In: *ABD* III: 670-673.

Thiele, E.R. 1983. *The Mysterious Numbers of the Hebrew Kings.* New Revised Ed. Grand Rapids.

Thomas, P.P. 2003. *Jeroboam II the King and Amos the Prophet: A Social-Scientific Study on the Israelite Society during the 8th Century BCE.* Delhi.

Thompson, T.L. 1974. *The Historicity of the Patriarchal Narratives.* (BZAW 133). Berlin.

—— 1992. *Early History of the Israelite People from the Written and Archaeological Sources.* (SHANE 11). Leiden.

—— 1995. Dissonance and Disconnections: Notes on the BYTDWD and HMLK.HDD Fragments from Tel Dan. *SJOT* 9: 236-240.

—— 1999. *The Mythic Past: Biblical Archaeology and the Myth of Israel.* London.

Thureau-Dangin, F., Barrois, A., Dossin, G., and Dunand, M. 1931. *Arslan Tash*. (Biblothèque archéologique et historique 16). Paris.

Timm, S. 1982. *Die Dynastie Omri. Quellen und Untersuchungen zur Geschichte Israels im 9. Jahrhundert vor Christus*. (FRLANT 124). Göttingen.

—— 1993. König Hesion II. von Damaskus. *WO* 24: 55-84.

Trebolle Barrera, J.C. 1984. *Jehú y Joás. Texto y composición literaria de 2 Reyes 9-11*. (Institución San Jerónimo 17). Valencia.

Tropper, J. 1993. Eine altaramäische Steleinschrift aus Dan. *UF* 25: 395-406.

—— 1994. Paläographische und linguistische Anmerkungen zur Steleninschrift aus Dan. *UF* 26: 487-492.

Tsukimoto, A., Hasegawa, S., and Onozuka, T. Eds. 2009. *Tel 'En Gev on the Eastern Shore of the Sea of Galilee: Report of the Archaeological Excavations (1998– 2004)*. Tokyo. (Japanese).

Tsukimoto, A. and Kuwabara, H. Eds. *forthcoming*. *Excavations at Tel 'En Gev: Seasons 1990–2004*. Tokyo.

Unger, E. 1916. *Reliefstele Adadniraris III. aus Saba'a und Semiramis* (Publicationen der Kaiserlich Osmanischen Museen 2). Konstantinopel.

Unger, M.F. 1957. *Israel and the Aramaeans of Damascus*. Grand Rapids.

Ungnad, A. 1906. Jaua, mār Humrî. *OLZ* 9: 224-226.

Ussishkin, D. 1994. Gate 1567 at Megiddo and the Seal of Shema, Servant of Jeroboam. In: Coogan, M.D., Exum, J.C. and Stager, L.E. Eds. *Scripture and Other Artifacts. Essays on the Bible and Archaeology in Honor of Philip J. King*. Louisville: 410-428.

—— 2000. The Credibility of the Tel Jezreel Excavations: A Rejoinder to Amnon Ben-Tor. *TA* 27: 248-256.

—— 2009. On the So-called Aramaean 'Siege Trench' in Tell eş-Şafi, Ancient Gath. *IEJ* 59: 137-157.

Ussishkin, D. and Woodhead, J. 1992. Excavations at Tel Jezreel, 1990–1991: Preliminary Report. *TA* 19: 3-56.

—— 1994. Excavations at Tel Jezreel, 1992-1993: Preliminary Report. *Levant* 26: 1-48.

—— 1997. Excavations at Tel Jezreel, 1994-1996: Preliminary Report. *TA* 24: 6-72.

Van der Plicht, J. and Bruins, H.J. 2005. Quality Control of Groningen [14]C Results from Tel Reḥov: Repeatability and Intercomparison of Proportional

Gas Counting and AMS. In: Levy, T.E. and Higham, T. Eds. *The Bible and Radiocarbon Dating: Archaeology, Text and Science.* London: 256-270.

Van der Plicht, J., Bruins, H.J., and Nijboer, A.J. 2009. The Iron Age around the Mediterranean: A High Chronology Perspective from the Groningen Radiocarbon Database. *Radiocarbon* 51: 213-242.

Van Seters, J. 1975. *Abraham in History and Tradition.* New Haven.

―――― 1983. *In Search of History. Historiography in the Ancient World and the Origins of Biblical History.* New Haven/London.

Vaux, R. de. 1934. La chronologie de Hazaël et de Benhadad III, rois de Damas. *RB* 43: 512-518.

―――― 1951. La troisième campagne de fouilles à Tell el Farʿah, près Naplouse. *RB* 58: 393-430, 566-590.

―――― 1952. La quatrième campagne de fouilles à Tell el Farʿah, près Naplouse. *RB* 59: 551-583.

―――― 1955. Les fouilles de Tell el Farʿah, près Naplouse. *RB* 62: 541-589.

―――― 1956. The Excavations at Tell el-Farʿah and the Site of Ancient Tirzah. *PEQ* 88: 125-140.

―――― 1957. Les fouilles de Tell el Farʿah, près Naplouse. *RB* 64: 552-580.

―――― 1961. Les fouilles de Tell el Farʿah, près Naplouse. *RB* 68: 557-592.

―――― 1962. Les fouilles de Tell el Farʿah, près Naplouse. *RB* 69: 212-253.

Vaux, R. de. and Steve, A.M. 1947. La première campagne de fouilles à Tell el Farʿah, près Naplouse. *RB* 54: 394-433, 573-589.

―――― 1948. La seconde campagne de fouilles à Tell el Farʿah, près Naplouse. *RB* 55: 544-580.

―――― 1949. La deuxième campagne de fouilles à Tell el Farʿah, près Naplouse. *RB* 56: 102-138.

Vielhauer, R. 2007. *Das Werden des Buches Hosea: Eine redaktionsgeschichtliche Untersuchung.* (BZAW 349). Berlin/New York.

Vitto, F. and Davis, D. 1976. Har ʿAdir. *HA-ESI* 59-60: 9-10.

Vogelstein, M. 1945. *Jeroboam II. The Rise and Fall of His Empire.* Cincinnati.

von Nordheim, E. 1992. *Die Selbstbehauptung Israels in der Welt des Alten Orients. Religionsgeschichtelicher Vergleich anhand von Gen 15/22/28, dem Aufenthalt Israels in Ägypten, 2 Sam 7, 1 Kön 19 und Psalm 104.* (OBO 115). Freiburg/Göttingen.

Weinfeld, M. 1972. *Deuteronomy and the Deuteronomic School.* Oxford.

―――― 1984. Kuntillet ʿAjrud Inscriptions and Their Significance. *SEL* 1: 121-130.

Weippert, M. 1978. Jau(a) mar Humri. *Joram* oder Jehu von Israel?. *VT 28*: 113-118.

—— 1992. Die Feldzüge Adadnararis III. nach Syrien Voraussetzungen, Verlauf, Folgen. *ZDPV* 108: 42-67.

—— 1998. Ar und Kir in Jesaja 15,1. Mit Erwägungen zur historischen Geographie Moabs. *ZAW* 110: 547-555.

Weißbach, F.A. 1922. *Die Denkmäler und Inschriften an der Mündung des Nahr el-Kelb.* Leipzig/Berlin.

Wellhausen, J. 1885. *Prolegomena to the History of Israel.* (Reprinted 1994). Atlanta.

—— 1898. *Die kleinen Propheten: übersetzt und erklärt.* 4th Ed. (Reprinted 1963). Berlin.

—— 1899. *Die Composition des Hexateuchs und der Historischen Bücher des Alten Testaments.* 3rd Ed. Berlin.

—— 1905. *Prolegomena zur Geschichte Israels.* 6th Ed. Berlin.

Wesselius, J.-W. 1999. The First Royal Inscription from Ancient Israel: The Tel Dan Inscription Reconsidered. *SJOT* 13: 163-186.

—— 2001. The Road to Jezreel: Primary History and the Tel Dan Inscription. *SJOT* 15: 83-103.

White, M.C. 1997. *The Eliah Legends and Jehu's Coup*, (BJS 311). Atlanta.

Whitley, C.F. 1952. The Deuteronomic Presentation of the House of Omri. *VT* 2: 137-152.

Willoughby, B.E. 1992. Amos, Book of. *ABD* I: 203-212.

Winckler, H. 1889. *Die Keilschrifttexte Sargons nach den Papierabklatschen und Originalen.* Vol. 1. Leipzig.

—— 1909. *Das Vorgebirge am Nahr-el-Kelb und seine Denkmäler*, Leipzig.

Wiseman, D.J. 1956. A Fragmentary Inscription of Tiglath-pileser III from Nimrud. *Iraq* 18: 117-129.

Witte, M. 2005. Von den Anfängen der Geschichtswerke im Alten Testament – Eine forschungsgeschichtliche Diskussion neuerer Gesamtentwürfe. In: Becker, E.-M. Ed. *Die antike Historiographie und die Anfänge der christlichen Geschichtsschreibung.* (BZNW 129). Berlin/New York: 53-81.

Wolff, H.W. 1956. Hoseas geistige Heimat. *TLZ* 81: 83-94.

—— 1964. *Amos geistige Heimat.* Göttingen

—— 1969. *Dodekapropheton 2. Joel und Amos.* Neukirchen-Vluyn.

—— 1974. *Hosea. A Commentary on the Book of the Prophet Hosea.* Trasnlated by Stansell, G. from *Dodekapropheton 1 Hosea.* Philadelphia.

Wolff, S. 1998. Archaeology in Israel. *AJA* 102: 757-807.

Wolters, A. 1988. The Balaamites of Deir 'Alla as Aramean Deportees. *HUCA* 59: 101-113.

Wray Beal, L.M. 2007. *The Deuteronomist's Prophet: Narrative Control of Approval and Disapproval in the Story of Jehu (2 Kings 9 and 10)*. (LHOTS 478). New York/London.

Wright, G.E. 1959. Israelite Samaria and Iron Age Chronology. *BASOR* 155: 13-29.

Wright, J.L. 2008. Warfare and Wanton Destruction: A Reexamination of Deuteronomy 20:19-20 in Relation to Ancient Siegecraft. *JBL* 127: 423-458.

Würthwein, E. 1984. *Die Bücher der Könige. 1. Kön. 17 – 2. Kön. 25*. (ATD 11, 2). Göttingen.

Yadin, Y. 1960. New Light on Solomon's Megiddo. *BA* 23: 62-68.

—— 1970. Megiddo of the Kings of Israel. *BA* 33: 66-96.

—— 1972a. *Hazor: The Schweich Lectures of the British Academy, 1970*. London.

—— 1972b. *Hazor: The Head of All Those Kingdoms*. London.

—— 1975. *Hazor: The Recovery of a Great Citadel of the Bible*. London.

Yadin, Y., Aharoni, Y., Amiran, R., Dothan, T., Dunayevsky, I., and Perrot, J. 1958. *Hazor I: The James A. Rothschild Expedition at Hazor: An Account of the First Season of Excavations, 1955*. Jerusalem.

—— 1960. *Hazor II: The James A. Rothschild Expedition at Hazor: An Account of the Second Season of Excavations at Hazor, 1956*. Jerusalem.

Yadin, Y., Aharoni, Y., Dunayevsky, I., Dothan, T., Amiran, R., and Perrot, J. 1961. *Hazor III-IV (Plates): The James A. Rothschild Expedition at Hazor: An Account of the Third and Fourth Seasons of Excavation, 1957–1958*. Jerusalem.

Yamada, S. 1995. Aram-Israel Relations as Reflected in the Aramaic Inscription from Tel Dan. *UF* 27: 611-625.

—— 1998. The Manipulative Counting of the Euphrates Crossings in the Later Inscriptions of Shalmaneser III. *JCS* 50: 87-94.

—— 2000a. *The Construction of the Assyrian Empire: A Historical Study of the Inscriptions of Shalmaneser III (859–824 B.C.) Relating to His Campaigns to the West*. (CHANE 3). Leiden/Boston/Köln.

—— 2000b. Peter Hulin's Hand Copies of Shalmaneser III's Inscriptions. *Iraq* 62: 65-87.

—— 2003. Stylistic Changes in Assyrian Annals of the Ninth Century B.C. and Their Historical-Ideological Background. *Oriento* (Bulletin of the Society for the Near Eastern Studies in Japan) 46-2: 71-91 (Japanese).

Yee, G.A. 1987. *Composition and Tradition in the Book of Hosea: A Redaction Critical Investigation*. (SBLDS 102). Atlanta.

Yeivin, S. 1960. The Date of the Seal "Belonging to Shemaʿ (the) Servant (of) Jeroboam". *JNES* 19: 205-212.

Younger, K.L., Jr. 1990. *Ancient Conquest Accounts: A Study in Ancient Near Eastern and Biblical History Writing*. (JSOTS 98). Sheffield.

—— 1998. The Deportations of the Israelites. *JBL* 117: 201-227.

—— 2005. 'Hazael, Son of a Nobody': Some Reflections in Light of Recent Study. In: Bienkowski, P., Mee, C., and Slater, E. Eds. *Writing and Ancient Near Eastern Society. Papers in Honour of Alan R. Millard*. (LHBOTS 426). New York/London: 245-270.

Zaccagnini, C. 1993. Notes on the Pazarcık Stela. *SAAB* 7: 53-72.

Zadok, R. 1977. *On West Semites in Babylonia during the Chaldean and Achaemenian Periods. An Onomastic Study*. Jerusalem.

—— 1997. Historical and Ethno-Linguistic Notes. *UF* 29: 797-814.

Zarzeki-Peleg, A. 1997. Hazor, Jokneam and Megiddo in the Tenth Century B.C.E. *TA* 24: 258-288.

—— 2005a. Trajectories of Iron Age Settlement in North Israel and Their Implications for Chronology. In: Levy, T.E. and Higham, T. Eds. *The Bible and Radiocarbon Dating: Archaeology, Text and Science*. London: 367-378.

—— 2005b. The Iron Age IIA-B Transitional Period (Stratum XIII). In: Ben-Tor, A., Zarzecki-Peleg, A., and Cohen-Anidjar, S. 2005. *Yoqneʿam II: The Iron Age and the Persian Period. Final Report of the Archaeological Excavations (1977–1988)*. (Qedem Reports 6). Jerusalem: 169-183.

Zayadine, F. 1967-68. Samaria-Sebaste, Clearance and Excavations (October 1965–June 1967). *ADAJ* 12–13: 77-80.

Zimhoni, O. 1992. The Iron Age Potter from Tel Jezreel – An Interim Report. *TA* 19: 57-70.

—— 1997. Clues from the Enclosure-Fills: Pre-Omride Settlement at Tel Jezreel. *TA* 24: 83-109.

Zwickel, W. 2000. Überlegungen zur wirtschaftlichen und historischen Funktion von Kuntillet ʿAğrūd. *ZDPV* 116: 139-142.

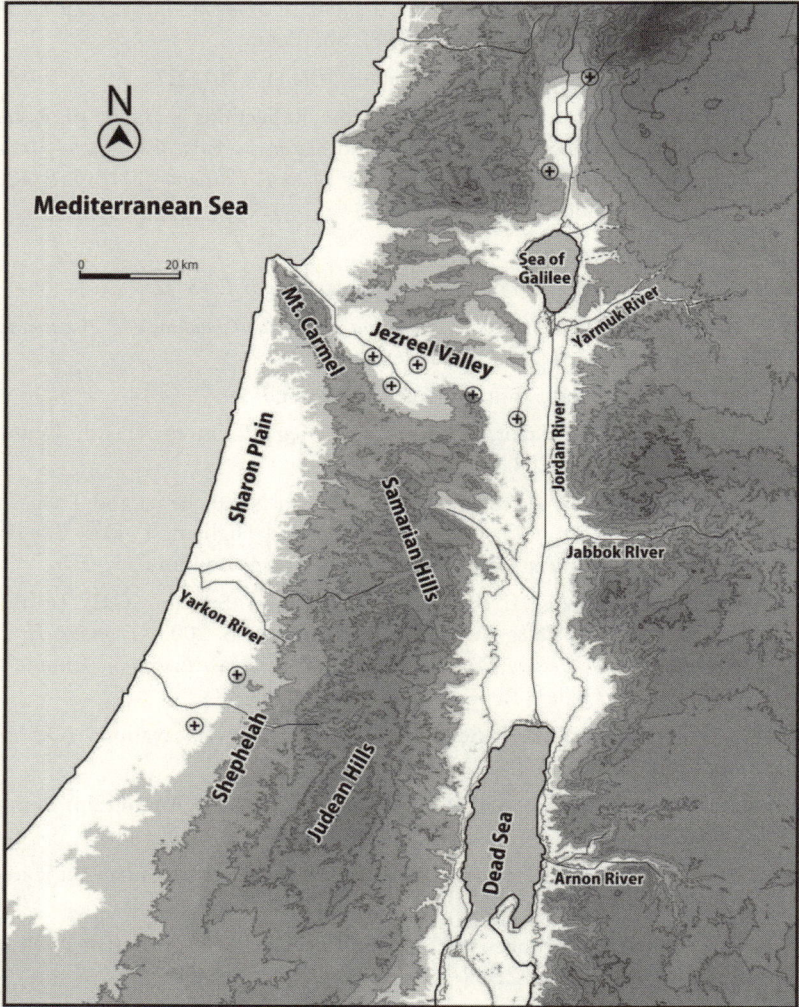

Map 1. The Cities Destroyed by Hazael

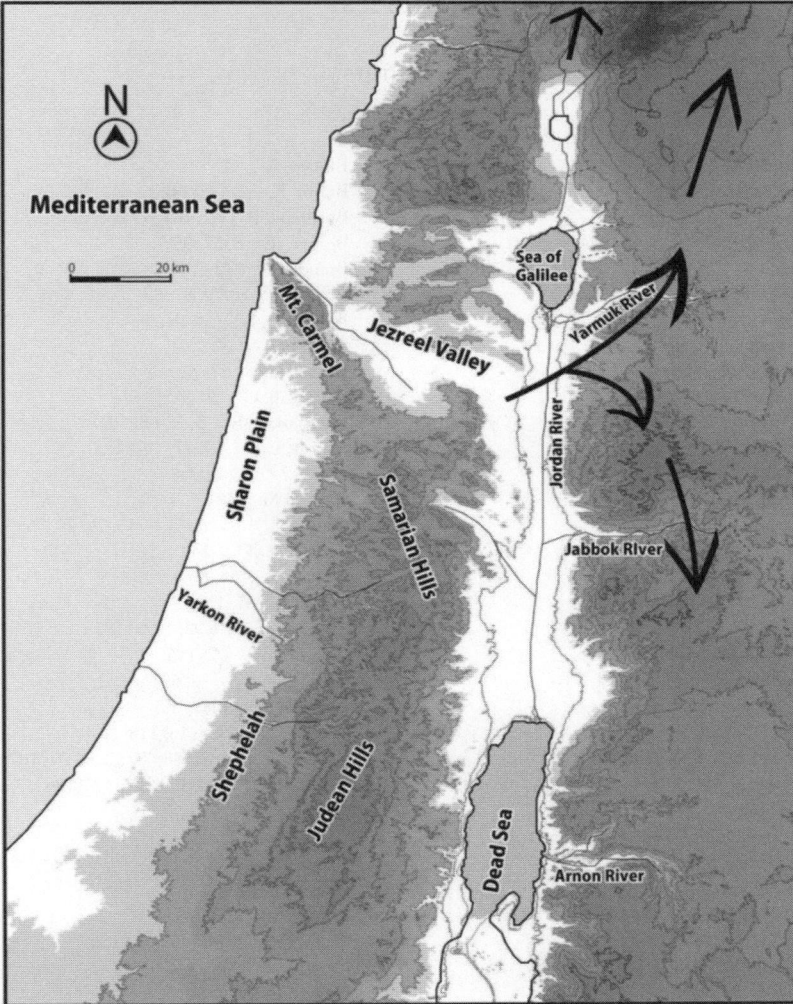

Map 2. The Israelite Expansion under Jeroboam II

Indices

Authors

Hebrew Bible

10:21aβb-25a	25	13:10-13	80, 107
10:25b-27	23-25	13:11	108
10:26	24	13:12	88
10:27	24	13:12-13	107, 110
10:27b	23	13:13	107
10:28	23-25	13:14-17	82, 108
10:28-29	84	13:14-19	82, 107-108
10:28-31a	24	13:15-17	82
10:28-36	85	13:15b	82
10:29	84-85	13:17	81-82
10:29-31	24, 84	13:18	82
10:29-36	12	13:18-19	82, 108
10:30	148	13:20	111
10:30-33	84	13:20-21	105, 107-108
10:31	87	13:20b	108
10:32a	85	13:22	79-81, 83, 87-88, 105, 109
10:32	85-86	13:22-25	75, 80, 82
10:32-33	46, 75, 84-85, 105	13:23	78-79, 81
10:32b	85	13:24	81, 83
10:33aα	85	13:24-25	80-81, 109
10:33a	85	13:25a	82
10:33	81, 85-86	13:25	82-83, 107-108
10:33aβ-b	85	13:25b	82
10:33b	85	14:1	9, 107, 110-111
10:34	86, 88	14:2	111
10:34-36	84, 86	14:3	24
10:35	86	14:7	109-110, 139
10:36	9, 86	14:8	110
11:18	24	14:8-14	107, 109
12:3	24	14:9	109
12:18	78, 110	14:10	109-110
12:18-19	75, 78, 83	14:11	109-110
12:19	78, 109	14:14	109, 122
12:21-22	19	14:15	88
13:1	9, 107	14:15-16	80, 107, 110
13:1-2	78, 87	14:17	107, 111
13:1-8	78	14:19	20
13:1-9	84	14:19-20	19
13:2	87	14:22	109-110, 139
13:3	46, 75, 78-80, 83, 85, 87-88	14:23	9, 123
13:3-5	78-79, 87	14:23-24	123
13:3-6	78-79	14:23-29	123
13:3-7	78	14:24	123
13:4	81, 87	14:25a	123
13:4-6	78-79, 87	14:25	81, 123, 125-126, 129-130
13:5	78, 87, 103	14:25-27	123
13:6	85, 87	14:25b	123
13:7	78-80, 83, 88, 105	14:25b-27	125
13:8	87	14:26-27	78, 81, 125
13:8-9	78, 87	14:27	125, 130
13:10	9, 107	14:28	88, 125-126, 130
13:10-11	107	14:28-29	123

Semitic Sources

Personal Names

Geographical Names